The B-17 Tomahawk Warrior: A WWII Final Honor

A TRUE STORY OF HONOR AND SACRIFICE

▲▲▲▲

By
David E. Huntley

The B-17 Tomahawk Warrior: A WWII Final Honor

Copyright 2016-2023 By David E. Huntley
Published by Huntley Associates Dallas, Inc.
ISBN 978-1-7346899-1-4
Book Cover by Stunningbookcovers.com –
(Crew photo by 398th.org and colorized by Colin Kimball)

ALL RIGHTS RESERVED
No part of this manuscript may be reproduced in any manner without the express written consent of the author, except with brief excerpts in critical reviews and articles, and subject to crediting the author.

DISCLAIMER and IMPORTANT NOTES
My book contains numerous quotations and citations from many sources, some of which may contain errors, omissions, or typographical errors. Some of these anomalies might be found in airmen's diaries, official documents, and in newspaper reports in wartime. Where I felt it was appropriate, I have inserted either a (sic), an Author's Note, or a footnote to correct the anomaly. Generally, however, I have not edited wartime quotations or extracted citations.

The navigator's diary details each mission. There are certain days where he may have recorded observing a certain plane being shot down, I have provided further extensive reports of what happened from official records. Of crews who bailed out, got captured, interrogated and their experiences as P.O.W.'s. My additional material gives the diary a wider window of dramatic events on certain days, particularly Chapter 9, 19th Mission June 21, 1944.

I have used with permission extensive historical data and photographs from the 398th Bomb Group Memorial Association website, and in some of the credits I abbreviate this to, 398th BGMA.

One of the more common misrepresentations found in historical records, is the misnaming of the Army Air Corps and the Army Air Forces which were both part of the 8th Air Force in Europe. I have summarized the distinction between them here:

During World War II, the United States Army Air Corps was reorganized and renamed as the United States Army Air Forces in 1941. This change was made to give the air arm of the U.S. military a greater degree of autonomy and to emphasize the importance of air power in modern warfare. Despite this reorganization, the Army Air Corps would remain the air combat arm of the Air Force during the period of the European Theater of Operations (ETO), which lasted from 1942 to 1945. The Army Air Forces continued to operate as an independent branch of the U.S. military until it was merged with the United States Army to form the United States Air Force in 1947.

During World War II, the Army Air Forces included both the Army Air Corps and other components, such as the Army Air Forces Combat Command. The 8th Air Force was a component of the Army Air Forces, and its units included both Army Air Corps and Army Air Forces Combat Command units. The Army Air Corps provided bomber and fighter groups to the 8th Air Force, which flew bombing missions over Europe. The Army Air Forces Combat Command provided fighter and reconnaissance units, among others, to the 8th Air Force. So, both Army Air Corps and Army Air Forces Combat Command units were part of the 8th Air Force.

▲ ▲ ▲ ▲

EPIGRAPH AND DEDICATION

▲ ▲ ▲ ▲

DON'T LET THE GREATEST GENERATION OF THEIR
TIME BECOME THE FORGOTTEN GENERATION OF
OUR TIME
David E. Huntley – Author (2012)

The author survived the London blitz in WWII, and his late wife lived under the Nazi occupation of France. He dedicates this book to the Americans and Allies who landed on Normandy beaches and those in air combat who helped save Europe from tyranny. The author especially dedicates this book to the 398th Bomb Group Memorial Association, who preserves the memories of everyone attached to the Group from 1943 to 1945.

Dedicated also to my children, Martine, Nicole, Alan, and Dean, and to their children. Those who fought in WWII, especially the Tomahawk Warrior crew who saved my life, made their current lives possible.

▲ ▲ ▲ ▲

ADVANCE PRAISE

▲ ▲ ▲ ▲

I am amazed at the time and effort David Huntley put into this book. His tenacity at getting the story out there and ensuring its accuracy is awe-inspiring.

My biggest regret is that my father Davis Charles Searl is not alive to read it. He would have so enjoyed the story! He was very proud of his cousin 1st Lt. Charles J. Searl. However, at least my brother Charles Searl and his son Cullin Charles Searl will be able to experience the honor that he had brought to my family and so many others, with his tribute to the Tomahawk Warriors.

I learned so much by reading the ARC. It was so well written that many times I got lost in the narrative and I felt as if I was being taken back to that time and that era and those places. Amazing! Finally, it serves as an honor to the fallen crew as well as a source of comfort and closure for the families of these heroes.

As a member of the Searl dynasty and a descendant relative of the Tomahawk Warrior crew, I am humbled to have been even a small part of this journey.

- **Kathy Searl, 2nd cousin of the Tomahawk Warrior pilot, Lt. Charles Searl**

On August 12, 1944 a B-17 Flying Fortress, flown by the Charles J. Searl Crew of the 398th Bomb Group, mysteriously crashed and exploded near Penn, England shortly after takeoff. David E. Huntley, a 9-year-old boy at the time, recalls in vivid detail waking to the deafening roar of that 4-engined plane passing "frighteningly low" just over the roof of his cottage as it came crashing down in a nearby field. He witnessed the immediate horrific aftermath and the image of the auxiliary personnel retrieving the crew's remains stayed with him all his life. Huntley's *The B-17 Tomahawk Warrior: A WWII Final Honor* is a brilliantly investigated account of this crew's fateful final day. For many years there has been much speculation as to the cause of that fiery crash but thanks to Huntley, we now have a truly plausible explanation. But the author did not stop there. Recently he has brought posthumous honor and recognition for each crew member as well as long awaited closure for their relatives.

Excellent! It was a very good read and extremely hard to put down. This book is the best account of what happened that I have seen. A fine tribute to the crew known as "The Tomahawk Warriors." **– Lee Anne Bradley Historian, 398th Bomb Group Memorial Association**

As a B17 combat pilot of WWII with the Bloody One Hundredth Bomb Group, I was pleased to be asked by David Huntley to review his manuscript for the "Tomahawk Warriors." As a result, let me simply say that this book represents a Herculean effort to properly commemorate the memory of the valiant bomber crew who tragically lost their lives while attempting to join their Group to confront the evil Nazi regime in their effort to inflict their will on the world. Unfortunately, in wartime we seldom had the time or resources to properly investigate the circumstances and probable causes of accidents such as this. Nevertheless, Huntley's unrelenting pursuit of the facts and circumstances surrounding this particular incident and its impact upon the friends and relatives of this heroic crew, is highly commendable and rewarding. – **102-year-old Major Lucky Luckadoo, US Air Force (Ret)**

I greatly enjoyed your book and congratulate you on the extraordinary quest and labour of love that lies behind it. It really is a unique story. – **The Earl, Lord Frederick Howe. United Kingdom**

"This phenomenally researched story, written from the heart and with sincere appreciation, is a gem among the books dedicated to the memory of American airmen who sacrificed their lives to free the world from the evil of Nazism." – **Marina Osipova, an award-winning author of WWII historical fiction**

"Everything you have researched and written here is outstanding. My father would be so proud of the depth and nature of your portrayal of his brother Joe, despite having such limited sources to draw upon. Joe's sons and daughters will be so thankful for your thoughtful writing. I speak for the entire Chvala family in giving you our deepest thanks and appreciation for your invaluable work." – **Chuck Chvala**

▲ ▲ ▲ ▲

CONTENTS

▲ ▲ ▲ ▲

Epigraph and Dedication v
Advance Praise vii
Foreword xvii

Part 1: Preface, Prologue & Probing Mysteries 1
Preface 3
Prologue..7
Chapter One: Good-Bye to the Blitz – Leaving London 11
Chapter Two: A Safe Home – "Hello," Loudwater, Buckinghamshire....18
    Life in High Wycombe..22
Chapter Three: A New Life in the USA – Life in Dallas, Texas and
        then a Discovery...24
Chapter Four: Discoveries – Introducing Martin Ginther 37
    The First Connection to a Relative of the Crew.................................39
Chapter Five: The Pilot's Daughter 59
    Meeting Cheryl Surfus in Wisconsin April 20-22, 2019....................59
    A Visit to the City of Tomahawk 64
    A Dedication by Kathy and Chuck Searl 69
Chapter Six: The Navigator's Nieces 75
    The Search for the Kempner Descendants......................................75
    Meeting the Kempner Family 79
    Lt. Irving "Hank" Kempner 83
    Lt. George Kempner 85

Chapter Seven: The Pilot, 1st Lt. Charles J. Searl 86
   My Imaginary Conversation with Charles J. Searl...................86
   The Likely Cause of the Crash 92
   The Weather and Plane Identification for August 12, 1944...............98
   Plane Identification...................105
   Searl's Early Life...................111
   Enlistment and Officer Pre-Pilot Testing 115
   Training, Graduation and Deployment...................117
Chapter Eight: The Navigator, 2nd Lt. Saul Kempner...................127
   Saul Kempner History and Basic Training...................127
   Marshall Stelzdfried: (Citation)...................128
   Family Efforts to Communicate with the Army after the War.........140
   The Return of the Kempner Diary 148
Chapter Nine: The Diary Kept by 2nd Lt. Saul Kempner 152
   Sub-Chapter: May 1944 – Missions #1-8...................152
   Why O'Neal went down on Mission to Berlin...................158
   1,200 U.S. Fighters Escort 1,000 Bombers Over Reich, France......177
   Rail Yards in Germany are Blasted. 179
   Sub-Chapter: June 1944 180
   Story of Lt. Rohrer & Crew Shot Down 205
   Purple Heart 215
   Sub-Chapter: August 1944 224
   The Last And Final Mission of the Tomahawk Warrior Crew
      August 12th, 1944 229
Chapter Ten: Tracing Crew Descendants and the 'Snyder Mystery'.....236
   Sub-Chapter: The Co-Pilot 2nd Lt. Albert L. Dion 236
   Albert W. Knight – Waist Gunner 239
   The Frank Snyder Mystery – Part One 254
   The Mistaken Snyder 254
   The Frank Snyder Mystery – Part Two...................258
   The Real Frank Snyder...................258
   St. Sgt. Frank Allen Snyder -Tail Gunner 258

Sub-Chapter: The Crew's Descendants Who Have Not Been
   Found 267
Tech Sgt. James A. Beatty, D.o.b. 10/3/1923 267
S Sgt. Alfred Beuffel – Ball Turret Gunner, D.o.b. 9/9/1923............268
Sgt. Cecil E. Kennedy – Radio Operator, D.o.b. 5/27/1919 270
Lt. Leo C. Walsh – Bombardier, D.o.b. 10/3/1923..........................270
Sgt. Orville M/ Wilson, Waist Gunner, D.o.b. 7/18/1924.................271

Part 2: Wwii Air Combat History 273
Chapter Eleven: The B-17 Flying Fortress and Wwii 275
   398th Bombardment Group History (Citation) 277
   An Example of the Tough Airworthiness of the B-17g and the
      Men Who Flew Them 284
   B-17g #42-38050 Thunderbird 292
   Tribute to the Texas Raiders of the Commemorative Air Force
      (CAF)..307
   Other Aspects of Air Combat in Wwii 310
   Path Finder Force Bombing Method (Pff) (Citation) 312
   Types of Explosives Used in Wwii (Citation) 314
   It Should Have Been a Milk Run: Bombs Kissed in Mid-Air
      by Paul Brown 601 Radio Operator....................................315

Part 3: Honor-A Historical Moment-& A Link to America's
   Independence 319
Chapter Twelve: Request for Posthumous Honors............................321
   An Application to Request a Us Honor For 1st
      Lt. Charles Searl 321
   Request for a British Posthumous Honor.................................322
   Presentation of the Scrolls of Honour 325
Chapter Thirteen: The Commemorative Marker..............................340
   Designing, Making, and Placing of the Commemorative Marker ...340
   Why is this Story Important to So Many People?.....................349

Chapter Fourteen: A Moment in American History 353
    Joseph Kennedy Jr. and the Tomahawk Warrior Connection 353
    A Broader and More Detailed Description of the Aphrodite
        Project 362
Chapter Fifteen: Tribute to Lord Howe 379

Acknowledgments 385
About the Author 389
Index 391

▲ ▲ ▲ ▲

FOREWORD

▲ ▲ ▲ ▲

By Brigadier General, Mitchell A. Hanson,
United States Air Force

- "It is, I believe, the greatest generation any society has ever produced." – Tom Brokaw in his book, The Greatest Generation, describing the men and women of WWII.
- "Anyone who doesn't have fear is an idiot. It's just that you must make the fear work for you. Hell, when somebody shot at me, it made me madder than hell, and all I wanted to do was shoot back." – Brig Gen Robin Olds, US Air Force "Triple" Ace.

The 398th Bomb Group was formed for one purpose and one purpose only: to defeat Nazi Germany and to help end a brutal war that cost countless thousands of lives. The 398th was activated on 1 March 1943 and prepared for war in the dependable and magnificent Boeing B-17 Flying Fortress heavy bomber. 12,732 B-17s were produced between 1935 and May 1945: of the aircraft that were produced, over 4,735 were lost during combat missions.* The average life expectancy of an Eighth Air Force B-17 in late 1943 was 11 missions.** The numbers vary depending on the source, but over 50,000 airmen died in combat during World War II, with over 25,000 being killed in training accidents. The 25-mission tour of duty was set sometime prior to 1944 and it was estimated that the average crewman had only a one in four chance of actually completing his tour of duty.*** Yet, through all of the figures, the odds and statistics, these young individuals strapped on their flying gear and did what had to be done.

I first met Mr. David Huntley at a Roll Call Luncheon at Birchman Baptist Church in Fort Worth, Texas. The Roll Call organization is a group of extremely patriotic individuals whose mission is to honor and serve our veterans by providing a regular venue for fellowship and camaraderie. They meet the 4th Friday of every month. Mr. Huntley introduced himself and explained what he had been working on for some time. Intrigued, I asked him numerous questions about his project. As he described his research and his desire to honor the crew of the Tomahawk Warrior, Mr. Huntley had a gleam in his eye like the same nine-year-old boy who had witnessed this horrific accident. His enthusiasm, warmth, sense of purpose and desire was captivating. I was truly honored when he eventually asked me to pen the Foreword for this excellent book.

In Huntley's "The B-17 Tomahawk Warrior: A WWII Final Honor," his research, investigation, historical references, and personal accounts are unlike anything I ever saw or read previously. His passion for uncovering the real story, finding the data behind the tales and detailing the history of the crew members and their families is unmatched. His description of the individuals in England who honored and continue to honor the Tomahawk Warrior crew is heartwarming and shows the deep appreciation and admiration of the locals who know this tale. Huntley's personal recollection as a nine-year-old boy—the sounds, the sights, and the horrific discovery of the crash are brought to life in his incredibly detailed writing. The fact that Mr. Huntley spent many years, countless hours, and multiple trips to various destinations to recognize and bring honor to the Tomahawk Warrior crew speaks volumes about the individual who wrote this story. He not only honors these individuals, but has brought closure and relief to the families of the crew members he was able to locate through his exhaustive research.

No one knows what went through the minds of 1st Lt. Charles Searl (pilot) and 2nd Lt. Albert Dion (co-pilot) as they sat behind the controls of their stricken aircraft on that fateful day. As a military pilot myself, I feel quite sure they knew their fate well beforehand. Since England's open fields were littered with impediments to landing (to thwart the Nazi gliders), this B-17 crews' only option was to either crash land into a village or take their chances elsewhere. Military men and women, especially pilots, are trained to make split second decisions. Facing the prospect of taking innocent civilian lives, I believe they made the honorable decision to point their stricken aircraft in another direction and avoid any unnecessary loss of life. These were special people, individuals who unquestionably loved their country and believed in what they were doing. I believe they saved countless lives on the ground because of their heroic actions. These are the type of individuals that Tom Brokaw referred to as "The Greatest Generation," without a doubt.

Every time these young men got into their aircraft, there was fear of what lay ahead, some doubt as to whether they would return, and some hope that the mission would be successful, and they would return unharmed. As referenced in the quote from Brig Gen Robin Olds, only fools would not have any fear. The one thing this band of brothers did not doubt, was their belief in each other and what they were fighting for. When you train with, live with, and fly with the same group of individuals day after day you become a family. Each family has its individual idiosyncrasies, but that's what makes each one unique and each one special in its own way.

The Tomahawk Warrior crew was no different, and it is very evident they were a special family. Their ultimate hope was that their efforts would help to end the bloody war, a hope that eventually came true, but only after the demise of this group of warriors.

A resounding thanks to the British authorities for their remembrance of the Tomahawk Warrior Crew. The posthumous scroll, commemorative marker, and the yearly recognition of the crew is an enormous testimony to the fine individuals who live in the villages of Loudwater and Penn, Buckinghamshire, England. A special thank you to Mr. David Huntley, whose impeccable research and devotion to this noble cause brought about all these accolades to the crew.

1st Lt. Charles J. Searl; 2nd Lt. Albert L. Dion; 2nd Lt. Leo C. Walsh, bombardier; 2nd Lt. Saul J. Kempner, navigator; Sgt. Orville M. Wilson, waist gunner; Staff Sgt. James A. Beatty, engineer; Sgt. Alfred Bueffel, ball turret; Sgt. Albert W. Knight, waist gunner; Sgt. Cecil E. Kennedy, radio; and although not on the final fateful flight, Sgt. F.A. Snyder, tail gunner… we all salute you and thank you for your service to our great nation. I also salute the families that raised such fine young men. The men who made the ultimate sacrifice in the defense of this great nation and against an evil empire. May God bless you all and may God bless the United States of America and the United Kingdom.

- *   Website: https://eaa.org/eaa/events-and-experiences/aluminum-overcast-eaa-b-17-bomber-tour/b-17-hisotry-with-boeing-and-eaa
- ** Website: https://www.airandspaceforces.com/article/valor-the-right-touch/
- *** Website: https://eyewitnesstohistory.com/b17.html

▲ ▲ ▲ ▲

PART 1

PREFACE
PROLOGUE
&
PROBING MYSTERIES

▲▲▲▲

PREFACE

▲ ▲ ▲ ▲

Time brings alternative stories of WWII to light almost every day. Yet, occasionally, an incident that was buried in the archives of history untouched and unseen and then suddenly, discovered, is brought from obscurity by ethereal forces of unusual coincidences and circumstances. It becomes a mystery of such significance as to warrant further attention and investigation.

The fate of the B-17 American bomber that crashed and exploded in a field in England, on August 12, 1944, killing all nine of the crew known as the Tomahawk Warriors, is one of those mysteries of the Second World War. It would have lain in partial obscurity, if it were not for my initial involuntary involvement. As a child, I witnessed of what would become a dogged determination in my lifetime later to tell this story. By securing Secret Declassified Operational Records, I resolved the mystery that had arisen over this incident and the securing of a posthumous honor[1] to the deceased crew. It brought relief and closure to the descendants' relatives.

The crew of the Tomahawk Warrior were part of the 600th Squadron of the 398th Bomb Group of the United States Army Air Corps, 8th Air Force. They were stationed at Nuthampstead in the county of Hertfordshire in England. The base was also home to the 601, 602, and 603 Squadrons. On

---

[1] The local community and church do pay homage to the crew each year on Remembrance Day but the full details of how and why the plane crashed has never been fully explored, until now. I was able to get the British to issue a posthumous honor to the crew.

the early morning of August 12, 1944, the Tomahawk Warrior crew took off from Nuthampstead at 6:18 a.m. British Double Summer Time to form part of a massive daylight bomber raid on a German target near Versailles, France. Some difficulties prevented the plane from forming with the rest of the squadron. It crashed and exploded with a full load of high explosive munitions in a field near the village of Penn, Buckinghamshire.

Several questions about what happened that day have remained a mystery until answered in my book; The souls of the Tomahawk Warrior crew will last forever in a peaceful slumber. Not as dismembered bodies lost in the universe of the forgotten.

- One: While it has been recorded as losing the Tomahawk Warrior and its nine-crew, my book discloses that the crew were flying a different plane in place of their usual aircraft. The evidence reveals not only the identity[2] of the aircraft which crashed on that fateful day, but also the identity and serial number of the crew's usual aircraft.[3]
- Two: Based on official records, you will find why the crew could not fly their usual aircraft that day.
- Three: The crash destroyed the plane with such force that all the crew members except one were unidentifiable. Eight of the crew were interred together at the National Cemetery in Arlington, USA. The military buried the ninth identified crew member at the American Cemetery in Cambridge, England. You will find my explanation why the force of that explosion was greater than normally expected.
- Four: The number of missions the crew had completed before they perished was misreported on various websites. Using actual operational records, I have validated the number of missions they

---

[2] From Official Declassified Secret Operational Records
[3] Chapter 8 Weather & Plane Identification

undertook. After the war, I found information in the navigator's diary supporting this fact.
- Five: The story of how the navigator's diary came into my possession and its return to family descendants I describe in detail. They were unaware of the existence of a diary. The emotional impact to the family was palpable.
- Six: One of the strangest aspects of this saga relates to the member of the crew who did not take his place on that final fatal mission. It has been referred to as the 'Frank Snyder mystery.' The squadron usually flew with a crew of ten. On that day, the tail gunner, Snyder, wasn't on the aircraft. There has never been an official explanation of why. Unsuccessful efforts by others in the past had failed to locate him. This had perpetuated the myth of the 'Snyder Mystery.' My book, after intense research, finally reveals where he ended up and it forever linked the tragedy of his own death to the Tomahawk Warrior.
- Seven: There is one further strange coincidence that involved an important event in American history. It is my discovery of the link between the death of Lt. Joe Kennedy, (expected to be groomed for the American Presidency) in an explosion of his plane, and that of the Tomahawk Warrior, which occurred on *exactly* the same day, August 12, 1944. With supporting documentation, in the chapter,[4] "A Moment of American History," I reveal more about the Tomahawk Warrior connection than just the date.

The gruesome image I have as a nine-year-old child when that plane almost came down on top of my cottage that morning has forever remained with me. Something urged me to honor those brave men for saving my life and many others that day.

---

[4] Chapter 14

In my research, I traced the descendants of four of the deceased nine-man crew.[5] The resulting personal, historical, and biographical material, as well as interviews, helped me to reconstruct the lives of the four crew members.

The four men were Charles J. Searl, pilot, Albert L. Dion, co-pilot, Saul J. Kempner, navigator, and Albert W. Knight, the waist gunner. It was those men and their ethereal spirits which guided me in this quantum universe we live in. Their presence steered me toward providing an accurate picture of what happened on August 12, 1944, and to give loving closure to their deceased relatives and their current descendant relatives.

The Posthumous Scrolls of Honour I secured from the British Authorities will remember them. They were officially presented to their family descendants I had traced. At last, they are recognized for the sacrifice they made for saving not just my life, but hundreds of others in our area on that fateful day.

With the help of friends and officials in the U.K., I have established a Permanent Commemorative Marker next to the crash site in 2020 as a reminder of their sacrifice.

David E. Huntley – Author

▲ ▲ ▲ ▲

---

[5] I should note that the officers in the crew were originally 2nd Lieutenants and referred as that rank for the duration of the narrative. The exception was 1st Lt. Charles Searl, because his promotion recorded in the Operational Records came halfway through their mission assignments. At the time of burial, however, Walsh and Dion were also recorded as 1st lieutenants.

PROLOGUE

▲ ▲ ▲ ▲

A Vivid Image

My bed faced the window of our cottage, and the noise from the plane became louder and louder as it drew nearer, causing me to wake up. I could see the faintest light from the dawn as this terrible noise and vibration passed over our roof. I could not see the plane as it went directly overhead. The sky was not lit up or showed any sign of reflected flame in the cloud or atmosphere. The noise, vibration, and the darkness stood out to me over the years.

The massive explosion[6] of such an impact with the ground that rocked the entire area and broke windows for miles around was bigger than most bombs we had experienced in London, except for the German V1 rockets and the V2 menace, which came a month later.

Bob, my older brother, had jumped out of bed and exclaimed, "That plane is down. Come on, let's see."

Later, I remember my own thoughts were, "I'm going to be adding something to my shrapnel collection for showing off to my schoolmates." Me being a 'foreigner' from London, the local children at the Loudwater village school didn't easily accept the funny-talking Cockney kid. This would help my acceptance into the local milieu.

I was running as fast as my nine-year-old legs could carry me, but my older brother Bob and my stepbrother Tom were several yards ahead of

---

[6] The reason for the enormity of the explosion is explained in Chapter 9 the final Mission #28

me. We had run up Derehams Lane. I could see smoke to the right. Bob shouted to me, "Come on, David, keep up!" He then led us onto the adjacent field, and we followed the public footpath to the next stile. We hopped over and ran across another field until we reached Whitehorse Lane, which forked left into Gatemoor Lane.

We couldn't see the smoke coming from the field because of the high hedges. It was dissipating now. Suddenly, there was a break in the hedgerow, revealing an iron fence, or maybe it was a metal gate. I don't remember exactly, but what I saw next became etched into my brain for the rest of my life.

As I stood there with my brothers, my inexperienced eyes could barely grasp the enormity of what I was seeing. The blackened field was covered in small pieces of debris. Could it be the remnants of the plane that had twenty or thirty minutes earlier in the dawn light roared frighteningly low over our cottage? The plane had crashed in the adjacent area of Penn, next to our village of Loudwater, Buckinghamshire. We knew it was in trouble when we heard the coughing and the stuttering of an aircraft's engines. The vibrations of its impending descent shook every wall and window in our home as it flew right over us.

So, here we were in the chilly air and near to a farm, which I later learned was Lude Farm in the nearby village of Penn. Frozen in horror, I stared at the auxiliary personnel who were already on the scene, hurrying around the field with galvanized metal bins and picking up bloody body parts. I had seen victims carried out of bombed buildings during the blitz in London, but while limp and sometimes bloodied, they were whole human beings. This was something much different. With a clear view of the field from the metal fence or gate, I could see open parachute silks on the ground, and one embedded in the hedge on the lane itself. I said to my brothers, "Surely, they could not have parachuted from such a low height?"

I don't remember their reply. It was much later when I realized the parachutes were simply shrouds covering human remains. One of the auxiliary personnel came quite close to where we were standing and gaping. As he picked up what looked like a bloody arm with a piece of cloth sticking to a part of it and placed it in his bin, he spotted us. He gave a shout to someone and a man ran to our side of the field. He told us to "bugger off, you're not allowed here, now go back home."

We, of course, reluctantly slunk off. I never considered picking up a souvenir of the debris. Maybe subconsciously, I may have been afraid of what I might have touched. All I could think about were the bins the men were carrying around that field and what they contained.

The 398th Bomb Group, who was alerted to the crash, sent Flight Surgeon Captain Robert Kelly[7] to the scene to assist in identification. Recalling the incident, the retired Los Angeles Gynecologist said, "The plane and crew were practically vaporized, nothing left larger than a fist. It was not pretty."

I certainly saw bloody parts larger than a fist being picked up and transferred into those galvanized bins. The captain was right, it was not pretty!

Those scenes and images would have a big impact on me later in life. It never occurred to me, as a young schoolboy who had himself survived the nightly bombing raids on London, that somehow, the soul of one of those poor airmen would stay with me and guide me on a mission to connect with his just-born child. In fact, another of the airmen who perished that day would leave a written legacy as a diary. By some twist of fate it would come into my hands and strongly reinforce my mission to tell their story.

On that fateful morning, there were strange and indistinct shadows that entered my mind. Yes, I had seen bloody body parts, and yes, the overall image of that scene would remain with me forever. Yet, there was something else, and it was the sense of these indistinct images that seemed linked to the crash site. I would tell my wife and children about the crash many years later.

Then seventy-five years further on, the crew's descendants would come to consider me nothing less than a messenger from God. I would

---

[7] Extract of official report from the 398th Bomb Group Memorial Association website.

never consider myself in that role. I have to admit, there were succeeding revelations of incidents, of dates, and coincidences which, for each one, drew me in to conclude that I must write this story. The dead crew and their souls made a kind of connection to me as a little boy. It would manifest itself to guide me on a mission to honor their sacrifice for saving many lives that fateful day, including my own.

▲ ▲ ▲ ▲

CHAPTER ONE

Good-bye To the Blitz – Leaving London

▲ ▲ ▲ ▲

That day, in 1944, as I walked down Edgeley Road in Clapham, London on my way to school carrying, as always, my Mickey Mouse gas mask, and my lunch of bread and dripping[8] wrapped in a newspaper, I was thinking about the fact that we were going to move to a place outside the city. I had hoped I would not have to take the gas mask. Whilst we never had to use it, the school made us practice with it. Plus, it was the ugliest one you ever saw! One could wear it and terrify every cat in the neighborhood. We Londoners never trusted Hitler to not use gas on us, but always thought the dictator might one day.

We had air raid drills at least once a week. The teacher marched us diligently to the special shelter in the school playground. The interior stank to high heaven of pee. After some minimal time, the teacher, unable to tolerate the smell any longer, ordered us back to the classroom. We always received a lecture about not using the shelter as a lavatory.

Of course, when we were let out for playtime, for some, the urge became too much and they couldn't make it to the lavatories. Thus, would sneak into the shelter for a quick relief. We had an unwritten rule that banned number two's, so we had our own punishment for miscreants, although rarely instituted.

I enjoyed going to school, not because I liked the lessons, but for many

---

[8] Plain bread covered with congealed fat from whatever the Sunday roast meat had been, flavored with pepper & salt, then wrapped in newspaper.

other distractions it offered compared to being at home and having to endure unpleasant chores. It was a place where there were always discussions about food in our lives. Sharing experiences of what happened to who or what, swapping shrapnel, and yes, using some milder swear words, which was a rite of passage at an early age.

During playtime, we used to exchange jokes we had heard from the radio program ITMA, which was the acronym for "It's That Man Again" (meaning Hitler!) starring Tommy Handley, the comedian. It was also the period when we arranged swaps of our shrapnel collection with other boys. These were small pieces; we could carry in our pockets. Larger pieces we hid at home, often in the garden. It was lucky we found no unexploded incendiaries to hide in the backyard! (Or under the bed!).

After school, some of us, who were more adventuresome, rambled through bombed-out buildings while risking the ire of Auxiliary Personnel. They'd tell us to "clear off", and often in a saltier language.

On weekends, I rode around on a scooter made of scrap wood and wheels that came from steel ball bearing races. Noisy as hell! Another activity carried out in the cellar was helping my brothers make toy soldiers with molten lead and molds. We had a blowtorch to melt the lead in a crucible before pouring it into the forms. My job was to file or sandpaper the mold joint marks on the figures and then paint them according to the type of the soldier. (More than likely, that paint was also lead based).

Scooters made of scrap wood. Credit Beetley Pete.

I liked to go with my brothers to Clapham Common, to watch the men inflating and winching up and down the barrage balloons, inspecting or maintaining the anti-aircraft guns and searchlights.

Day after day, my father's earlier comment about the necessity of us boys leaving London became more urgent because the V1 rockets the 'Jerries' (Germans) were sending over were killing more and more people.

We had survived the worst of the blitz, and we were lucky because our house had a coal cellar we could retreat to. The government had also issued us a Morrison Shelter[9], which we installed in the living room. There was also an Anderson Shelter[10] in the back garden, but they forbade us kids to go in it.

My father, after being wounded and evacuated from Dunkirk, took on the role of an Air Raid Precaution Warden (ARP). This position ensured that the blackout got enforced, and he reported to a central post of any bomb damage as it occurred.

My father had tolerated the V1s or doodlebugs, also known as buzz bombs, because one could hear them coming and when the engine stopped, everyone ducked or took shelter because one knew it was coming down. The V2s[11] that started in September of '44 were devastatingly different because you neither heard them nor saw them as they descended at supersonic speed from a height of 55 miles in the stratosphere. The V2s killed 7250[12] people before the war ended.

The Londoners weren't on the terrible beaches of Normandy. Nor were they at the battles of Market Garden, or Bastogne. Still, 43,000[13]

---

[9] A Morrison Shelter was a very large table with a thick solid steel slab on top from which we ate our meals, and the sides had wire mesh to protect against flying debris if a bomb hit the house while we slept underneath it.

[10] A hole dug in the ground and covered with corrugated iron and heavy soil placed on top.

[11] See videos and details of the German V rockets http://www.stelzriede.com/ms/html/sub/marshwvr.htm

[12] Source Daily Mail.com

[13] Civilian War Dead Honour Roll 1939-1945 Westminster Abbey

men, women and even more horrifying many children were lost in the years of the bombings and rockets. Approximately 85,000 civilians got badly injured during these bombings and rocket attacks. Almost 70% of the 2 million homes destroyed during the war were in London. The total fatalities caused by enemy actions as recorded in the Westminster Abbey War Dead Honour Roll were 66,375.

This map shows the locations where bombs fell on London during World War II

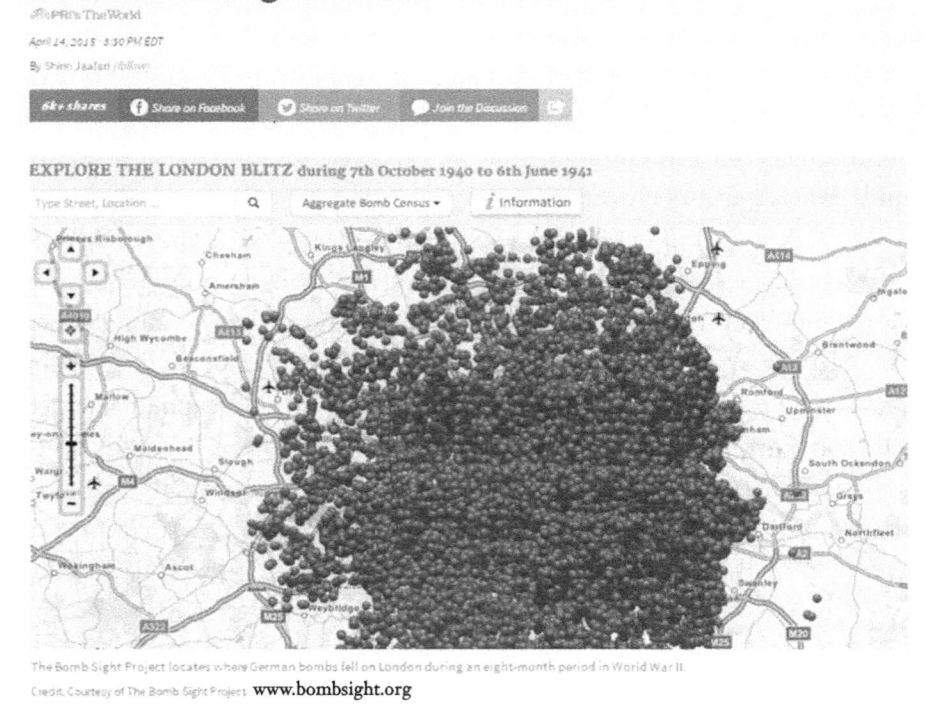

The Bomb Sight Project locates where German bombs fell on London during an eight-month period in World War II.
Credit: Courtesy of The Bomb Sight Project **www.bombsight.org**

Us Huntley children didn't have the same fears as adults in war time. However, my heart was beating in my chest as I thought about what it will be like to have the house fall on me, especially after having seen a woman pulled out of the rubble of a house, in the aftermath of a German raid.

The worst sight came one morning after a nighttime direct hit took out a house across the street from us on Voltaire Road. Ambulance crews were recovering the bodies of the elderly couple who lived there. The limpness and contorted positions, and the blood coming from their ears, was a horrible sight, but what made me cry was when someone told me their dog had died in the rubble. I used to play with that dog, whose name sadly I cannot remember, but whose image I can still picture, a short, sturdy, black and tan terrier of some sort.

When huddled in the coal cellar during a raid, amid the deafening noise of the bombs exploding and ack-ack guns on Clapham Common, I wondered if the next one would hit our house.

In the morning, all the horrors of the night raid forgotten, I was off to school to meet my mates, to share jokes and laugh. It was another night coming home from school, and I never knew if my house would still be there.

THE HOUSE WE OCCUPIED IN WAR TIME AT EDGELEY RD., CLAPHAM. THE SIDE ADDITION AND DOOR HAS BEEN ADDED SINCE THE WAR. HOUSES OPPOSITE WERE DESTROYED.

Copyright Huntley Associates Dallas, Inc.

(Mysteriously, in 2019, I contacted the current owner of the house, a Mrs Francine Vella-Roccia. Her family had bought the property in 1945 after we had left London. She became a good friend and assisted me during my visit for the Tomahawk Warrior project in England).

That brings me to a story that happened to one of my classmates. The following memory is a rough recollection of a conversation I have had as a schoolboy in London during the war. The names are vaguely remembered, but their images are clear to me like it was yesterday. For the record, my Cockney nickname in those days was Spud. (Slang for potato, usually because of a hole in the heel of a sock)

"Allo Bert, whadya get fer lunch t'day?"

"Well, me Mum was gonna give me bread and jam today, but she ran out of jam. She gave me the jar to scrape the side wi me finger, but there was not enough to put on the bread. So I got drippin' again instead."

"Yeah, me too – I got some of the brown bits. I got some of the newspaper to wrap me lunch in before they tore up the paper for the lavatory. Course, we always saved the pictures of Hitler or Jerries for the lavatory."

"Jerry was busy last night wernt he? He dropped a packet or two near Golders Green and I heard Putney got 'ammerd last night too. I fink it nearly got Putney Bridge"

"Oi Spud, Nobby Clark told Chalky that he never knew why Jim never came to school last week. Well, it turns out that Chalky's mum found out that Jim's house bought it when it got a direct hit on last Tuesday's raid. Jimmy's gone, and so's his mum. His Dad had to pull them out of the rubble. Their entire street was a bloody mess. The dad saved Jim's little sister, Kathleen. Now, it's just dad and the girl. I ope the ack-ack guns, got some of the Jerries, the bastards."

"Yeah, me too. The guns were makin an ellova row on Clapham Common last night. Dad told me to get down in the cellar after I saw the searchlights in the sky."

"Did you get any shrapnel for your collection, Spud?"

"I got a couple of sharp pieces but me dad keeps tellin me its dangerous cos if yer cut yerself wiv a piece of incendiary, it could have some phosfery stuff on it which could get in the cut and bloody kill yer."

"Well, I'm off to get me tea. See yer at school tomorrow, if we are lucky."

"Don't forget yer gas mask, cos Ms. Thompson gets all nasty if yer leaves it at 'ome."

"Yer know ye ave to practice wiv it, and I put it on the other night and the cat ran fer its life. HA HA."

What prompted me to remember the basis of that conversation recently was when a stranger had spotted "WWII Survivor London Blitz" embroidered on my cap, and asked, "So you went through the blitz then?"

I replied, "I did yes."

"Pretty horrible, but better than being in combat, though, I suppose."

"I beg your pardon? So, you think the period between 1940 and 1945 in London was not combat? In the sense that we didn't have the weapons to fight back at the enemy, you're right. We just had to hope we wouldn't be next when a bomb or rocket fell. At least in combat you're not a sitting duck, and your children are not in the front line with you."

I told him the story you just read above. In the modern context, tell the civilians of Ukraine they are not in combat!

And so, it was with all my experiences in London. I prepared myself for the move with my two brothers, in July 1944, to an aunt's cottage twenty miles away in the village of Loudwater.

▲ ▲ ▲ ▲

CHAPTER TWO

A SAFE HOME – "Hello," Loudwater, Buckinghamshire

▲ ▲ ▲ ▲

LOUDWATER VILLAGE IN 1944 HAD a population of around 3000, and its major employer, Cossor's radio factory[14], was engaged in producing wartime communications systems. My father got a position there after we moved from London. We stayed in my step-mother's sister Annie's cottage on Station Road, which was situated on the corner of Station Road and the A40, the main road leading from the industrial and market town of High Wycombe to the City of London. Annie's home was a part of a larger two-story building containing several of these "cottages," as they were called.

This tiny cottage had a scullery/kitchen, and an adjoining front room, there were stairs leading from the kitchen to two upstairs bedrooms. Us three boys, my older brother Bob, step-brother Tom, and myself, occupied the back bedroom and my father and step-mother occupied a bedroom on the same floor. Aunt Annie had a makeshift bed in the downstairs front room.

---

[14] The story of A.C. Cossor Ltd. began in 1859 when the company was established by Alfred Charles Cossor in Clerkenwell, London to manufacture scientific glassware. His eldest son, also called Alfred Charles Cossor, joined the company in 1875, and it was he who founded the A.C. Cossor electronics company. The company's expertise in the manufacture of electrical glassware, such as early cathode ray tubes and X-ray tubes, led the company to diversify into electronics. https://en.wikipedia.org/wiki/A.C._Cossor

There was no electricity, and light came from gas lamps on the walls downstairs and candles upstairs. Cooking was by gas. There was no heating in the cottage and only a single fireplace in the front room. Coal, of course, being rationed, we didn't burn too much for heat.

We had enough food, but we would never become obese with the rationing and shortages during this period. I was as hungry in Loudwater as I was in London. I remember eating a lot of greens, which I didn't mind; in fact, my brothers would encourage me to eat theirs. The one luxury I distinctly remember was having my first egg, boiled, and sitting in an egg cup with the top lopped off. Dipping a piece of toast into the golden yellow yolk with a little pepper and salt, was the most wonderful and delicious thing I had ever tasted, except for a bread pudding, which I loved.

Because there were no indoor facilities, the entire community of several cottages had to share some drop-type lavatories further away in the backyard. There was no flushing water, but everything dropped into a large common drain below each seat. There were several seats each separated by a privacy door. A special truck came by each week or fortnight, I can't remember exactly, and pumped out the sewage into its big tank. The truck parked in the street with a large pipe snaking through the pathways to the cottages and into the lavatories. This generated a pretty awful smell in the entire neighborhood. I should mention, of course, that there was no toilet paper. We used a newspaper, torn into sheets which were stuck on a hooked metal spike. This was a standard practice even several years after the war.

We missed our house in London with its electricity, two flushing lavatories, and big rooms.

Dad used to say, "Never mind, it's for a short time, and we will get a house in High Wycombe soon."

I could not wait, but wait, we did. Meantime, I had to register for the local school, which I was not looking forward to at all. The school looked more like a church, and I remember the children in my class were of varying ages. My lack of academic capabilities was further exposed by my ignorance of anything the teacher was trying to instill in us. Whatever they had taught me in London had not permeated down to the rural county of Buckinghamshire, and thus the curriculum they presented me with seemed as foreign to me as the Sumerian alphabet was to modern man.

I survived the brief time we spent in Loudwater by keeping my wits about me and my head low in the classroom. My time in the playground proved well spent, and I made one or two friends. I had honed some pretty good playground skills in London, especially in fisticuffs, which became handy here. There were a few local yokels who thought this Cockney kid who talked funny needed to be tamed but soon found, to their chagrin, I was a little more than they had bargained for.

My popularity at school increased exponentially from zero to significant proportions when, after the summer holidays, school began and the word went out that I had seen an American plane crash. Other than detailing the grisly scene, I could not embellish my story with hard evidence of debris from the site. I showed them my shrapnel collection from the London bombings, which made a suitable impression.

We stayed in Loudwater through the Christmas holidays, and I enjoyed a children's party at the Cossors' factory, where a traditional pantomime took place with the usual comedic fun. Lots of cake, blancmange, trifle, mince pies, and a present or two handed out by Father Christmas, as they know Santa Claus in England.

Soon after Christmas, we moved to our new address at Cologne Villa, 93 Queens Road in High Wycombe. Yes, it's ironic that we should live in a house with the name of a German city[15] that the RAF was bombing into rubble and ruin at this moment in time.

---

[15] The RAF flew 262 bombing raids on Cologne, dropping 34,700 tons of explosives and killing 20,000 civilians. This was the first of the 1000 bomber raids on Germany. Source: wikipedia

Cologne Cathedral and surrounding area www.worldwarphotos.org

    In today's progressive world, we hear a lot about the British bombings of Dresden. I grew up under the typical English way of life of fair play, rules of cricket, and Marquis of Queensbury rules. However, if I walk down the street or in a dark alley and a thug comes out of the shadows and attacks me by surprise with a lethal weapon, all rules are out. My opponent just broke all the rules, and my life is in danger. I show no mercy. Many people forget Dresden was a major munitions center and a gateway to the East, which Russia wanted neutralized for their advance. That is war, and I hate it too, but survival means winning or dying. Remember too, Britain was alone for the early part of the war, and no one was coming down that alley to help. The fact the Americans came to help eventually is the main reason I am writing this book. It's showing my gratitude to them for turning up to face that tyranny, and to help defeat it.

▲ ▲ ▲ ▲

Life in High Wycombe

In 1945, High Wycombe had a population of 40,000. It was 25 miles from London and it became my new home. It was a market town, famous for its furniture factories. The area featured many beechwood forests, a highly prized wood for making chairs and other pieces of furniture. A unique characteristic of this part of Buckinghamshire was the chair bodger. He was an artisan who, skillfully, using time-honored techniques and dexterity in his tiny home workshop, used a hand lathe to turn out beautiful chair legs for the local factories. Famous names like Gomm, Ercol, Hands Furniture, and others.

Another feature of High Wycombe, but buried deep in underground bunkers of the surrounding hills, was the HQ of the U.S. Army Air Force Bomber Command. General Jimmy Doolittle was the Commander. The General had become famous for leading a formation of B-25 bombers to bomb Tokyo not long after Pearl Harbor. It was to show Japan they were not invincible. The base in High Wycombe was code-named Pinetree[16] and responsible for directing the bombing missions of the 8th U.S. Air Force over Germany and France.

This, of course, meant there were many 'Yanks' in and around the town who we could ask, "got any gum, chum?" Invariably, we got rewarded by our generous visitors with a stick of Wrigley's chewing gum. We would keep the precious wrapper as a convincing souvenir to show off to our mates at school.

In 1945, after the war when the WWII Bomber Command was closed and the 8th Air Force left for the United States, American personnel took some of the local women with them, as there had been many marriages during the war. This was much to the dismay of the local menfolk, who felt the Yanks were oversexed, overpaid and over here!

After the base was closed, the underground bunkers got sealed. The

---

[16] I write extensively about this period in my book Deathwatch Beetle: A Historical Post WWII Spy Thriller. https://deathwatchbeetle.net/

Abbey School, where the base was located, and its beautiful grounds were returned to the owners. This elite place of learning for girls resumed taking in boarders after the school reopened. Ironically, it was at this historic academy where my future wife Sophie had come from France with other French and Danish girls to work as a domestic help in 1954.

At this point, let me draw the curtain on my narrative and open a much later chapter of my life where the vivid images of the bomber crash got re-kindled by a chance, to form an irrevocable connection to the ghosts or souls of the plane's crew, their unknown relatives, and myself.

▲ ▲ ▲ ▲

CHAPTER THREE

A NEW LIFE IN THE USA
– Life in Dallas, Texas and then a Discovery

▲ ▲ ▲ ▲

Drawing aside the curtain of time as if it were a Jules Verne time traveler's episode, I bring this story to a different life and world. In those ensuing years, I grew up in High Wycombe and met and, in 1955, married a beautiful French girl by the name of Sophie.

Sophie was also a WWII survivor, having lived under German occupation in France. We had both known the hardships and difficulties of those times.

We had lived in Paris and London, and found post-war Europe stimulating to some extent but financially barren, and with limited prospects. People were leaving England by the thousands and heading to Canada, Australia, New Zealand, and other parts of the Commonwealth. We started a new life in Africa, Rhodesia initially, and then South Africa for a combined 21 years, where, eventually, we had grown our family to include four children. The USA was calling, where Sophie and I thought we could still fulfill our own destiny and our children could reach their individual potential. So, as Africa was becoming more unstable, we again boarded the 'ferry to the future' and arrived in Dallas, Texas, in October 1978, with four children and two cats. No, we would never leave our beloved cats behind!

As our time travel portal carried us forward at warp speed from 1978 to 2016, we had found ourselves with our four children, now married, spread across the country from Texas to Florida to California, and our clan expanded with the addition of seven grandchildren. I was semi-retired from business and had written my first book, a post WWII historical spy thriller.

Pleased with the success of this first attempt at historical fiction about the search for a missing prominent Nazi war criminal, I was researching for my next project when I came across the website of the 398th Bombardment Group Memorial Association of the US Army 8th Air Force, 1st Air Division. As I was browsing through the site, the familiar name of Penn caught my eye.

Penn was the village just above Loudwater in England. On closer scrutiny, the article was referring to a B-17 American bomber that crashed in this Buckinghamshire village in the UK during the Second World War.

As I continued to read the account, it quickly dawned on me that this was, in fact, the very aircraft I had witnessed as a child. The article referred to the plane by its nickname, The Tomahawk Warrior[17], and the date of the crash was **August 12, 1944**. Coincidentally, that day was **August 12, 2016**, **exactly seventy-two years** since the incident had occurred. I thought this was rather strange, but little did I realize that many more coincidences would arise, which I would find ever more mystifying.

I felt the information I was reading on the 398th.org website, together with a few supporting words of mine, would make an interesting anecdote on my current book's website. I told Sophie about my find because she and I used to talk about our respective experiences during the war. Sophie thought it interesting that I had discovered the actual story of the plane and the area of the crash.

I thought this would be an opportune time to let my children know

---

[17] This was the nickname of the plane which I am repeating here.

that here was a personal example of why we should be grateful to the Americans and Allies for the sacrifice they made for us in WWII. I posted the following Open Letter on my website addressed to my children. The content and my description of the event were based on the version that I had read from the 398th Bombardment Group Memorial Association website, (398th BGMA) together with errors of fact, which I discovered later.

(Huntley, 2016) A NOTE TO MY CHILDREN AND GRANDCHILDREN

It would probably surprise you if I said that a 30 to 40-second sliver of time and distance separates you all from what you are today, to nothing at all, to a non-existence, to not even be a thought in someone's mind. A little dramatic perhaps, but true. Let me explain. I have in the past mentioned to you that as a small boy; I had just been through the blitz in London and later the V1, and finally, the V2s were coming in when we left the city and came to live temporarily at my aunt's cottage in the village of Loudwater. This was a small village near the larger town of High Wycombe, Buckinghamshire.

Early one morning, just as it was getting light, a plane roared overhead, flying extremely low with its engines spluttering, and in less than a minute, a massive explosion rocked the building and the total area. My brother Bob and stepbrother Tom said there was a plane crash, and we should all get up out of bed and go to investigate. We ran up the hill of Derehams Lane toward where the crash occurred, and it was there that I saw the remains of a plane, virtually unrecognizable as a plane at all. There were people running around with galvanized metal tubs, picking up bloody body parts, and I recall parachute silk being used to cover bodies or remains. As an almost nine-year-old, it made a deep impression on me. My brothers were trying to shield me from the gruesome scene, although I had seen plenty of wartime in London. I was asking how could the airmen have been using parachutes? Obviously, the plane had been too low for the crew to bail out. I now have the answer to that question. The chutes were now shrouds!

It was an amazing coincidence that I should stumble on the written history of the plane crash on exactly the **72nd** anniversary of the event. Although it is seventy-two years later, the story validated it was the plane I saw that fateful morning. It read, 'A B-17 bomber of the USAAF 398th Bomb Group nicknamed Tomahawk Warrior, took off from Nuthampstead for their bombing mission, when two of the four engines caught fire. This caused them to crash at Lude Farm in Penn just above Loudwater.'

(Author's Note: My later research[18] and investigation showed this statement about engine fires to have been possibly mistaken, or at least unconfirmed)

When you read the 398th BGMA account of the flight that I have attached below, you learn that the pilot, Charles Searl, tried to avoid crashing his plane in a populated area. My research, observation, and my knowledge of the area showed that he could not crash-land in the large meadows near our cottages because, like many other large open spaces, they were covered in massive concrete pillars to prevent German invaders from using gliders to land troops. Lt. Searl saw the farmland and flew right over our cottage to get to Lude Farm, which was 1.5 miles from where we were staying. At the speed the plane was flying, probably around 150 miles per hour, it seemed to have been approximately forty seconds later it hit the ground.

The effect of this planeload of bombs exploding on impact was, of course, far greater than any single bomb I had experienced in London. I heard the noise and felt the blast for miles around. Had that plane not made it to the open farmland and had dropped on us in Loudwater, it would have killed many people, including ourselves.

So, we should all be thankful that America came to the rescue of Europe in WWII. For our family, in particular, we remember that Lt. Charles

---

[18] Records and a final witness filmed interview indicate there was no fire.

Searl and his crew bravely diverted his plane that morning so that we could enjoy the fruits of freedom from an oppressive government had the Nazis prevailed. I had written my first book and dedicated it to WWII veterans long before I came across the record about this plane. Maybe it is part of my quest to thank those who served in helping to save Europe from tyranny.

Your father – August 15, 2016 (End of citation)

I felt the information which I had published on my website, should include an extract from the 398th BGMA, which carries the story of Ron Setter, who was the son of the resident farmer at Lude Farm and was at the scene of the crash. He made certain statements which he could not have known at that time were in error. The following is a citation courtesy of the 398th BGMA, with footnote corrections by the author based on official archival sources.

Citation (398th Bomb Group Memorial Association, n.d.)
"TOMAHAWK WARRIOR", A TRIBUTE TO CHARLES J. SEARL AND CREW BY RONALD (RON) M. SETTER

Saturday, 12 August 1944 – a B-17 bomber named the Tomahawk Warrior and nine young men came into the history of Penn forever. Many years have gone by – some elders of Penn who remembered that day have passed away and a new generation born. They can only read of the sacrifice made by the Tomahawk Warrior and her crew. The nine young men who flew that morning died long before their time on their twenty-fifth mission[19]. Only a few more to fly and they would have been going home to loved ones and a full and happy life ahead.

This is their story. The 398th Bomb Group was one of the last to arrive in England during March of 1944. They flew their B-17's from

---

[19] According to the declassified Secret Operational Records in the author's possession, this fatal flight was the crew's 30th mission but only 28 were fully accredited.

Newfoundland to England to the allotted aerodrome of Nuthampstead near Royston in Herts where the countryside was very similar to that which surrounds Penn. To one crew their B-17 was special to them and as was usual the Pilot, Charles Searl named it the Tomahawk Warrior after the small town where he lived. There was a crew of ten to fly her and a skilled ground crew to care for her.

The first mission[20] was to Berlin on the 19th of May.

They returned safely and one can only feel that they were relieved and jubilant. Charles Searl was married with a daughter of eighteen months and he and his wife were expecting another addition to the family in July. He was 23 and had enlisted in the Air Force soon after Pearl Harbor. As far as records show, none of the other nine crew members were married and their ages ranged[21] from 20 to 27.

They had come from many states across the USA. Wisconsin, Massachusetts, Michigan, Washington, D.C., Arkansas, Virginia, Ohio, and New York.

The Tomahawk Warrior flew many missions, including one on D-Day, to targets at Caen and Courseulles, France. Missions were interposed with leave which one supposes they spent in London. Their evenings would be spent at the local Inn just on the edge of the airfield and at Royston, the nearest small town. Entertainment would have been laid on at the base along with dances and there must have been invitations from the local population.

---

[20] The first mission was on May 7th to Berlin. Lt. Kempner mistakenly entered May 8th in his diary as their first mission. May 8th was, in fact, their second mission to bomb Berlin. May 7th was not credited because of mechanical problems and it returned to base.

[21] Their ages, according to the personnel records in this author's possession, were from 20 to 26 years of age, with Lt. Dion the eldest.

(Photo courtesy of the 398th BGMA)

Searl's Crew – 600th Squadron – Early 1944
Back Row (viewer's left to right)
2nd Lt. Leo C. Walsh, Bombardier;
2nd Lt. Albert L. Dion, co-Pilot;
2nd Lt. Charles J. Searl, pilot;
2nd Lt. Saul J. Kempner, navigator

Front Row (viewer's left to right)
Sgt. Orville M. Wilson, waist gunner;
S/Sgt. James A. Beaty, engineer;
Sgt. Alfred Bueffel, ball turret;
Sgt. Albert W. Knight, waist gunner;
Sgt. Cecil E. Kennedy, radio;
Sgt. F.A. Snyder, tail gunner
(Snyder was not on the fateful mission)[22]

---

[22] A 6-7-1990 report in the Bucks Free Press local newspaper said he had a dental appointment that day. The paper gave no source for that statement. I was not able to find any official sick leave reports.

Continuing the narrative of Ron Setter (citation)

The crew of nine took off at 0618. The formation was hazardous with the bad weather as the plane climbed to reach height. By 0700 the Tomahawk Warrior[23] was heading out Southeast and already in trouble. One engine was seen to be on fire,[24] and as it turned over the town of High Wycombe to return to base, a second engine[25] was seen also on fire. Below in the town was the HQ of the 8th Air Force and most likely monitoring the mission.

It has always been accepted that the pilot was trying to find open ground to attempt a landing when he had no chance of reaching his base or even Bovington airfield which was only ten miles away to the North. He would have seen the populated area he was flying over and realized the devastation the plane would cause if it crashed there. It skimmed over the farmhouse of Lude Farm and crashed into open fields opposite.

Tomahawk Warrior and its crew of nine young men ended life in a massive explosion and fire. No one had bailed out of the stricken plane and no distress signal was ever traced. They stayed together, comrades now for all eternity. One of the crew was found in the lane and two at the edge of the fields. The rest were identified by their dog tags. A short entry in official records at their base read, 'Takeoff 0618 hours, 0720 no return'. Such a short epitaph.

No investigation took place as to the reason for the crash. It was just one more casualty of war. General Doolittle, who was at the HQ in High

---

[23] It will be noted in later pages that this aircraft was not the Tomahawk Warrior, and it was a different plane the crew flew that day.

[24] No reference is given as to who formally witnessed an engine fire. In fact, Mr. Len Howard, who had spotted the plane in trouble seconds before it crashed, said in a 2013 video interview that there was no fire from the engines. He saw it plunge toward the ground and heard it explode, but he did not proceed to the crash site. In a later personal interview Mr Howard reiterated that comment. Len Howard Interview B-17 crash (2018_12_02 15_57_36 UTC) 398th Bomb Group Memorial Association.

[25] William Setter, the father of Ron Setter, in a much earlier publication, The Flak News by the 398th Bomb Group Association, is reported to have said, "the engines were on fire and smoking."

Wycombe, visited the scene of the crash later in the day. The field where the Tomahawk Warrior crashed is the same today as it was (fifty-seven years)[26] ago. Beautiful, peaceful, and the seasons come and go. It is an everlasting memorial to duty and sacrifice. They that died need no other.

The following are the names of those who died that morning:

Pilot: Charles J. Searl, Wisconsin Co-Pilot: Albert L. Dion, Massachusetts Navigator: Saul J. Kempner, Michigan Bombardier: Leo C. Walsh, Washington, D.C. Radio/Gunner: Cecil E. Kennedy, Virginia Eng / TT Gunner: James A. Beaty, Arkansas Ball Turret Gunner: Alfred Bueffel, New York Right Waist Gunner: Albert W. Knight, Ohio Tail Gunner: Orville M. Wilson, Washington, D.C.

Credit: Arlington National Cemetery   *Knight's grave, Cambridge, UK*

They were all buried in Cambridge Cemetery, but after the war, in accordance with the wishes of their relatives, eight of them were re-interred in Arlington Cemetery, America. They sleep amongst the highly honored in America. The Chiltern Aircraft Research Group honors the one who was left behind, Albert Knight yearly on the anniversary of the crash with flowers and thoughts of the eight lying in their home country.

Each Armistice Day, the Holy Trinity Church in the village of Penn,

---

[26] Seventy-eight years at the time of writing this book.

remembers them in a service and reads their names out along with others from the village who gave their lives in wars. Small American Flags are placed along the path by the church door, each with the name of the Tomahawk Warrior's crew, and usually the Battle Hymn of the Republic is sung in honor. The Book of Remembrance in Penn Church has their names inscribed in glorious memory. To all who read this tribute, remember... they gave their lives just as bravely and in sacrifice for peace, just as those who were lost on and over the battlefields of Europe. (**End of citation**)

1st Lt. Charles Searl
(Photo Courtesy of Searl's daughter Mrs Cheryl Surfus)

(Photo & ensuing comment courtesy of the 398th BGMA)

Walsh standing and Searl:
1. Lt. Leo C. Walsh, Bombardier (Searl crew)
Seated: 1. Lt. Charles J. Searl, Pilot

Notes: 1. Photo contributed by: George E. Schatz, Elwood Crew Bombardier.
2. Written by George in 1944 on the back of his original photo: "Three days after our Elwood crew completed our combat tour (August 8, 1944) We played ball with Charlie and Leo. The next day they were dead!"

Following the detailed information above, I included the map showing how my brothers and I had scrambled to get to the crash site, which turned out to be Lude Farm.

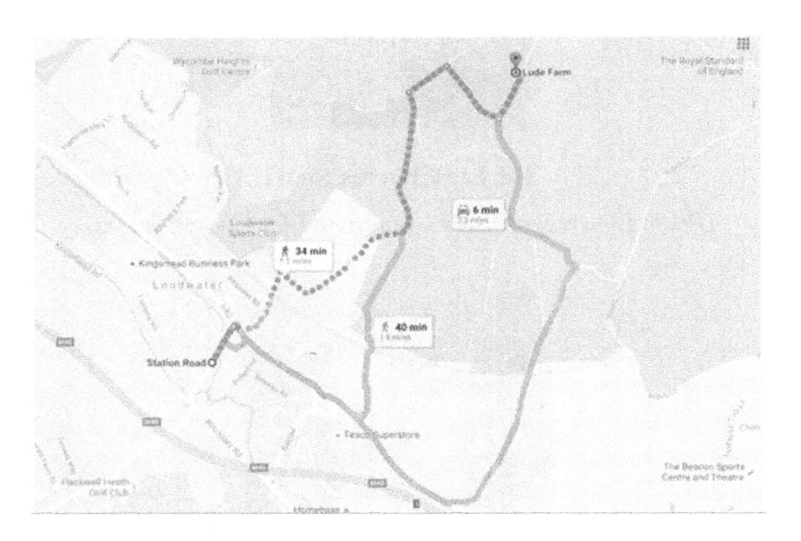

The route[27] that my brothers and I ran from the cottages on Station Road to the Lude Farm crash site. Credit Google Maps.

---

[27] Of course the map here is of modern times. There would have been no Motorway M4 and no built up area around our cottage. Only meadows.

The B-17 Tomahawk Warrior: A WWII Final Honor

These were the cottages we stayed in after leaving London. Ours was the one with the black door. (Copyright Huntley Associates, Inc. photo)

Old Forge Road, which ran parallel to the cottages on the opposite side of Station Road, had a blacksmith and his forge. I liked to stand and watch the blacksmith shoeing horses. Every day, he was busy making things in his fiery work area. He created a lot of clanging noises and produced huge sparks as he hammered the iron into shape. I mention this because beyond the Old Forge Road, there were only meadows and the meandering River Wye.

These were the meadows, which I had described in my "Note to my Children." There were a significant number of concrete pillars which had been installed by the government to prevent German troop gliders from landing during any attempted invasion. I am convinced therefore that Lt. Charles Searl directed his plane to the open fields of Lude Farm near the village of Penn, about a mile away, as he could not make a forced landing on the meadows in Loudwater because of these obstacles[28]. No one has mentioned this aspect in any other report, and it provides additional support to the evidence of Lt.. Searl's effort to save lives in both villages.

Since the pilot's actions had saved my life and many others in the village, as well as of my future family, I felt I owed him and his crew some effort to get recognition for their sacrifice. (See chapter 12.)

---

[28] See Chapter 12 for an explanation of British defenses against German invasion.

My discovery about the Tomahawk Warrior in 2016 was indeed fascinating, and for me that year, on a personal level, was eventful and full of joy. However, there were very different and painful times to come.

The year of 2017 began with shocking news that my lovely wife Sophie was diagnosed with cancer that we both found hard to accept. She had been through so much in the last ten to twelve years with a significant number of medical conditions. I was a dedicated caregiver, providing Sophie with the moral and physical support to keep her motivated and deeply loved.

Neither of us could imagine the battle she would face in the coming months, as this beautiful life was rapidly drained out of her. Sophie passed away on February 15, 2018, and life changed forever.

▲ ▲ ▲ ▲

CHAPTER FOUR
DISCOVERIES – Introducing Martin Ginther

▲ ▲ ▲ ▲

IT WAS IN SEPTEMBER 2018, while I was still trying to cope with the loss of my wife Sophie, when I received a voice message on my phone by someone named Martin Ginther from Beverly, Ohio. Mr. Ginther, said that he had been searching on the Internet for information about the Tomahawk Warrior. He also mentioned that he had a remarkable story to tell me. It was after I called him back, that the Tomahawk Warrior tragedy took on a life of its own.

Martin's father, Ed Ginther, had been in the US Army Air Corps 325 Complementary Squadron assigned to the 398th Bombardment Group at Nuthampstead, in England. This was the base from which the Tomahawk Warrior crew of the 600th Squadron flew all their missions including their last and fatal one.

According to Martin, his father had found an unidentified diary in a trash bin soon after the belongings of the deceased crew got collected and recorded by the attending officer. Ed brought the diary with him back to the USA when he left the USAAC. It had lain forgotten among his old papers. While rummaging through them in 2013, almost 70 years later, Ed came across the forgotten diary and he showed it to his son, Martin, saying, "Did I ever show you this diary? I had buried it in my old archives for years."

Martin was astounded when he saw that the navigator of a plane nicknamed "Tomahawk Warrior" had written it describing each of the planes' bombing missions from May 8th to August 6th 1944. He also pasted newspaper cuttings related to those same targets for each day. Martin immediately told his dad, "We should find a home for this amazing piece of history."

They set about trying to make a copy. In fact, they made twelve copies. These were simply crude xerox copies, which were not excellent reproductions. However, they wanted to find a suitable home for the diary. They approached the 8th Air Force Museum in Savannah, GA, and several other entities but received no firm interest.

Martin tried to locate any living relatives of Lt. Saul Kempner, the diary's author, without success, and so, it remained at the Ginther residence. Without using the Freedom of Information Act (FOIA) to gain information from the Army of that period, it was virtually impossible to find anything which would lead them to any living relatives. It was in 2018 when Martin stumbled upon my website, where I had a section telling the story of the Tomahawk Warrior from my perspective as a living witness of the event back in 1944.

In September and again in October 2018, Martin Ginther telephoned me, or I should say, he left a couple of messages on my voice mail. He said it was a matter of importance that we should talk. In fact, he mentioned that a member of the deceased crew had left a diary behind, and his father had this item in his possession.

Of course, recognizing its significance, I returned Martin's call immediately. Upon hearing his description of the diary and how it came into his father's possession, it became of even greater interest to me as I had been so intimately involved with this incident as a child. When I asked if I could get a copy, Martin said they had made twelve copies of them. They had distributed these among various groups who they thought may have an interest, including a local newspaper in Ohio. Unfortunately, there were no further copies available, but he would send one to me if one turned up. I made no further comment, because without the actual diary, I'd have nothing to compliment the story with on my website.

In late January 2019, I received a large parcel in the mail with Martin Ginther's name on the return address. It contained a copy of the 2nd Lt. Saul Kempner's diary. Upon examination, it became obvious this was of great historical value. Not only did Kempner describe each of their bombing missions, he had carefully culled corresponding news items from published sources of the time, which described a broader view of those same targets. My connection to the crash of the Tomahawk Warrior, compelled me to write a book about the event.

In my next telephone discussion with Martin, I asked if his father would consider allowing me to have publishing rights in return for giving him full acknowledgment of his connection to the diary and its origin? He said he would ask his dad and get back to me. Martin also mentioned that he and his father had attempted to locate the family or relatives of the late Lt. Kempner, but had been unsuccessful. When I inquired if he thought his father would return the diary to surviving relatives if I located them, Martin felt strongly he would agree. The Ginthers' acknowledged that the diary should be returned to the family if possible.

I spoke with the Ed Ginther on the telephone a few weeks later. He was willing, in principle, to allow me to have exclusive rights to publish the diary, but would confirm it when we meet in person. I agreed to draw up a written contract and bring it with me for the meeting at his home in Beverly, Ohio, on March 2, 2019.

▲ ▲ ▲ ▲

The First Connection to a Relative of the Crew

It was in August 2018, six months after my wife Sophie had passed away, and I had just finished reading a book by a well-known author by the name of Ellie Midwood, a historical fiction depicting wartime in France, and it was powerful and beautifully written. I felt bound to accept her invitation at the end of the book for her readers to write to her. From this small beginning and later, when she had read my book of historical fiction,

"Deathwatch Beetle: A Post WWII Historical Spy Thriller," Ellie invited me to join her Facebook Group.

It was on that Facebook group that I posted an extract from the story of the Tomahawk Warrior from my website, and it drew a lot of interest from my fellow authors and others. It became even more interesting in December 2018, when a young lady, Shelly Surfus Loe, contacted me and said that the pilot, Lt. Charles Searl, was her grandfather. After messaging each other, I contacted her mother, Mrs. Cheryl Surfus of Weston, Wisconsin.

Cheryl is the second daughter of Lt. Charles Searl and his wife Arlie. Both Arlie, and his first daughter, Charlene, were deceased. The first conversation I had with Cheryl was very emotional. For the first time in almost seventy-five years, Cheryl was talking with someone who had been at the site of her father's demise, on that foreign field so many thousands of miles from home. As I described the horrific scene of what I saw that day, I found it very difficult to hold . . . my own emotions in check. I thought of the torn and broken bodies I had witnessed. Knowing that her father had given his life in such a violent way, I imagined what this must mean to Cheryl. I realized, too, that I was simply a chosen messenger of sorts as an ethereal connection from the soul of Searl to his living daughter, and bringing his spirit home to her for safekeeping.

Cheryl told me that she felt a stronger connection with her father. She had never known him, and he had never known her because she was born one month before her father died. So, my link between them must have helped merge their familial relationship. Cheryl has since made it clear frequently that she considered me to be a part of the Searl family. And, of course, I am indeed gratified and honored.

After that telephone conversation, Cheryl had sent me several e-mails together with artifacts and memorabilia to help me to draw a picture of her father's character and personality. An extract of one of her e-mails reads:

The B-17 Tomahawk Warrior: A WWII Final Honor

11/29/2018.

"It's amazing to be in contact with someone who has firsthand information about the crash. I am so sorry . . . you had to experience something so horrific at such a young age. My father was an amazing young man, and I wish he could have survived the war."

"But he definitely didn't die in vain. He loved his country. I will send you more information about my father. I so appreciate that you will sign and send copies of your current book to my two daughters."

Thank you, Cheryl

I replied;

"Dear Cheryl, I was the guest speaker at a veterans' group in Fort Worth, Texas, on Pearl Harbor Day and I gave a full PowerPoint presentation of my current book. It touches on the story of the Tomahawk Warrior. At that point in the presentation, I mentioned I had just received a call while I was in San Diego last week from a lady in Wisconsin. When I told the audience without mentioning your name, you were the daughter of the pilot, Lt. Charles Searl, the 400 people in the crowd, most of whom were veterans, audibly gasped in astonishment. It truly is an amazing story, Cheryl, and I am so happy to have connected with you and your family. Let's hope your daughters like the book I gave them as well as the inscription. While looking forward to receiving any additional information about your father, based on my observation and description of events so far, your dad should receive a medal for avoiding our village like he did. This deserves an investigation."

David

One interesting item and one, which Cheryl had given me a permission to publish on my website, was a letter[29] that Charles wrote to his wife, Arlie, that strikes a chord in whoever reads it.

Cheryl's e-mail refers to the letter;

"You have my permission to post Dad's letter. It is amazing to find someone who lived in the village where my father crashed. I have shared your story and our connection with many friends. I look forward to hearing more about you and your own family."

Cheryl.

I don't know the date Charles wrote the letter. It must have been close to the time when he felt a premonition he was not coming back home. And maybe it was on that field that he had passed his soul to the little boy staring wide eyed at the devastation in front of him. Could it be that Charles had guided me through the next seventy-seven years of my life to help bring a peaceful closure to his daughter and future grandchildren, who were never to see him?

In the meantime, I had set in motion an effort to determine if it was possible to get a posthumous bravery award for Searl and his crew by appealing to the current Senator in Searls' home State of Wisconsin.

During this period, I had many conversations and e-mail exchanges with Cheryl including plans to visit her in Wisconsin.

---

[29] The letter is reproduced in Chapter 7 about 1st Lt. Charles J. Searl.

1st Lt. Charles Searl – photo courtesy of Cheryl Surfus.

There were several more electronic communications between myself and Cheryl, which provided her with more detailed information about her father. Some was new to her. The following e-mails and telephone conversations helped pave the way for me to meet her in Wisconsin personally, and to interview her.

"Hi Cheryl, I hope you have received the copy of the communication I sent to Senator Ron Johnson. His office called me to elaborate on the procedure for obtaining a posthumous honor, and I am now trying to fill out the required forms.

Do you know the name of your dad's commanding officer or any other senior officers in his 600th Squadron? Of course, there is no one who can sign the citation which I am drawing up but I can at least, specify their name as deceased.

By the way, will you remember the strange coincidences I have mentioned regarding the Tomahawk Warrior? Well, here are two more.

*Your father's birthday is the **18th of March**, 1921. My twin sons were born on the **18th March**.*

"Dear Cheryl, as you may remember, I have been dealing with the son of the owner of the diary and today, I spoke to the father. He is 92 years old, and he

cleared the perished crew's lockers. We got on well and I am drawing up a contractual agreement for him to review. If he likes what he sees and agrees, in principle, I will fly to Ohio to complete the matter. Of course, I have promised I will tell his story and get some family background from him to include in the general narrative of my book. I will try to get him to draw on his memory about Lt. Searl's locker as well. Don't faint, Cheryl, guess what his birthday is? **18th of March!** Something has made me do this. Sincerely, David."

"Cheryl replied:

David, that is incredible. This has been an amazing time for me, as well as you. Thank you again, keep in touch. Cheryl"

A further e-mail from me

"Hi Cheryl, the various unofficial reports show your dad was on his 25th mission when he went down. Well, I now have the diary of Saul Kempner, the navigator, and his last entry was a successful twenty-seventh mission over Germany on the 6th of August 1944. I have attached a copy of the page for that mission and my transcription of his handwritten entry."

"This will show you what your dad and his crew went through. So, his last mission was, in fact, the twenty-eighth that they went down. The diary gives a description of all twenty-seven missions.[30] David."

A heartfelt reply from Cheryl:

"Hi David, you have had me in tears again today, but not sad tears, just emotional ones. Looking forward to talking to you soon. Cheryl"

---

[30] After a full analysis of the Operational Records, I have determined there were a total of 30 missions undertaken but two not credited. The first one on May 7th due to Mechanical failure, and the last one on August 12th which crashed.

A further e-mail from Cheryl:

> "David, I was just able to open the file with the copy of the diary page. Oh my gosh, this is amazing. It is like history being rewritten. It is sad that there isn't anyone alive who knows my dad. I am going to contact one of my old neighbors from Tomahawk, who is very involved with the chamber. They may know where I can find some contacts with relatives who knew him. I am keen to read the rest of the diary. Again, all I can say is thank you. Cheryl."
>
> "Dear Cheryl, I will more than likely attend a Memorial Service that the Penn village puts on this year, 2019: If I go, may I let them know at the time that I shall represent you and your family? Perhaps I could read a letter from you at the service? I will meet the owner of the diary in Ohio. He has agreed in principle to sign an agreement for me to have exclusive publishing rights to incorporate the diary in my book. Kind Regards, David."

As I prepared to visit Martin Ginther and his father Ed, I kept in touch with Cheryl on my various plans. She was looking forward to when I could get to meet her in Wisconsin.

2/8/2019

> "David, very nice to hear from you. I opened the attachment and very much enjoyed the pictures. I will send pictures of my family soon. Have been experiencing miserable weather the past few days. Freezing and now, a lot of snow. Hopefully, we will have a pleasant spring and warm summer. I am very much looking forward to meeting you."
>
> "I would love to have you represent me at the memorial service. I would also hope you would share with them what you have shared with me. I will stay in touch. Cheryl."

3/14/2019
Subject: Proposed Visit

"Dear Cheryl, I am working with the Kempner's regarding my proposed visit to Detroit. I could do so during the period of April 15th to the 29th. I would need one or two days to spend with them to get as much information as they would want me to have. In the meantime, I will compile a list of questions that might be helpful to me in telling their family's story as it relates to Saul Kempner. I will also do the same for you. I would like to combine any travel to Detroit with a connecting visit to Wisconsin. I have asked them to let me know as soon as possible because, if I am to travel in April, I need to know soon to facilitate the travel planning. If these dates are not suitable, we can leave it until I get back from Normandy in June, July or August. I would hope the snow will be finished by April. David."

A positive response from Cheryl:

3/23/2019
"Subject: Re: Proposed visit

Those dates in April sound fine. It is obvious you are very busy, but that keeps us young. Have a great day. Cheryl."

▲ ▲ ▲ ▲

Meeting Mr. Ed Ginther, Sr.

It was an overcast day when I took off from Dallas/Fort Worth International Airport on the afternoon of March 1st, 2019. This flight to Detroit was the first leg of my journey to Ohio, where I was to meet Ed Ginther, the WWII veteran of the U.S. Army Air Corps. Arriving in Detroit the walk between gates for my connection the airport in Columbus, Ohio was not too long, although my 83-year-old legs were less responsive than a few years ago.

On arriving in Columbus, I made a phone contact with Martin, one of Ed Ginther's nine children. He had arranged to pick me up after work. I made my way to the curbside where I found him and introduced myself.

Martin was tall and slim and looked younger than his given age of sixty years. As a highly skilled motor mechanic, he works long hours to help keep the United States Post Office fleet of vehicles in Columbus viable with minimal breakdowns.

The ride to Marietta from Columbus was, of course, full of animated conversation. We discussed the story of the Tomahawk Warrior and its crew. It unfolded as if peeling away the many years of mystery regarding the war-time crash. We were both excited to be engaged in this process of discovery of the enigma of the Tomahawk Warrior. Each of us connected by our own unique relationship to it.

The advent and discovery of the diary had changed my attitude to this 1944 incident, from just a shocking interlude in my life, to something of much greater significance. By tracing the relatives of the navigator, 2nd Lt. Saul Kempner,[31] the author of the diary, the matter had become more than simply a posting on my web page, or other social media. It was now something of historical significance. In fact, it was a story that needed telling partly from my personal connection to it, but also to help certain descendants get some additional closure over the manner in which their relatives met their end. Having tracked down two nieces of the navigator, Janice Morgan, and Andrea Blake, prior to my meeting with Mr. Ginther Sr., it made the subject of returning the diary to the Kempner family, even more relevant than before.

It amazed Martin that I had traced the Kempners and we agreed we should bring it to his father's attention for a future return of the diary to the family.

---

[31] Re. Chapter 6 search for the Kempner family

He was amazed too, that the pilot, 1st Lt. Charles Searl, had flown his crippled craft over my cottage and over the complete village before crashing in a farm field a mile and a half away. It made the story even more dramatic. The results would have been catastrophic if he hadn't done it. I have also told Martin that I had already set in motion on January 6th 2019,[32] my personal effort to get a posthumous award for Searl and his crew for the sacrifice they made that day.

As we drove toward Marietta, the sky was a dull gray with high cloud cover and it was cold. Martin said that they had had snow falling the previous week. I could see pockets of it scattered where small amounts had accumulated here and there as we sped by.

Martin told me his dad was not in the best of health and needed oxygen help, but was otherwise sturdy and had good faculties. I told Martin that I was looking forward to speaking with his mom and dad the following day. After the two-hour drive, we arrived in Marietta, OH, where I had booked a BnB for the weekend. It was a double story with wood sidings and composite roof, with some remnants of last week's snowfall still visible. There were tall trees on the one side of the house, whose branches were still bare. These bare limbs would soon seek the spring sunshine to encourage the rebirth of leaves. For me, that was going to be a few weeks off yet. I felt the chill in the air when stepping out of the car and exploring the front door that had been left open for my late arrival.

Martin assisted me with my case inside to the kitchen area. We arranged for him to pick me up the next morning around 10:30 am to take me over to his parents' house. I bade him goodnight and carried my luggage up the stairs to my designated bedroom.

It froze that night, and I could not find extra blankets or a duvet. The next morning, I spoke with the host, who provided me with extra bedding for the following night.

---

[32] Ref; Chapter 12 Initial effort to obtain recognition for the Tomahawk Warrior crew.

Martin arrived after I had breakfasted on some cereal and a cup of tea. The morning was crisp but continued to be overcast and we set out for the 30-minute drive to the small village of Beverly, population 1,313. This was where Mr. Ginther senior lived with his wife Alma and their 28-year-old grandson, Jonathan Ginther. The countryside was bleak in the greyness of winter, with bare-limbed trees reaching upward as if seeking any glimmer of sun that may have broken through the cloud layer above us.

On the way to his dad's house, I mentioned to Martin that I had spoken to Janice Morgan, one of Saul Kempner's nieces in Detroit the previous night, and she had told me she might try to drive down to meet with us. It would depend on the weather as it had forecast snowfall.

We turned down a side road which led to the Ginther property. Ed and Alma Ginther's house was set back from the road in a wooded clearing on about two acres of land. It looked picturesque even in the gloom of this wintry day. One could imagine the same scene in the spring or summer months when the maple trees had filled out their complete foliage, casting sunlight and shadows in all directions. There were also several very tall pine trees, which Martin told me were trees from previous Christmas celebrations, and planted outside after the festivities had ended each year.

Martin parked the car near to a barn situated away from the house by about 100 ft. As we neared the door to what appeared to be a covered porch or extension to the house, a dog began announcing our arrival with some important barking. Upon entering, the dog, a pit bull named Myah, could not decide if he was excited to see Martin and me or more intent on getting outside to explore. Martin kept him in check while I closed the screen door.

After suitable canine introductions, Martin led me into the kitchen and further into the living room where I met Ed Ginther and his wife Alma, both of whom were sitting in their respective recliners. Ed Ginther prepared to stand up. I attempted to advise him it was unnecessary, and that he should continue sitting, but he was having none of that, and got to his feet together with his oxygen lines attached.

Ed and I shook hands, and although I stood tall above him, I could tell he had been a much bigger man earlier in life and certainly his handshake was strong, beguiling his current frail stature. At ninety-two, Ed still had his faculties in good order, and his conversation with me, interspersed with humorous anecdotes, was very engaging. We enjoyed each other's company, and his wife Alma sat contentedly in her recliner with a smile, while Ed re-counted his days in wartime England. Alma, Martin informed me earlier, had suffered a few minor strokes and, whilst she was quite cognizant of our conversations, she made few comments of her own.

Ed's birthday, the **18th of March**, was the same day as Charles Searl's, the pilot of the Tomahawk Warrior. Was it an omen or coincidence that it was the same date as my own twin sons? Life is strange indeed.

I was eager to discover how Ed had come into possession of the navigator's diary. Also, whether he had made a contact with any of the Tomahawk Warrior crew. Our conversation flowed back and forth about England and of Ed's time there during the war. He talked of the nice people he had met. Especially those who he would spend time with in London, when he was on leave to go from the airfield at Nuthampstead.

Ed had originally registered for Service on his birthday, March 18, 1943. (***Again, that March 18!***) He was called up eventually for basic training then transferred to Camp Kilmer in New Jersey. After his basic training he boarded the "Louis Pasteur"[33], a French ship being used as a troop carrier. The ship headed out of New York harbor and sailed to England while evading German U- boats.

And how stunning it is that Ed celebrated his 19th birthday on the ship, on **March 18, 1944.**

---

[33] This vessel had transported the French gold reserves to Canada at the beginning of hostilities.

The ship troop carrier that took Ed Ginther to Europe without a convoy

Photo By Marius Bar – carte postale, Public Domain, https://commons.wikimedia.org/w/index.php?curid=12339995

They arrived in Liverpool, England on March 22, 1944. After spending a few uneventful weeks there, they posted Ed to the Air Force station #131 at Nuthampstead in Hertfordshire on April 17th, which was the home of the 398th Bomb Group. Ed volunteered for the anti-aircraft gunnery training and was sent to a gunnery school in Ireland on May 18th. He began his training on 50 caliber anti-aircraft gun. On June 3rd, he became formerly attached to the 305 Complimentary Squadron and returned to Nuthampstead to begin his duties.

During my discussion with Ed, he had produced some photographs and some handwritten notes. It was only when I returned home to Dallas, did I decipher his notes and found that as a part of his duties in the 305th Squadron, he was to accompany mechanics and technicians on check flights, after the planes damaged during the bombing missions were repaired.

The first of these B-17 check flights was on July 14, 1944 and the pilot was Lt. Brown (the official records in my possession show that it was probably Capt Brown), but I could not identify which aircraft it was.

The second flight was on July 18, 1944, with Lt. Alhadeff in a B-17 serial #42-102599. I believe Ed either got this date wrong, or the serial # was wrong because according to the official records, this plane was MIA (missing in action) on July 16, 1944 piloted by Lt. Lovelace. 2 KIA (killed in action) and 7 taken POW (Prisoners of war)

Later I had found, that the third check flight that Ed had joined, he flew with **Lt. Searl** as the pilot on August 3, 1944. As I have pointed out elsewhere in this book, it was the plane the crew regularly flew as the Tomahawk Warrior, serial #42-102507. Searl was checking this plane as he was being assigned this ship for the August 6th mission to Berlin and which ultimately received heavy flak damage that day. This had a significance to what happened on their next mission on August 12, 1944.

By telephone later that month after I discovered this information in my interview material, I asked Ed, if he could recollect anything about that check flight or anything personal about Charles Searl. I also asked him if he could see any nose art on the front of the plane that identified it as the Tomahawk Warrior. Unfortunately, at nine-two, Ed's memory was clear on certain things in his life, and less on others.

Ed signed my contract, allowing me to publish the diary in my future book. He also agreed that I could assure the Kempner family the diary would go back to them at a future mutually determined date.

Ed Ginther in Dress Uniform and in work overalls

Ed and Alma Ginther on their 60th Anniversary
(Photo's courtesy Ginther archives)

Citing Ed Ginther's Notes:

6/6/1944 was D-Day
Certain duties required equipment checking flights in B-17 Fortresses. Did three of these;
7/14/1944 Flew check flight with Lt. Brown B-17 #unknown
7/18/1944 Flew check flight with Lt. Alhadeff B-17 #599
8/3/1944 Flew Flight check with Lt. Searl B-17 (Note: Author Huntley disclosing tail #)
8/14/1944 Instructed to remove belongings of a B-17 bomber crew who had perished on 8/12/1944

While stationed in England, Ed Ginther and a fellow airman made trips to London on 48-hour passes. They would visit a family in Dagenham in the East End of London where a Mrs. Denton hosted them or at her sister's house nearby. Mrs. Denton began a correspondence with Ed's mother, Mrs. Ginther, back in the States. These letters describe the life of an average family during the blitz in London with all the hardships of the blackout, rationing and the German raids with V1 rockets or "Buzz bombs" as they were called. Here are extracts from those letters.

I transcribed these letters verbatim without corrections, except for readability.

September 29, 1944 Mrs. Denton, 36, Hayon Road Dagenham London

Hello Mrs. Ginther,
Well, here I am again. I hope you and your little family are well, the same as it leaves myself Rose & Alan, at the time of writing this letter.

Thank you so much for sending me the paper along dear. I was out shopping when it came but I found it in the letter box when I went to the door for Alan. He had just come home from school, well I opened the paper then I shook it, thinking you had put a note inside but instead I found my own letter to you in print. Well, well I went all hot and bothered because they never do things like that here, but thank you darling, I will treasure that paper for every day to come.

Well dear now to talk about Edgar. We had a letter from him this morning saying he is coming up this week end and he has got a 48 hrs. leave. Won't that be fine but I expect you wishing he was coming home to you dear. I know because I had a lovely letter from my Len today and he tells me he is doing a lot of flying now, night as well as day. He says he won't be home till after Xmas. I was hurt when I read that but will keep my fingers have crossed, one never knows. Well dear I wrote to Edgar and Teddy this morning and to Len but I will keep this letter open till I see the lads on Friday or Saturday. Then I will be able to tell everything about that sweet boy of you because I know you are just waiting to hear how he is. Good night, dear!

Well, here I am again dear after a week waiting, I still have not seen Edgar but Teddy came up on his own, he said Edgar is well and had his day off in the week. I expect he's too shy to come up on his own. So, I told him next time he has day off to come and fetch a pal with him if he's too shy to come alone for I don't mind. So long as they are happy and it makes a break for them.

Well dear the nights are getting longer that means we have to black out early now. I thought we were going to have our lights on again but no, we are still, having old Jerry visiting us but its not so bad now. We had a warning at 4 am this morning but didn't bother to get up. I heard him overhead. They make an awful din. I put the light out and went to sleep again.

Wont it be nice when the war is over and we can go to bed every night without the siren waking us all up. We won't know what to make of it. \ Well dear I think I have told you all the news this time so I will close now with all the best and cheers from Mrs. Denton.

November 21, 1944

Dear Mrs. Ginther
I was so pleased to get your letter, but I'm rather late in answering it, you see dear I have been waiting to see if Edgar would turn up but on the last time, we saw him was when he had a 48-hr. pass. That was good we had a good time we all spent the Saturday at my house then we all went up to my sisters on Sunday for dinner and tea. So that was the end of the 48.

Well dear, please don't worry over him dear I know he is well because Edward saw Edgar for a few minutes last week. I expect you have heard from him by now I hope so anyway because I know what a worrying time it is when you don't hear often. You want to know if I do much canning no dear, there is nothing to can. I haven't even made any jam this year. They did let us have a little extra sugar for jam but I was right out are of sugar so of course I had to fall back on that. You see dear we are allowed ½ Ib on each book so I have 1 ½ ib each week that's for the table and cooking as well. So, you can see it doesn't go, far

I thought it would drive me nuts but no, it's like everything else, you get used to it in time. Our biggest problem is our clothing coupons believe me I've never used darning cottons so much in my life as I do now. But we are all in the same boat. But at times it's quite laughable that one has to do especially when you can't get elastic. When you do got to the shops to buy anything its never wrapped up. After you have been caught once it makes you think to take your own paper but with it all we still manage to laugh.

I'm glad my sister isn't over here because I'm sure she wouldn't have been able to stand up to it all. I wonder how we have managed to go through all the dreadful raids. Edgar and Edward have often stood out in the garden with us watching the buzz bombs till they get quite near then we would all make a B line for the dugout. The kids would start singing at the top of their voices. Poor kids I think that are very brave they hardly take any notice of the raids at all but they still play war and believe me they play just where the places are down.

Well, here I am ramping on I reckon your get bored with this letter if I keep on so as it is so near the Xmas holidays, I don't suppose I shall be writing to again till afterwards, so I wish you and your family a merry Xmas and I do hope this dreadful war will be over soon. I am going to ask Edgar up for the holiday that's if he can get the time off. Well cheerio my dear friend and all the best from Mrs. Denton and family."

"January 5, 1945

Dear Mrs. Ginther,
Many thanks for your nice letter and before I go any further, I want to thank you for that parcel you sent me. Edgar brought it down to me a week before Xmas. I was very pleased with-it dear; the stockings were grand they are just the shade and sizes we wear that is when we can get them.

Thank you for everything because everything you sent me is on coupons. The soap is very acceptable because we can't get Lux now. We are not short of soap dear, there is plenty of the washing kind and its true we are rationed with it but you never see the best toilet soap now. Why did you send me all those things dear? You know I am grateful for your kindness You should not have done it dear for what I do for Edgar.

I expect it will be a few weeks before we see Edgar again. I am pleased you have heard from my sister. She does worry over Edward. I have told her how the boys have a good time when they are here. Also, at my other sister's house and we see Edward nearly every week but she still worries.

I always ask the boys if they have written home when I see them. I expect it's some fault at the base.

Since I wrote to you last my young sister has been blasted out by a rocket. It sure made a mess of her house. There's no roof and the bedrooms are not fit to sleep in any more so they have to sleep in the shelter. Fancy camping out in this weather. Well, we had to also for a year but we don't grumble, we thank our lucky stars we are alive.

Edgar has been to our house lots of times.

Well dear I think I better bring this letter to a close before you get bored. One last word, I had a very nice letter from Gertrude and a pretty Xmas card. I got them on Xmas morning. I was pleased. Well, I will say goodnight, dear friend and a happy New Year to you all.

Love Mrs. Denton."

In these letters, one gets a strong sense of how the Brits faced the adversity of war. With the deprivation, the rationing, and the bombing, they bore it with a sense of humor and tolerance. Their optimism convinced them the war would be over soon. The huge raids on German targets in France and in Germany by the Americans during the day and the massive night-time bombers of the British RAF at night, comforted them.

▲ ▲ ▲ ▲

CHAPTER FIVE
THE PILOT'S DAUGHTER

▲ ▲ ▲ ▲

Meeting Cheryl Surfus in Wisconsin April 20-22, 2019

FOLLOWING OUR INITIAL CONTACT, AS well as many e-mails and telephone calls, I arranged with Cheryl Surfus to visit her in Wisconsin for an interview. I was planning to attend the 75th anniversary of D-Day in Normandy on June 6th 2019, so I needed to see Cheryl before then, if possible.

Since tracing the Kempner nieces and talking to them about a potential date to visit them in Detroit for an interview, Cheryl and I settled on potential dates in April or March. The purpose was to coordinate a combined journey between Texas, Wisconsin, and Michigan where I could have detailed discussions and research with both the Searl and Kempner's descendants.

And so, it was April 20, 2019. I wanted to learn more about the lives of the Tomahawk Warrior crew. It was a beautiful sunny morning in Dallas at around seventy-three degrees Fahrenheit as I headed to the airport. I was prepared for a long day with a change of planes in Bloomington, Minnesota. Cheryl Surfus had kindly offered to meet me at my final destination, in Mosinee, Wisconsin.

I could see a gray, overcast sky as the flight arrived in Mosinee and taxied to the gate. I sent a text to Cheryl, letting her know I had landed and there she was, a stately lady in her seventies, patiently waiting for me, and with a big smile. We greeted each other with warm handshakes.

Cheryl led me over to the parking lot to her car, and so I began learning about her father, Charles J. Searl, as well as the Searl dynasty. The drive to her retirement home took 15 or 20 minutes, which was a relief, as it had been a long day of traveling. During that brief journey, Cheryl expressed her gratitude for coming to see her, and for what I was doing to bring recognition for her father and his crew. She said that one of her daughters, Shelly, would come the next day and bring her family with her.

I had booked to stay at the special guest apartment of Cheryl's retirement home. It proved to be very comfortable, as well as convenient for visiting Cheryl's apartment a few long corridors away. We met in her own rooms, where we chatted for a short while. Cheryl appeared to have a nice, roomy accommodation.

Cheryl was very excited to show me a brief history of the Searl family and of Charles himself. It affected her. She was talking to a person who was close to where her father died. It was me bringing some solace home to his daughter.

We planned to meet again the next day, Sunday, for a lunch in Cheryl's apartment with her daughter, Shelly Loe, and her family. Cheryl was to cook a turkey for this special occasion. She explained that her other daughter Rachel and her husband Terry, their three children, Jake 21, Ashley 18, and Amanda 17, lived too far away to make a one-day trip.

After a long day of traveling and talking, I was ready to take advantage of the delightful guest suite at my disposal. I got to sleep that night quickly.

The next day, at the agreed time, Cheryl invited me to examine some of the archival material, which she had kindly assembled for my review. Shelly and her family had not yet arrived, so I could examine and photograph several items of interest, which were of historical significance to the Tomahawk Warrior story.

A turkey was already cooking in the oven, and the aroma stimulated my appetite.

Before I proceed further, I am providing a family tree to facilitate a clearer understanding of the Searl clan as I introduce the names of Charles' relatives in this story.

Nile Wesley Searl, Charles' father, had made a detailed study of family[34] history. He discovered that there were three brothers who had come from Warwick in England and landed in Boston in 1634. The three were John, Edward and Andrew. Charles' part of the Searl family came from the progeny of John. Previous generations of Searls had served in the Revolutionary and Indian wars. So, they had quite a tradition of military service. Nile Searl served and was wounded in the First World War.

In the family tree below, Nile Wesley Searl and his younger brother, Arthur Albert, were partners in a flour and feed business together. Nile named Charles after both of his grandfathers, Charles and Joseph. At the time he was born in 1921, the family lived above Jones Grocery Store on Wisconsin Avenue in Tomahawk.

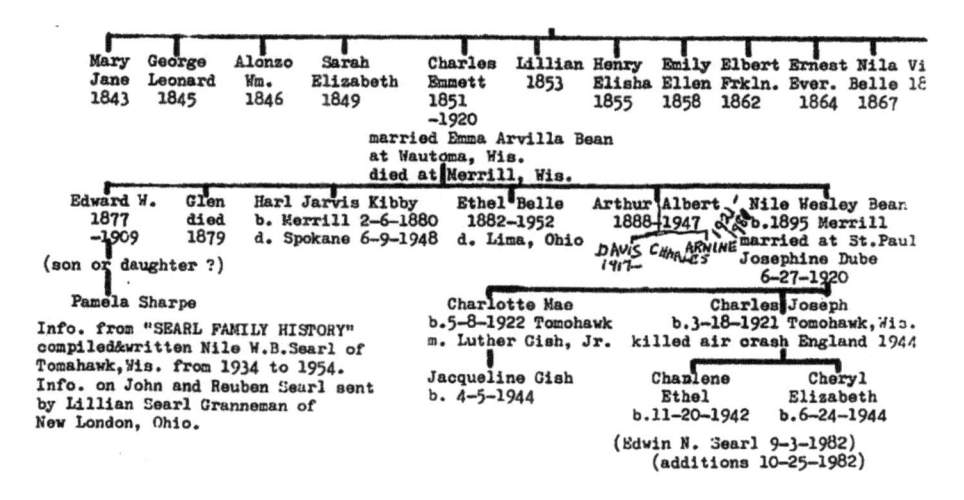

```
Mary    George   Alonzo   Sarah      Charles   Lillian Henry   Emily  Elbert   Ernest  Nila  Vi
Jane    Leonard  Wm.      Elizabeth  Emmett    1853    Elisha  Ellen  Frkln.   Ever.   Belle 18
1843    1845     1846     1849       1851              1855    1858   1862     1864    1867
                                     -1920
                                     married Emma Arvilla Bean
                                     at Wautoma, Wis.
                                     died at Merrill, Wis.

Edward W.   Glen    Harl Jarvis Kibby    Ethel Belle    Arthur Albert    Nile Wesley Bear
1877        died    b. Merrill 2-6-1880  1882-1952      1888-1947        b.1895 Merrill
-1909       1879    d. Spokane 6-9-1948  d. Lima, Ohio  DAVIS CHARLES    married at St.Paul
(son or daughter ?)                                     1917-  ARWINE    Josephine Dube
                                                                         6-27-1920

Pamela Sharpe                           Charlotte Mae              Charles Joseph
Info. from "SEARL FAMILY HISTORY"       b.5-8-1922 Tomahawk        b.3-18-1921 Tomahawk,Wis.
compiled&written Nile W.B.Searl of      m. Luther Gish, Jr.        killed air crash England 1944
Tomahawk,Wis. from 1934 to 1954.
Info. on John and Reuben Searl sent     Jacqueline Gish            Charlene            Cheryl
by Lillian Searl Granneman of           b. 4-5-1944                Ethel               Elizabeth
New London, Ohio.                                                  b.11-20-1942        b.6-24-1944

                                        (Edwin N. Searl 9-3-1982)
                                        (additions 10-25-1982)
```

The Family Tree. Courtesy of the Searl families.

Nile and his wife Josephine had another child in 1922, a sister of Charles named Charlotte. The two of them became very close in their time growing up together. Charlotte passed away in 2003, leaving behind a daughter, Jacqueline (Jackie). Charles had married Arlie Irene Peterson

---

[34] A document compiled by Nile Wesley Searl of the complete ancestry of the Searl family since 1610.

from Irma, Wisconsin, on May 6, 1942. Irma was about 10 miles from the city of Tomahawk.

My study of the archival material put out for me became interrupted by a knocking on the front door, and Cheryl exclaiming, "Ah, this must be Shelly and her family!"

Shelly came in, accompanied by her husband Mark, followed by her three children Kacey 23, Jarret 20, and young Jack at 11. After formal introductions and while we were all relaxing around the living room, I gave them a briefing about what I was trying to accomplish. Shelly, of course, was thrilled not only that she had found me on Facebook but also that now I was in direct contact with her mother.

From the sense of wonder on their faces, I could tell that they were excited to meet a person who had been at the place of their grandfather's last journey in life. I was now part of their own family history. It seemed quite surreal to me thinking back to the day of the fatal crash, that I am now meeting and speaking directly with Charles's children, grandchildren, and great grandchildren, and connecting it with here and now.

I spent time with Shelly and her two eldest children, answering their questions about what it was like in London during the war. They took keen interest in the photographs of the bombing, the German V1 and V2 rockets, food rationing, and bomb shelters. My description of how my late wife Sophie and her family had to flee from the Germans when they invaded her country of France shocked them. I described how she and her family got shot at by German Stuka dive-bombers. It forced them to dive into road-side ditches to escape the bullets. While my audience understood how hard this may have been for those in Europe, they couldn't fully grasp the reality of those times.

Now it was time for Cheryl's roast turkey. We all gathered at the table to enjoy a delicious meal and the family conversation. Afterward, I took pictures of a significant number of family heirlooms, photographs, and memorabilia, while making audio recordings of the general conversation.

Cheryl told me some nicknames given to certain members of the family and a couple of interesting anecdotes about Charles. His father Nile, once wrote the following about Charles for the family history archives:

"My son Charles Joseph Searl (named for both grand-fathers) was born March 18, 1921, at Tomahawk, Wisconsin. We were then living in an apartment above the then Jones Grocery store on Wisconsin Ave. I was a partner with my brother, Art, in the Flour & Feed business. Charles was an unusually large and handsome boy, a storehouse of information, and had two years of college, when war broke out in 1941. In 1942, he enlisted just before he was 21 years old in the Army Air Corps, and he graduated with honors at the head of his class, and given a permanent commission as a pilot. In April, 1944 he left for combat duty in England, and on his 29th mission as a pilot killed in action with the rest of his crew, near Penn, Buckinghamshire, England, and in March 1949 re-interred at Arlington, National Cemetery."

Josephine with baby Charles    *Nile -Josephine -Charles-Charlotte*

Charles at 18 years of age.

The story of Charles growing up, going to college, and enlisting in the Army Air Corps unfolded for me as I steadily noted and photographed the family historical material offered to me by Cheryl. As the afternoon progressed, I felt a strong connection to this family. I realized, as a father myself, just what impact the loss of a son on a foreign soil must have had on Nile and Josephine.

Soon, it was time for Shelly, Mark, and their children to depart for home. I promised to keep the Searl family informed of whatever progress I'd make in developing the story of the Tomahawk Warrior.

Cheryl and I chatted for a while to discuss our plans for the next day. We decided on a visit to the American Legion post in Tomahawk, as well as the small museum there. She offered to show to me the ancestral home where she grew up.

▲ ▲ ▲ ▲

A Visit to the City of Tomahawk

The City of Tomahawk

The city of Tomahawk sprang into being almost over night. The locality was practically uninhabited wilderness previous to 1886, in which year the Tomahawk Land & Boom Company began operations here. In the spring of 1887 this company laid out the site of the city of Tomahawk; the survey of the plat, made under the direction of Thomas M. Doyle was recorded June 1, 1887. And the first lots were offered for sale at auction in Mikwaukee on June 25th of the same year. September 15, 1887, the tracks of the Wisconsin Valley Division of the Chicago Milwaukee & St. Paul railroad, then in process of extension from Merrill to Minocqua, reached Tomahawk. Saw mills and other industries sprang up at once, and the census of 1890, just four years after the city was laid out and settlement began, found Tomahawk with a population of 1,816.

Courtesy of the Tomahawk Area Historical Society[35]

---

[35] Visit http://tomahawkhistoricalsoc.org/

After a sturdy breakfast at a local cafe, Cheryl and I set out to visit some prominent historical landmarks in Tomahawk. First, we stopped at the war memorial to pay tribute to the local citizens who had died in the various world conflicts, including Searl. In another section of this chapter, I will relate how a separate branch of the Searl family has also honored Charles at this **memorial** site.

For a small community like Tomahawk, the loss of every local citizen in service to their country is significant. In 2020, the population was 3,049 and in 1940,[36] it was 3,365.

Cheryl Surfus   *Tomahawk War Memorial*
(Author's photo's)

After touring the Tomahawk War Memorial and paying our respects to the fallen in all wars, Cheryl and I made our way to the American Legion named the Bronstead-Searl Post 93, but recently renamed as Bronstead-Ingman-Searl Post 93. We met a few key people associated with the Post, and the small museum across the street.

The Post well represented Charles Searl's photographs and artifacts illustrating his service and sacrifice to his country. Cheryl is proud to see her

---

[36] US government census 1950 comparing to 1940

father's name honored in the title of the Post besides the Medal of Honor Korean War hero, Einar Harol Ingman Jr.

Braving the little drizzle of rain, we left the American Legion Post and crossed the street immediately opposite and entered the small museum of Tomahawk.

Cheryl was pleased to show me the one room primary school she had attended in her early years in Tomahawk, and which has been carefully preserved. Such schools were typical from the 1800s to the 1940s.

Seeing the heavy wooden desks and chairs supported by solid cast-iron frames and chalk slates prominently displayed on each desk, I imagined Cheryl and her fellow students were busy with their work. It must have been rather awkward for the children to turn their heads to see the blackboard on their right side, instead of traditionally looking forward. Maybe the room arrangement differed in the old days?

The teacher, however, must have had a good view of the classroom from her desk. A black potbelly stove in the far corner provided a blessing in the cold of a Wisconsin winter. On the wall above the stove, hung an American flag to receive the pupil's Pledge of Allegiance each morning.

In the museum, I saw the City's history unfold in front of my eyes. The images of many prominent citizens, Charles Searl among them carefully preserved.

There was a particular exhibit; a photograph of Charles in his uniform, which I had never seen before. I took a picture of it and, back in Dallas; I had this professionally enhanced so Cheryl could have it framed. (Chapter 9 contains this photo.)

We had time to go to that part of Tomahawk where the Searl family grew up. As we passed some of the rural fields in the area, Cheryl explained how this part of Wisconsin was primarily a timber and lumber industry. She said it was also a major grower of ginseng. Her family owned a small parcel of land for growing this crop.

The cultivation of American ginseng started over a hundred years ago in Wisconsin when the Fromm brothers[37] transplanted one hundred wild specimens from nearby forests into prepared plots carefully replicating the plant's natural environment.

It takes four years[38] to bring ginseng root to harvest. The Wisconsin's way of cultivating ginseng replicates the way the wild ginseng grows in the forest. During those four years, the farmers work to save the precious plant from the harsh winter conditions and the strong summer light. They place a layer of straw on the beds to protect the plant. In the summer, they place some shade structures over the ginseng, so that the plant grows in a forest like state. During these four years, the farmer must observe a variety of things that can ruin the plant. It includes animals, getting into the garden, or it is unusually dry or wet. There are many factors that can affect the final ginseng root.

Cheryl said the crop can make good money, but it is very hard work. In the four years it takes to bring it to harvest, many problems can occur, resulting in a complete loss of the crop.

As we passed the Harley-Davidson plant on E. Somo Avenue or Highway 86, Cheryl slowed down and turned onto Charlotte Street. In what she said was the Hiawatha Heights development, her grandfather, Nile Searl, had purchased a large tract of land to build houses on in the 1950s. He had set out to honor his children and grandchildren in the plans for the Town Planning authority, by naming streets and avenues after them.

Thus, as we continued on Charlotte Street, named after Charles's sister, we passed the intersection on the left of Charlene Avenue, Charles's eldest daughter. Further on, we crossed over Charles Avenue to reach Cheryl Avenue, Charles's youngest daughter (my chauffer and guide that day) which had a 'No Outlet' at each end. On the latter, Cheryl pointed out her grandfather's house, and where she herself had lived for a while. Quite a unique anecdote of personal history to say that you once lived on the street named just for you.

My time with Cheryl was most gratifying, and I had enjoyed her

---

[37] Source: Ginseng Growers Association of America.
[38] Source: The Ginseng Board of Wisconsin

hospitality and meeting some of her family. Now, I had some interesting archival material to work with. However, unknown to me, I was soon to meet another side of the family. They would provide even more material on the life of Lt. Charles J. Searl.

Art and Josephine, friends and Charles.
Courtesy of Kathy Searl

Charles with cousin,   *Davis Searl and*   *Charles, Charlotte*
Davis Searl   *Charles Searl*   *and Davis*

All three photos courtesy of Kathy Searl

Charles Searl's sister, Charlotte, while on the 398th BGMA tour, stopped at Albert Knight's grave in Madingley, Cambridge U.K., 1990. Courtesy of Diane Plogger, Knight family historian.

▲ ▲ ▲ ▲

A Dedication by Kathy and Chuck Searl

It surprised me when another member of the Searl clan, Ms. Kathy Searl, a retired schoolteacher, contacted me through Facebook.

Kathy, her older sisters Susan, Christine, and her brother Chuck Searl, are the children of Davis Searl. Their grandfather, Art Searl, was the brother of Nile Searl. Davis, as mentioned earlier, was a first cousin of 1st Lt. Charles Searl, and they grew up together. According to Kathy, they were almost like brothers.

David E. Huntley

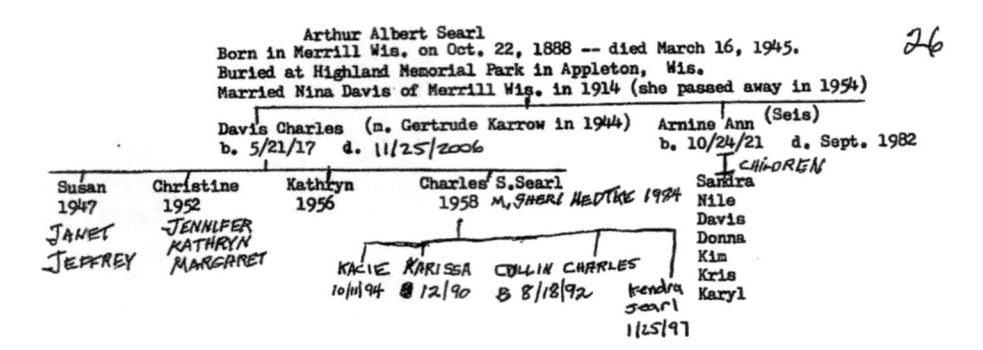

```
                    Arthur Albert Searl                                    26
           Born in Merrill Wis. on Oct. 22, 1888 -- died March 16, 1945.
           Buried at Highland Memorial Park in Appleton, Wis.
           Married Nina Davis of Merrill Wis. in 1914 (she passed away in 1954)
                                                              (Seis)
           Davis Charles  (m. Gertrude Karrow in 1944)   Arnine Ann
           b. 5/21/17    d. 11/25/2006                   b. 10/24/21   d. Sept. 1982
                                                              CHILDREN
 Susan    Christine    Kathryn      Charles S.Searl          Sandra
 1947     1952         1956         1958  M. SHERI HEDTKE 1984  Nile
 JANET    JENNIFER                                            Davis
 JEFFREY  KATHRYN                                             Donna
          MARGARET    KACIE  KARISSA   COLLIN CHARLES         Kim
                      10/11/94  8/12/90  B 8/18/92  Kendra    Kris
                                                    Searl     Karyl
                                                    1/25/97
```

Family tree courtesy of Kathy Searl

Kathy sent me a significant number of photos and memorabilia which, together with the material from Cheryl, helped me to build a comprehensive profile of her uncle Charles. These archives, as well as conversations with the two families, helped me to construct the life of Charles in Chapter Seven.

In 2022, after having visited the war memorial in the City of Tomahawk, Kathy, and her brother Charles (Chuck) Searl decided there should be a paving stone dedicated to 1st Lt. Charles Searl.

Kathy informed me that she had visited the Veterans Memorial Park in Tomahawk, Wisconsin, in a search for any specific paving tile honoring 1st Lt. Charles J. Searl. She could find none, but, after speaking with a member of the American Legion Post, she received a contact information for a Judy Haskins, who handled these matters.

Kathy and Judy had a delightful conversation about Charles Searl, and they discussed my upcoming book. The paver had to comprise a piece of granite with an appropriate inscription and measure twelve inches square.

After much communication and coordination, Kathy finally put together a memorial dedication in Tomahawk, Wisconsin, for Charles J. Searl. Kathy had the paving tile made in Tomahawk and planned to install it at the Memorial Park.

She had a discussion with Terry Baldowsky, the Commander of The Legion in Tomahawk, which is named Bronstead/Searl/ Ingman Post 93, who was very interested in the project. So together, they coordinated a memorial dedication for a date in the future of May 18 at 3 PM. The legion post would also contact the newspaper in Tomahawk and possibly the television station in Rhinelander for some publicity.

The following are two messages I received from Kathy preceding the Memorial Ceremony:

5//17/2022

I am going to sleep early tonight. Tomorrow is a big day. The culmination of over a year of planning. And you, my friend, were very instrumental in giving me the motivation and desire to see this through. It thrilled my whole family to attend this dedication. It is something that should have happened many years ago, but again, you can't turn back time. You can only move forward and do the best that you can! Kathy.

5/18/2022

We just arrived in Tomahawk and are having lunch. The weather is cold and damp. We are looking forward to tomorrow. On the way in, we drove down Charles, Charlotte, Cheryl, and Charlene Avenues. It was neat to see the land that my dad's uncle, Nile, owned so long ago. Kathy.

5/19/2022

I'm exhausted from the events of yesterday. Emotionally, I mean. Despite the weather, it was an absolutely perfect day. Far better than I even expected. I don't know where to begin.

My two sisters, Susan, and Chris, Chris's husband, Matt, and my significant other, Alan, traveled to Tomahawk (two plus hours).

We met up with my brother, Charles (he came from his cottage) and had lunch. Checked into our hotel. Most of us changed into our patriotic clothing. Charles changed into his honor guard uniform. The memorial park was across the bridge.

It amazed me at the number of people who had gathered. There was a whole printed program put together by Kevin Krueger of Generations Funeral Home. I have a couple to send to you. The posting of colors happened after the Welcome. A woman sang the National Anthem. She had an amazing voice! Then we all said the pledge of allegiance, followed by an opening prayer.

The historian gave his talk, and my brother Charles added some details, including your childhood experience(sic-of the crash), research and book, along with mention of the permanent commemorative marker at the crash site. After closing remarks and acknowledgments they did a Three Round Volley followed by TAPS. My brother took part with their Honor Guard. We closed with prayer and Retiring of Colors. It was an extremely moving moment.

Following the ceremony, many of us went to the Legion Post. The auxiliary had hot ham and cheese sandwiches, cole slaw, potato salad, chips and baked beans. Along with a special cake. My family provided 'open bar' for everyone. I have a few pictures I will try to send.

The paver is perfect. They placed it right up in front of the Memorial. There was a gentleman from the VFW who made sure of that. He told me more than once how important that was to him, because Charles was a hero.

People were able to view pictures and information my brother and I had laid out on a table. I had the little card that you gave me regarding your book. Several people asked me about that. They had a couple of different raffles that they were selling tickets for to raise money for the remodeling of the building. Of course we bought some! They also took us back into a room where they keep all their historical material. There were some things regarding Charles that I had not seen.

Everyone was so kind and so welcoming. There were 2 daughters of the Medal of Honor recipient that attended (last name Ingman). The

Legion is Bronstead/Searl/ Ingman. I just can't express the warmth and appreciation that I felt from everyone. I so wished that Cheryl [39]*could have been there.*

This morning, on the way home, we drove to the cemetery in Merrill where Nile and Josephine Searl are buried. Charles has a headstone placed between them, even though I know they buried him in Arlington Cemetery.

After almost a year of planning, it all came to fruition. I wish my dad was still alive to experience it all. He would have loved it. But I know he was there with us in spirit!

So, I won't rattle on any longer. I was just so excited to tell you how things went and to thank you again for helping to give me the idea and motivation to put this honor and tribute together. It was immensely rewarding.

Kathy

In my reply, I said,

Dear Kathy,

Thank you so much for your wonderful and descriptive narrative of the event in Tomahawk that you helped to arrange so diligently. It must have been very emotional for you.

Your description says it all, and I think Charles is now fully honored and remembered. For me, that is so gratifying. As a nine-year-old watching those remains being retrieved from that field on August 12, 1944, is an image which has remained in my head my whole life. I am glad I have

---

[39] Author's note: I had informed Cheryl Surfus of the impending ceremony in honor of her father but but I was not sure if she could make it.

helped to honor him and his crew, for being part of that great generation which gave us all our FREEDOM that we enjoy today.

Thank you and your brother Charles for mentioning my efforts and research, etc. I received an invitation to join another FB Group called Fans of the B-17 Flying Fortress, and today I posted about the TW. In a few scant hours, it drew 628 likes and still counting as I write this. Many, many comments and multiple shares. So, Kathy, as I continue to get the story published, I wish to thank you for all your efforts in Memorializing 1st Lt. Charles Searl.

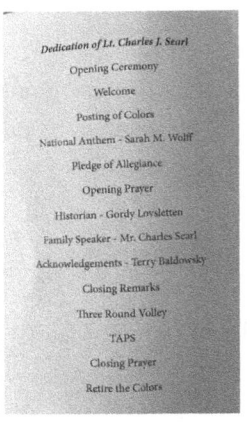

*The dedication ceremony of a paving stone at the War Memorial City of Tomahawk.
Photos, courtesy of Kathy Searl.*

▲ ▲ ▲ ▲

CHAPTER SIX

THE NAVIGATOR'S NIECES

▲ ▲ ▲ ▲

The Search for the Kempner Descendants

BECAUSE ED GINTHER HAD EXPRESSED a willingness eventually to return the diary to relatives of Lt. Kempner and I felt morally obligated to find these relatives to determine if they existed. I wanted to do this before flying out to Ohio to meet Mr. Ginther. The problem was, the crew of the Tomahawk Warrior were all single except for 1st Lt. Charles Searl. It would be almost impossible to locate the siblings with no widows or children.

Since my corporation, Huntley Associates Dallas, Inc., was in the business of executive recruiting and consulting, finding people was our specialty. Naturally, I set my search techniques in motion to begin the hunt for Kempner's surviving relatives. By that time, I already had obtained the documents with the names and addresses of all the crew, including their birth dates. From official records, I knew that Kempner was originally from Detroit. It was also my surmise that because his name was Saul; he was of Jewish background.

My research showed that the United States conducted a census in 1940. After carefully screening these detailed census records, I came up with a Kempner family in Detroit and Saul with his siblings. Saul's age at the time of the census was twenty, which matched his birth date on his service record. It showed he had an older brother George 26 years old at that time, but also a twin brother, Irving. His father,

Samuel, forty-nine, had immigrated to the USA from Poland, and his mother, Ida, forty-seven, was Russian. It also showed that there was a daughter, Frances Crane, a widow aged thirty-six. It seems impossible she could be Samuel's daughter based on her age. I assume she was mistakenly entered in the census column as a daughter in place of a lodger, perhaps? Recorded in the census as a cosmetologist, she worked in Beauty Shops.

Samuel, the father, was a sales agent for a bartender goods company. George, the eldest son, was a sales agent for a sports goods company. The twins were at college in 1940.

The census records showed the family lived in Ward 8 of Detroit City, Michigan/My assumption that the Kempners were of the Jewish faith proved correct, because when I contacted the Central Synagogue in Detroit, they confirmed that there were several families with that name. However, they pointed out that theirs was the last standing synagogue in downtown Detroit, although in the 1940s, there had been many more. The representative of the synagogue, Arlene Frank, suggested I should call the Jewish Historical Society, but it was a referral to a Ms. Robbie Terman of the Jewish Federation of Metropolitan Detroit that opened an avenue of possibilities.

Robbie had used some archival obituaries where she located names of children from the married members of the Kempner family. While Saul Kempner himself was single, his twin brother Irving was married and had two daughters, Andrea Blake and Janice Morgan, who were living in the Detroit area. Using my search resources, I traced their phone numbers and addresses.

At first I left messages at both sisters' phone numbers, asking for them to return my calls. By only leaving my name, I wanted to make sure I had correctly identified them. It must have sounded like a typical sales call or robot caller, and they were simply not responding. So, I left a more detailed message saying, I as a young boy, witnessed the crash of the Tomahawk

Warrior, and I believed they could be the relatives of the navigator, Lt. Saul J. Kempner.

This latter message definitely got their attention because Mrs. Andrea Blake called me back, cautiously asking me who I was. When I explained, and we got into a deeper conversation, Andrea began crying.

Then I asked her, "Andrea, were you aware your uncle wrote a diary?"

"No," she replied, "I did not know."

"Well," I said, "I have that diary and it is a remarkable piece of history in which Saul documented every bombing mission his plane was engaged in."

We both were very emotional by this time, and the tears were flowing on both sides. She had to come to terms with what I had seen in 1944. I was someone who had a direct link to her historical past and a connection to her uncle. I explained how I had come into possession of the diary and how it was to form the basis of a new book I was writing.

I told her I was going to visit Ed Ginther, the 92-year-old Air Force veteran who had found the diary, and I was going to ask him to confirm his previous statement to me that he wished to return the diary to the Kempner family. Martin, Ed's son, had already expressed their intention before, but had been unsuccessful in locating the Kempner family.

After exchanging our contact information, I sent to both sisters the details of the Tomahawk Warrior that I had discovered to date, together with information about Mrs. Cheryl Surfus, the daughter of 1st Lt. Charles Searl, the pilot of the crashed aircraft. I suggested they give Cheryl a call to connect their historical backgrounds to the Tomahawk Warrior crew.

My plans after visiting Ed Ginther, was to take a trip to the City of Tomahawk, Wisconsin to interview Mrs. Surfus and at the same time visit the birthplace of Lt. Searl, followed by a stopover in Detroit to interview Mrs Blake and Mrs Morgan.

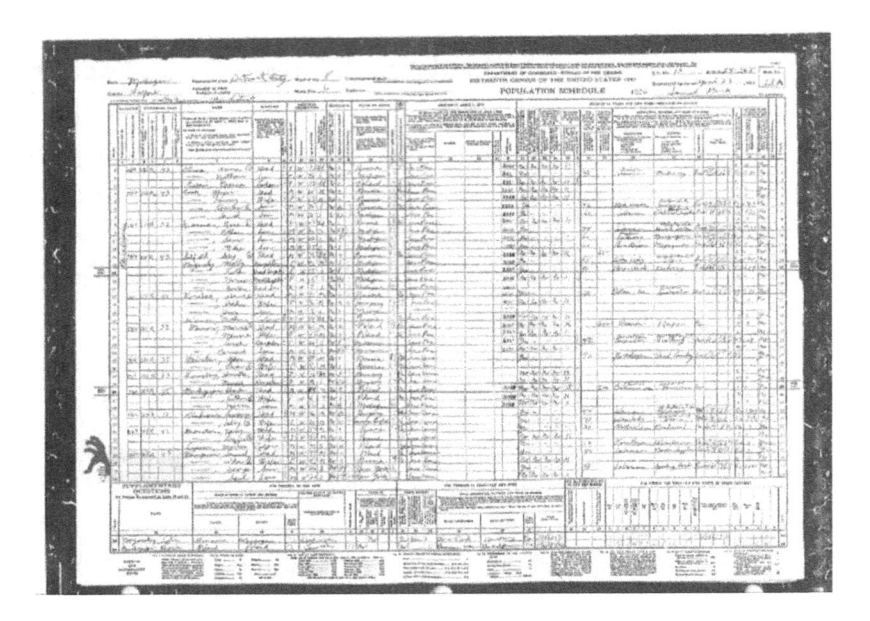

The original 1940 census records I discovered.

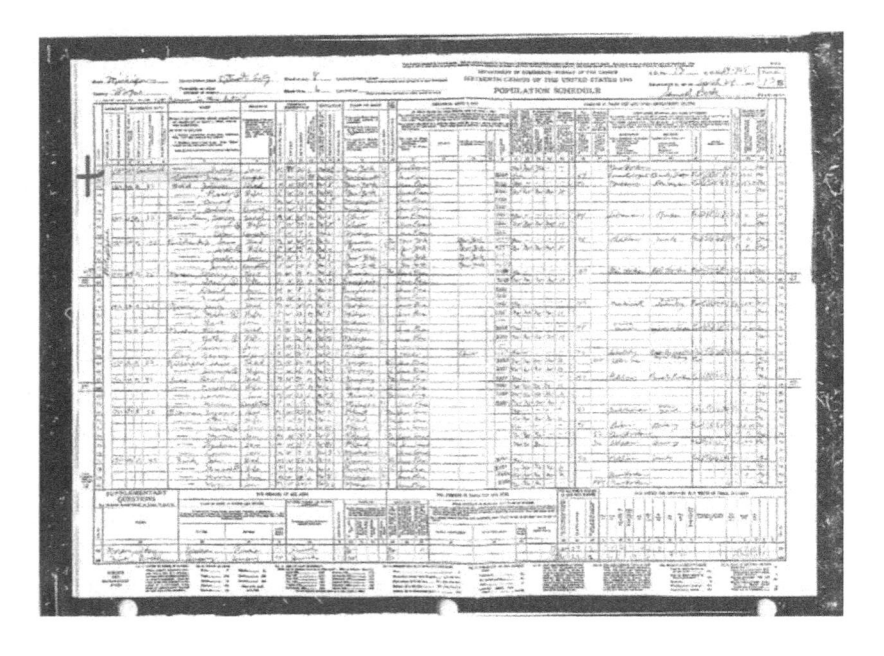

Meeting the Kempner Family

After finishing my interview with Cheryl Surfus, I took a plane to Detroit, Michigan. I arrived in time for Mrs. Janice Morgan to pick me up and transport me to a BnB close to her home in the suburb of Birmingham, where we later met.

She introduced me to her husband, Alec, a retired mathematician from the Ford Motor Company. Then we went to a Lebanese restaurant where I ate my first, most delicious, chicken shawarma sandwich. Of course, the subject of the Tomahawk Warrior and the part Janice's uncle Saul played as the navigator in this story took precedence over our conversation.

Janice's father, Irving Kempner, and Saul's twin brother, both deceased, had been the sole source of information about what happened to uncle Saul for Janice and her sister Andrea. Neither of them had any knowledge that their uncle Saul had written a diary during his period of service. Their father had never mentioned it while they were growing up.

After enjoying our meal, the three of us agreed to meet the next day when Andrea could join us at Janice's house. Alec and Janice drove me back to my temporary accommodation. I was glad to get a good night's rest after a day of traveling from Wisconsin.

I awoke early the next morning and enjoyed a leisurely breakfast. Janice had arranged to meet me at 10:00 AM. I was full of eager anticipation to know how much I might learn about the life of Lt. Saul Kempner.

Janice picked me up and drove me a short distance to her lovely double story home. The trees on either side of the street were just beginning to display new leaves and blossoms. I imagined that in a few weeks, a wonderful spring display would present itself.

Her house stood on a corner lot with a very large and well-established garden. There was a pagoda type area with a metal table and chairs, which was an obvious favorite spot to relax, read, or meditate with a cool lemonade on a lazy summer's afternoon.

With Janice-her husband Alec joined us; we settled down in the living room and talked about Irving Kempner. According to Janice, her father and his twin Saul were very close and, as both amateur playwrights even occasionally performed together on a local radio station.

Irving, in a letter[40] to his wife, Mary, in February 1945 referred to his brother Saul's death in combat as a tragedy which prevented his brother from reaching his greatest potential in a future radio career.

Andrea Blake, Janice's sister, joined us and we had a detailed discussion of how I had located Saul Kempner's diary. We thought about how and when I could help to get this family artifact returned to them.

Later that evening, I expected to receive more information and additional documents about Saul Kempner from another research source of mine, and I did. It turned out to be quite a surprise to the two sisters when I emailed the material to them.

The sisters were very close in some aspects, but different in others. Janice was the more conservative and quieter of the two and kept her emotions understated. Andrea was more outgoing, extroverted and especially ebullient of my discoveries about their uncle. They were both immensely grateful to me for virtually, as they said, bringing their uncle back to life and filling in gaps of family history. They eventually expressed their gratitude in heart-warming notes I received later, and which I share with my readers in this book.

(More information about Saul Kempner see Chapters 10 and 11)

The following photos are of the Kempner family, courtesy of Janice Morgan and Andrea Blake. Their father and mother were Irving and Mary Kempner. At the time of writing, an older sister Sally lives in Tennessee and I have had no contact with her.

---

[40] The letter is published at the end of this section.

*From L-R, Steve, Janice's son, Janice, David holding
the pic of Saul, and Andrea 2019*

Irving and Saul 　　　　　*Portrait of Saul*

David E. Huntley

Irving (left) in the radio booth    *Irving and his wife Mary*

George & his Wife Pat    *George as a Lt. In the Army Air Force 1943*

Irving   George   Saul
All previous photos are courtesy of the Kempner family.

All three sons of Samuel Kempner were officers in the Army Air Corps during WWII and fought with distinction. Although this author is writing about Lt. Saul Kempner and his part in the Tomahawk Warrior tragedy, I would like to pay a tribute to both George and Irving, who survived the war.

Lt. Irving "Hank" Kempner

In Irving's obituary: (A citation)

"Irving Henry "Hank" Kempner died November 3, 2004 at age 85.

Irving was a graduate of Cass Technical High School and Wayne State University. He was in the Army Air Corps during WWII, serving in the Flying Tigers in China; he retired from the Air Force as a lieutenant colonel. Mr. Kempner worked for 20 years as an investigator with the City of Detroit Human Rights Department. He was a long-standing member of the Masonic Lodge.

Mr Kempner is survived by his wife of 60 years. Mary (Tanenbaum) Kempner; daughters, and son-in-law, Sally Sklar of Linden, Andrea Blake of Oak Park, Janice and Alec Morgan of Birmingham: son, and daughter-in-law, Steven and Lisa Kempner of Royal Oak; grandchildren, Ian Sklar, Raphael, Ari, Miriam Blake, Abraham, Julia Morgan, Zachary Kempner.

Internment at Arlington National Cemetery in Virginia. (End of citation)

The Flying Tigers were an 'American Volunteer Group' (AVG) of American fighter pilots that flew for China in early 1942. An American, Colonel Claire Chennault, who devised special tactics against the Japanese, led them. The AVG achieved outstanding success and some reports in army archives show their kill ratio in battles with the Japanese was twelve to one. A separate report stated they lost twelve aircraft but downed three-hundred Japanese planes.

Interestingly, the nickname for the P-40's used by the Flying Tigers was the **'Tomahawks.'** Seemingly, a continuing array of coincidences which would arise throughout the life of this investigation.

The AVG was a small group and used around one-hundred Curtis Warhawk P-40s. Their planes were famous for having the noses painted with the red shark mouth.

Unfortunately, I have no direct historical military record for Irving, since my focus has been on his twin brother Saul. It was reported that Irving was a bombardier but if he flew with the Flying Tigers in China; he more likely flew as a pilot. That group operated P-40 Warhawks, which were single seat all metal fighters and ground-attack aircraft.

Remarkably, there were three Army Air Force Lieutenants in this one Kempner family. The parents, Samuel and Ida Kempner, must have been immensely proud of their sons.

3rd Squadron Hell's Angels, Flying Tigers over China, photographed in 1942 by AVG pilot Robert T. Smith, Repository San Diego Air and Space Museum Archive Catalog # 1606. On the ground guarded by a Chinese soldier. Army Archives.

While he was serving overseas, Irving, like many of his fellow combatants, would have periods of reflection and nostalgia, particularly during the breaks of a high level of intense combat. A poignant letter he wrote to his wife, Mary, illustrates his love for her, his frustration about the war, and losing his brother, Saul. As I publish this letter here, I am again reminded of my quest to recognize these heroes for the humanity they represent, rather than the inanimate machinery of the war.

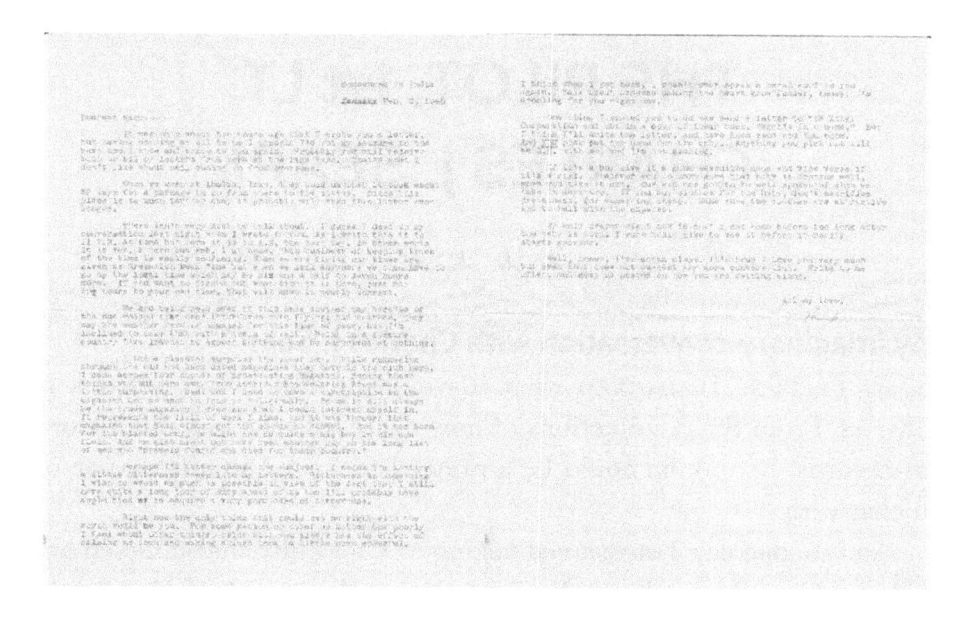

Courtesy of the Kempner family

Lt. George Kempner

There is only a brief record of George, the eldest of the three brothers. At the time of Saul's death, he was a Private in the Army Air Force and was training to be a pilot in Tucson, Arizona. He eventually served in the Army Air Transport Command as a 2nd lieutenant, although I have no official record of his service.

▲ ▲ ▲ ▲

CHAPTER SEVEN

THE PILOT, 1st LT. CHARLES J. SEARL

▲▲▲▲

My imaginary conversation with Charles J. Searl

IN MY PREFACE, I IMAGINED what it would be like if I could talk to Charles. From the recollections of now deceased relatives and historical records, I think he could be a pretty laid back and affable person to chat with.

And so, one day, I envisioned talking to him. I introduced myself and said that I saw the crash of a B-17 bomber on August 12, 1944, when he and his crew met their end.

As I saw his eyes misting over, I wondered if he, then far from home and about to die, thought about his mother and his wife and children.

I think I felt his emotional state, and couldn't help to tell him, but that I know his family loves and cherishes him and there are many people who remember and honor him and his crew.

"Charles, I am a witness to the evidence of your sacrifice is not forgotten in this area of Buckinghamshire, England, where your plane crashed. In fact, on each Remembrance Day, the local Holy Trinity Church pays tribute not only to their residents who fell in both world wars but also to you and your crew at the local Cenotaph. On the pathway leading to the church, they place American flags representing each member of the Tomahawk Warrior crew. Even before that, in 1948, the Vicar of Holy

Trinity Church and St Margaret's Church, Mr. Oscar Muspratt, wrote to your mother and advised her of a stone tablet to be placed with the names of the nine American airmen. In years past, some relatives and your sister Charlotte paid a visit."

In my almost hypnagogic state, I think I saw Charles placing his hand on his chest and his brows shooting up in surprise.

"I am moved. Really moved," he said.

I, watching his reaction, could not resist telling him that as a witness of the crash site, I was so horrified by the immediate aftermath that it became forever imprinted on my mind. "Even more, Charles, it became a journey on my part that pushed and guided me toward my several years-long efforts to obtain an official national honor for you and your comrades, for your sacrifice on that day."

"Honor?" he exclaimed. There was a long pause before he continued, "I understand. We did everything we could to avoid coming down on the village. I remember, we were fighting for altitude and trying to control our aircraft. We came very low over some cottages and then crashed thirty or forty seconds later in a field beyond them."

"Charles, I think I also should reveal to you that I am writing a book."

"A book? About what?"

"About you and your comrades' sacrifice."

I wanted to tell Charles more about what I have discovered and ask him questions, but since that day, the ethereal connection never returned.

While working on the project in the archives and meeting people, many open questions arose, and many coincidences revealed themselves. In 2019, for instance, I spoke to the deacon of the Holy Trinity Church about the Remembrance Day ceremony. In our conversation, I had enumerated some amazing coincidences about my connection to the Tomahawk Warrior event.

One of the most bizarre of the several coincidences was when I discovered the birth date of Lt. Charles Searl was on March 18th. My own twin sons were born on March 18th. One of them wanted to be a pilot since around the age of 7 when he would watch the jet airliners coming into land near our house, close to an airport. He is now a captain on one of America's national airlines. The really interesting thing was that the very first plane he ever flew when training to be a pilot was a Piper **TOMAHAWK.**

The Deacon responded to me. "David, these are not coincidences; this is God telling you that you must write this story."

1st Lt. Charles Searl
(Photo Courtesy of Searl's daughter Mrs Cheryl Surfus)

Regarding my imaginary conversation with Charles about the memorial in the village of Penn and the church there, the Reverend O. Muspratt, the local vicar at that period, was a driving force in getting the service established with the help of the neighborhood parish.

The following two letters dated 1946 and 1948 provide a glimpse of the vicar's dedication to having the crew of the "Tomahawk Warrior" recognized by his church and the village community.

The B-17 Tomahawk Warrior: A WWII Final Honor

> The Vicarage, Penn
> Nr. High Wycombe, Bucks
> 8th October 1946

PENN WAR MEMORIAL

The Officer in Charge,
American War Graves Registration Command

Dear Sir;

The American Embassy in London gave me your address in reply to an inquiry of mine regarding certain information about an American Bomber Crew from Bovingdon which crashed at Lude Farm, Penn, on August 12th 1944, we wish to include their names in our War Memorial in the Parish Church at Penn.

By some mischance I have not yet received a reply to the letter I addressed to you about August 17th last, and as the matter is becoming increasingly urgent I should like to see what you can do to expedite the matter. Actually since I wrote to you in August I have obtained a list of the names of the Crew which was given by General Doolittle himself to the local farmer where they crashed. They are as follows:

> 1st Lieutenant Charles J. Searl, 2nd Lieutenant Albert L. Dien, 2nd Lieutenant Saul J. Kepner, 2nd Lieutenant Leo C. Walsh, T/Sgt. James A. Beaty, T/Sgt. Cecil E. Kennedy, S/Sgt. Orville M. Wilson, S/Sgt. Albert W. Knight, S/Sgt. Alfred (MMI) Bueffel.

The position is that the draft plan of the Memorial drawn up by Mr. Edward Maufe, A.R.A., the distinguished Church Architect- is now being considered in detail by the Parish Authorities, who will be anxious to conclude these arrangements.

To enable us to complete the outline of our proposal we require the following particulars relating to each individual contained on the list herein:

> Full surname, Christian names, Decorations or Distinctions, Rank, Unit, Age, Place of burial, Summary of Service record, Home town or state; and Name and address of Next of kin

I would be very grateful if you would send me as soon as possible all the information you can from your records, and I will then apply to the Adjutant General in Washington for any further information necessary.

I am,

> Yours very sincerely,
>
> (Rev) O. Muspratt
> Secretary Penn War Memorial
> Committee

David E. Huntley

The Vicarage
PENN
Bucks
England

6 July 1948

Dear Mrs Searl,

I was deeply touched when I received your acknowledgment of my letter last year, your gratitude for the information I gave you moved me profoundly. It will interest you to know that my letter reached all the families concerned except Mrs Annie Iva Beaty, next-of-kin of Technical Sergeant James A. Beaty. Perhaps one of you may be able to give me her latest address.

I would have written again earlier but I have been hopelessly overworked on many other things, and besides I could not have told you anything further until now concerning the memorial here. After considering the matter very carefully, we have reached the conclusion that besides placing their names and records in our Book of Remembrance in Penn Church, there should be erected a simple stone on the roadside near the crash. An inscription could be engraved on this, recording their names, the date, &c. Will you please let me know if this suggestion meets with your approval, and I will make further enquiries regarding the details.

In the meantime, I am writing to you most urgently to let you know that I have just been able to arrange for the Bishop of Pennsylvania, who is over here for the Lambeth Conference, to visit the Parish next Sunday, July 11. He will join me in a Memorial Service at 3 p.m. on the site of the crash, and later, at 6.30-7 p.m. our Evening Service from Penn Church will be broadcast specially to the U.S.A. on the B.B.C. North American Service. I understand that this will be relayed through Radio Station WHP, Harrisburg, Pennsylvania, between 1.30 and 2 p.m. New York Time. I have no doubt that you will listen if you possibly can and will value greatly this unique opportunity to bridge the distance between us.

I enclose an account of the crash as some of you asked me to do so.

Yours sincerely,

O. Muspratt, Vicar.

The B-17 Tomahawk Warrior: A WWII Final Honor

There is also a hand-written letter from Rev. Muspratt to Mr. Nile Searl, the date of which is indistinct, but around 1947 or 1949, where he mentions a BBC radio program entitled, "An English County Christmas", in which the villages of Penn and Tyler's Green featured prominently. He even provided Mr. Searl the shortwave broadcast coordinates in meters and megacycles. Rev. Muspratt himself said he would be on that broadcast, which would mention the memorial to Charles Searl and his crew.

As an eyewitness to the immediate aftermath of the plane crash, but importantly, as a direct witness of those critical seconds before the impact in Penn just Northeast of us in Loudwater, I described our village of Loudwater and the surrounding meadows that the pilot had to traverse as he flew so incredibly low over our cottage.

I had mentioned this previously that beyond our cottage there were just meadows and the meandering River Wye, where a significant number of concrete pillars were installed by the government[41] as a deterrent to prevent German troop gliders from landing during any attempted invasion.

I am convinced, therefore, Lt. Searl had directed his plane to the open fields of Lude Farm near the village of Penn, about a mile away because he could not make a forced landing on those meadows in Loudwater. As they were heading Northeast over our cottage, Searl's co-pilot, 2nd Lt. Dion, being in the right-hand seat, would have had a better view of those fields and the pillars. No one had mentioned this aspect in any other report, and it provides additional support to the evidence that the crew's efforts to find open farm fields saved lives in both villages. (*I have since discovered, through a local historian, the names of residents who concur with my observations of concrete barriers*).

The village of Loudwater is at a lower elevation than Penn where the plane crashed, by about 155 ft. If they were as low as I think they were, they

---

[41] British anti-invasion preparations. May 1940, the directorate of Fortifications and Works (FW3) was set up at the War Office. The Air Ministry provided designs of fortifications intended to protect airfields from troops, landing or parachuting.

had to have gained some altitude to reach the farm fields. It was not much, but I think it was critical in their situation.

I have often wondered why none of the crew bailed out or whether Searl had issued a bailout order. I can only think that losing altitude in the short time frame since taking off at 6:18 a.m. from Nuthampstead left little or no time to bail out. His crew were used to Searl handling difficult flying conditions, so that day coming too low out of the cloud cover, they probably hoped for the best.

My layperson's estimate of the time for Searl to reach Loudwater would be around 25 minutes after takeoff, which had been at 6.18 a.m. Therefore, assuming a flying speed of 150 mph and a distance of around 44 miles, the plane would have been over us at around 6:40 to 6:45 a.m. Searl would have made a few turns trying to control the plane while looking for a place to land. This matches exactly the time I remember by the faint light from my bedroom window as dawn was just breaking. (*Sunrise*[42] *in London, UK 6:41 AM Saturday, August 12, 1944 (GMT+1) DST*)

The crash and explosion occurred less than a minute later, which would have been around around 6:46 a.m. The declassified[43] Accident Report (Chapter 9, 28th Mission) gives the time of the crash as 7:25 Hrs., which is highly unlikely based on the evidence and my personal observation at the scene.

▲ ▲ ▲ ▲

The Likely Cause of the Crash

In early January 2017, I received an e-mail from a Mr. David Hardie, in England, who had seen my website related to that part, which concerned the Tomahawk Warrior and my connection to it. He mentioned while at

---

[42] https://www.metoffice.gov.uk/
[43] The Official Secret Declassified Accident Report is shown in Chapter 9, Mission # 28

the church in Penn, with his wife, he noticed the Book of Remembrance for the crew of the Tomahawk Warrior and "often wondered what had happened." David Hardie had begun some searching on the Internet and afterwards found some articles, as well as, the 398th BGMA website. He was curious about why in the reports it stated that the plane's engines were on fire and what might have caused it to crash.

I had replied that,

On the same day, August 12, 1944, a B24 piloted by a Lt.. Ellis crashed near Nuthampstead. Some say it collided with another plane as they were gathering for a formation to bomb Germany. However, there is no direct evidence of this collision. Lt. Ellis has been honored posthumously with a special plaque for guiding his plane away from houses, etc. I have more data on this event, but in no way can it be concluded that it was directly connected with the Tomahawk Warrior. I will eventually put together some more info on this when I have time.

I also added,

As Lt. Searl saved my life that day and many others by diverting his aircraft to Lude Farm, I would like to explore ways on how he could be honored besides[44] the Book of Remembrance at Penn Church.

On April 27, 2017, I mentioned that,

I have a time of sunrise for that day, so my recollection of it just getting light with an overcast sky would give it about 7 a.m. or thereabouts[45].

---

[44] It seems this was the starting point of my driven quest to bring a more permanent Honor to these men of the Tomahawk Warrior.

[45] I was able to correlate the time more accurately from the records and my own observation on that specific day itself. Chapter 9, Mission #28

It was pretty dark in our bedroom when that plane went over, but there was a glimmer of daylight from the window. I am quite sure about this. We were up and scrambling to explore as soon as we heard the explosion, which was about 30 to 40 seconds or so after it went over us. 6:41 AM Saturday, August 12, 1944 (GMT+1) Sunrise in London,[46] *UK 6:42 AM Sunday, August 13, 1944 (GMT+1) Sunrise in London, UK*

David Hardie and I exchanged several additional e-mails over the ensuing months, in which he offered his understanding of aspects of the crash that he uncovered or surmised, based on research he had conducted. He thought that icing may have been a significant cause of the accident. Here is a verbatim quote from David that offers a possible reason for the crash. This was from David's e-mail to me dated May 17, 2017.

Here, I am citing the email from David Hardie, dated 5/17/2017.

Hello David,
I thought that you might be interested to know that I managed to interview Len Howard[47] *at his cottage in Beaconsfield last week.*

Len is now 94 and remembers the events of the August 12, 1944 clearly. Len is most probably the last living witness to the crash of The Tomahawk Warrior.

I spent about an hour in the company of Ian James[48]*, whilst interviewing Len about his recollections and to specifically about the details of the crash as seen from his vantage point and location that morning. I was very careful to let Len tell us the story without interjecting or proposing any theories or ideas so as to establish just the facts as he witnessed them.*

---

[46] Meteorological Office, UK, 1944, Double Summer Time (DST)
[47] An eyewitness, whose video interview, conducted many years earlier, can be found on the 398th Bomb Group Memorial Association https://398th.org/
[48] A Local historian and who had worked at Lude Farm in later years.

One detail which strikes me immediately, and Len was very sure of this, even when I asked him at several different times, was, that he is certain that there were no flames or smoke trails coming out from the aircraft before it hit the ground. This is quite significant because this would seem to discount reports that the aircraft was seen to be on fire.

One post-mission interrogation report from a pilot of the 398th, (of which I have a copy) states that he "saw an explosion in the clouds above him, at about 8000' looking towards London", whilst he was on a heading of 237Â°.

He further states it "may have been a doodlebug"[49] or it "may have been Searl."

This is interesting because if it had been Lt. Searl, then he would have been completely on the wrong side of the formation, according to the formation briefing charts for that mission. This would tend to discount the idea that Searl was seen to explode in the air, unless any other witness accounts appear.

We can never be 100% sure, but at the moment it may be the case that they were carrying heavy icing and dropped out of the formation and then stalled and spun in.

Len told me that the aircraft dropped its nose abruptly, then made three slow rotations, rapidly descending turns, and then hit the ground in a single tremendous explosion.

This seems very likely the "stall, spin, crash, burn" sequence of a loss of control due to heavy ice buildup. One other aircraft that morning aborted due to severe icing and also entered a violent spin, returning to Nuthampstead with a badly shaken crew.

Earlier in the week, I managed to visit the Woodman Pub at Nuthampstead and hosted Geoff Rice, the 398th historian[50] (sic) to lunch.

---

[49] A V1 rocket

[50] The museum's name is, 'Nuthamstead Airfield Museum' not the '398th Museum' and the late Geoff Rice was a Trustee of the Museum & the photo historian for the 398th Bomb Group Memorial Association.

He, later, allowed me to enter the 398th museum[51] and gave me a tour of the various artifacts and memorabilia. He even showed me a large ring recovered from the crash site of "The Tomahawk Warrior." Not sure though exactly what it is at this stage.

Anyway, my research continues and I remain hopeful that more details will gradually come to light.

I hope this is of some interest to you.

My kind regards to you.

I replied to David's e-mail on *5/17/2017.*

David Hardie, that is indeed very interesting. Well, Len Howard is consistent in his memory because his description is the same as the video interview he made years ago[52]. He does not mention any flames etc., and he gives the same description of rotating downward, but did not actually go and see the immediate crash site. He was with his father, maintaining the hedge-rows along the local lanes. I would be interested to know if his time-line matches my own? That plane was extremely low over our cottage, and the building shook severely when it flew overhead. One thing I find hard to believe is that there might have been icing on the wings. This was August! The air on the ground was certainly not cold. I will be back in touch. David Huntley

In another e-mail David Hardie stated:

One other aircraft returned to base on the same mission due to severe icing![53] One of the crew diaries reports that the aircraft subsequently en-

---

[51] See previous footnote

[52] The video interview is available on the 398th Bomb Group Memorial Association website.

[53] The author clarifies this statement with specific evidence from Declassified Operational Records in another Chapter

tered a violent spin, so much so that several bombs broke away from their shackles in the bomb bay and were resting on the others. They were lucky to land back at Nuthampstead alive.

The weather that morning at Nuthampstead was not too good, although further south where you were, the cloud base was much higher as the weather front was crossing the country.

Lt. Searl's was one of the first few aircraft to get airborne that morning at 06:18 a.m. The base record has it, so he was exposed to icing conditions in the clouds for much longer than the other aircraft. The adiabatic[54] lapse rate is about 2° C per 1000' of altitude, so even if the ground temperature was 10° C that morning, you would only need to be at 5000' to be in the freezing layer.

I have subsequently found that all of the B-17 deicing equipment as installed during manufacture, was subsequently removed because they were trying to save weight and get the center of gravity back within limits.

They had previously been flying the aircraft at high combat weights with the C of G too far aft, by about a foot, leading to controllability problems and several aborted missions. This is all mentioned in Cliff Bishop's fascinating book, "Fortresses over Nuthampstead."

Personally, I do not remember it being too cold, just a usual August summer's morning. Being young and not feeling the cold in those days, I would say it was 55° F or 13° C. However, it could also have been closer to 50° F or 10° C in which case freezing would have occurred at 5000 ft altitude.

David Hardie's assessment of icing problem is well founded as my own cross-referenced research on the subject[55] yields very similar conclusions based on what equipment the B-17G was delivered with. The rubber de-icing

---

[54] he rate at which atmospheric temperature decreases with increasing altitude in conditions of thermal equilibrium. Air will reduce by around 2 C every 1000 ft altitude.

[55] Page 51 in The B-17 Flying Fortress Story by Roger Freemen, Cassel 1998,

boots along the leading edges of the flight surfaces were removed due to the risk of damage and dislodgement in combat. Instead, a de-icing compound was used in their place. In April 1944, the thermal deicing of the wing was to be affected by directing warm air to the leading edge. However, around 1,700 B-17 Gs were delivered without heat exchangers, which were to solve such a problem. They only retrofitted these from December 1944. Therefore, the planes flown by the 600th Squadron of the 398th Bombardment Group, including those flown by the Tomahawk Warrior crew, would have been vulnerable to icing conditions. This documented history together with David Hardie's alternate independent research, and Len Howard's personal observation of the plane's attitude of descent gives a very strong credence, but not absolute confirmation, that the plane the Tomahawk Warrior crew were flying that day, suffered a loss of control because of icing. Further evidence[56] reinforces my inference in my next section.

▲ ▲ ▲ ▲

The Weather and Plane Identification for August 12, 1944

Although I cannot bring Charles Searl back by envisioning a further conversation with him, I can imagine how he would feel if he knew he was not the only one having trouble that day, which sadly, it ended badly for him and his crew.

I'm sure that Charles, in retrospect, would have recognized his own dilemma if he could see the following extracts from the 398th Operations Report[57] by Major Jean B. Miller, who reported that:

(Citation)

The Lead Group 602nd Squadron had a difficult assembly because of

---

discusses icing issue and de-icing equipment. The complete history of every B-17 ever built from the XB-15 prototype to postwar uses & Services

[56] I further postulated about icing of carburetors and this was subsequently verified as a very valid argument later by a veteran B-17 pilot in the next section.

[57] 398th History CD File B) 482d.pdf Page 60,61 Numbered Page: 1766,1767

adverse weather. They finally accomplished the assembly 5 miles southwest of Splasher #11. (*Author: A radio beacon*)

The High Group 600th Squadron (*Author: Charles Searl's Group*) had mist clouds up to 10,000 ft which were solid up to 30,000 ft. Visibility was less than 1/4 mile. They changed the assembly first to 23,000 ft over Debden,[58] and later changed to Splasher #11 at 18,000 ft. The 600th Group formation finally made the assembly four (4) minutes south of Splasher #11. (*Author's Note; Except Searl did not make it to the assembly*)

They also changed the Low Group 601st Squadron to Splasher #11 due to clouds assembly.

The Report says the following ships returned early:

"A/C 42-107080 went into a spin climbing to assembly altitude due to heavy accumulation of ice on wings. Bombs were shaken loose. A/C returned to the base."

"A/C 42-102596 did not receive instructions for change in assembly, returned to the base."

"A/C 42-107191 (Charles Searl's plane) exploded in mid-air[59] on route to assembly point. Reason unknown. No survivors." (End Citation)

As they cited it in the Operations Report above, Charles was not the only one at risk from icing on this mission. As illustrated in the full mission report, the Aircraft 42-107080 of the 601st Squadron, which was in the Low Group, went into a spin because of heavy icing, and their bombs shook loose in the holding shackles.

It would explain Len Howard's description of the slow spin into the ground of Charles's plane and the sheer impossibility of him maintaining any control as it plunged to earth. Charles' plane was one of the primary

---

[58] Splasher #11 a radio beacon at Habden Farm near Rogate, Hants, and Splasher #6 near Debden Essex

[59] It exploded on impact with the ground, not in mid-air.

groups that took off early that morning. Then, having to change to Splasher #11, put them in severe cloud cover for longer than he might have liked.

Could it have been iced up carburetors in one or two engines that caused a loss of power and vibration? The struggling engines would more than likely give off much smoke, providing some hearsay or undocumented witnesses with the impression of them being on fire.

(Author's Note: Since I postulated about iced up carburetors I had a recent discussion on this subject with Major, Lucky Luckadoo, a WWII who flew B-17s for the 'Bloody 100 Bomb Group, he said, "The greatest hazard we encountered was carburetor icing. This involved ice forming in the carburetor of the engines and preventing sufficient air to mix with the fuel. **It is much more likely to have occurred in this instance than wing icing at lower altitude in August.**" Author's emphasis).

I cannot imagine how Charles and the rest of the crew were feeling. John Comer[60], a Turret gunner, in the same Bomb Group, had observed in 1943, that the closer a crew got to their final number of missions, that the more apparent was the chance their ship will go down. I believe Charles must have had similar thoughts with every successful mission. He wrote a letter[61] to his wife Arlie, which seemed to reflect that sort of foreboding.

Crews accumulate superstitions as they fly on more and more missions. One cannot imagine what flashed through Charles's mind in those split seconds as the ground came up so fast toward him. I'm sure the letter he wrote to Arlie must have flashed before him.

An interesting aspect of the Major Miller's Official Report cited above is that, the only other reference of a ship from the 601st returning to base because of loose bombs on that mission on August 12th, could only be identified from the diary entry of Staff Sergeant Chilton[62] Jorgenson the Ball Turret Gunner of the 601st Squadron who wrote:

---

[60] John Comer, Author "Combat Crew" Simon & Schuster 1988
[61] Letter is published in Chapter 7 under Graduation and Deployment
[62] Diary entry Courtesy of the 398th.

August 12, 1944
(Citation)

Today we started on a mission to Bue, France [Versailles] but fate stopped us. It was just about the end of our crew when we took off. Climbing in the overcast, Jack saw a ship directly ahead of us and put us in a steep bank. This ended in our ship going over on its back and then into a spin. It threw everyone up to the roof and stuck there. Clark and I tried to get our chutes and get to the waist door, but I could not find mine. After being thrown around inside the ship, Markland's chute came sailing by me and I caught it and threw it back to him. I started again for the door. Another chute came by me and I grabbed it and put it on. By that time Clark was at the door. I was almost there.

By the grace of God, Jack pulled it out and leveled it off. Duff was having one hell of a time in the tail. Meanwhile, Andy and Danny Cohen, the toglier, likewise had a lot of trouble in the nose.

Pheiffer was doing his damnedest to hold Jack in his seat so he could control the ship. Some bombs pulled off the shackles and were rolling around in the bomb bay. We went out over the North Sea and opened the bomb bay doors to let them roll out. After getting back over land, Clark and Duff put the pins back in the rest of the bombs and we came home. Did I ever enjoy being on the ground? (End citation)

As this was the only ship from the 601st with loose bombs which returned to base on August 12th, we must assume it was Aircraft 42-107080. Therefore, we must accept the Official Report that the severe icing caused the return to base and not a near collision as described by Jorgenson in his diary. It's possible that Jorgenson, in the chaos for the struggle to maintain control, misheard what happened and recorded in his diary as a near collision. Is it possible that Jack, the unnamed pilot, reported the icing in his debriefing instead of a near collision? It is highly unlikely a pilot would misreport in a briefing. The diary entry must have been caused by a misunderstanding and confusion.

The author's research showed that Aircraft 42-107080 was usually flown by 1st Lt. Robert O. Taylor[63] and his crew. Their previous mission in that plane was on August the 6th on a bombing mission to Brandenburg, Germany. It appears based on the evidence of the Operations Report, that on August 12th the plane flew with a different crew, which included Jorgenson and the pilot 'Jack[64].'

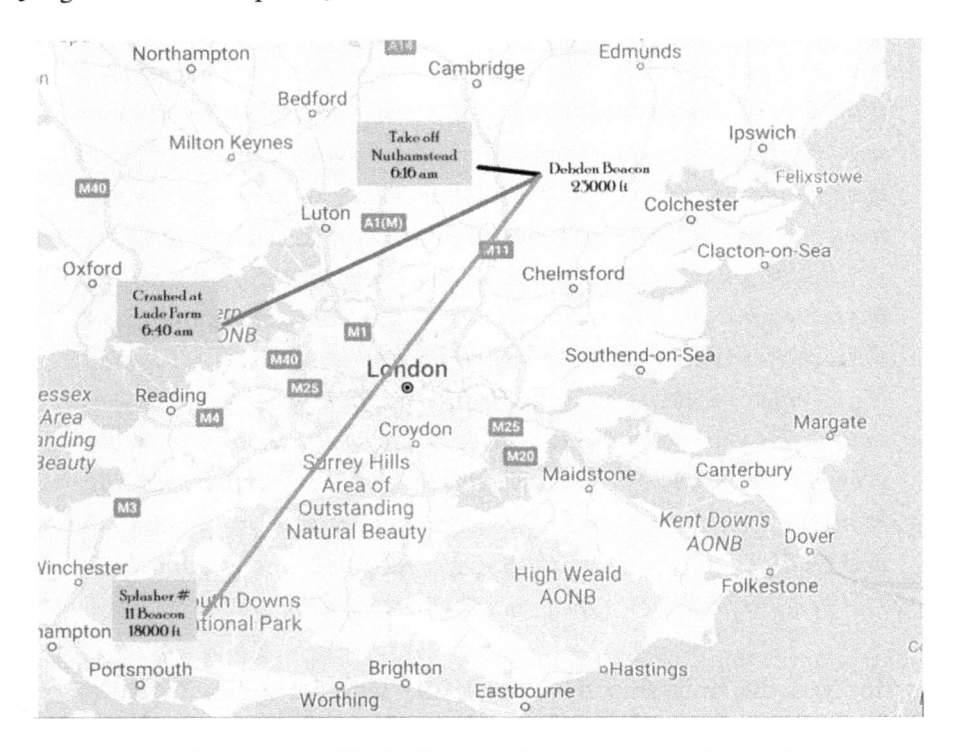

Author's Illustration of Radio Beacons for the August 12, 1944 mission
Credit Google Maps

---

[63] Courtesy of the 398th Bomb Group
[64] "Jack" was 601st SQ pilot, 1st Lt. John S. Falkenbach, aka: "Jack"

I think, with almost certainty, that the cause of Charles Searl's crash was the severe icing which prevented him from reaching the assembly point and caused the plane to be off course by several miles, when changing from Splasher #6 to the new Assembly point at Splasher #11, near Rogate.

Even those who could get in formation for the run to the target had comments, such as, the Diary[65] of 2nd L t. Charles J. Mellis, Jr. Co-Pilot, 603rd Squadron who noted:

(Citation)

August 12, 1944–Saturday [Mission #23: Versailles, France] "Went to (Versailles) Paris today. This time we hit the front over England and had trouble forming. Flew in the soup an hour and finally formed on the South Coast. Most of the ships got off ok, tho, and we did our bombing. Flak wasn't too bad and so it turned out to be a good mission except for the assembly. Flew a lot over friendly France today, but couldn't see any action on the ground as we crossed the lines." [Pilot Log entry] Mission: Station 131, England to Versailles, France and return Aircraft: B-17G Time: 7 hours. (End citation)

This is an imperfect copy of the declassified Combat Report that day, which clearly describes "Severe icing over England during assembly." (It also reports, erroneously though, "One plane exploded over England." It was referring to Searl's plane, which exploded on the ground)

---

[65] Courtesy of the 398 Bomb Group Memorial Association. https://www.398th.org/History/Diaries/Mellis/Diary_Mellis.html#anchor_19440806

```
                No nose x 1/40
   A/C LOST             TOTAL  1
   A. E/A    Nil
   B. A/A    Nil
   C. NON-ENEMY (CRASHES ON T/E OFF, ETC.) 1 exploded over England
   D. OTHER  Nil
5. CLAIMS:  E/A A/C DESTROYED  Nil  DAMAGED ___ Nil  PROBABLES  Nil
6. SORTIES  33
7. NO. OF A/C RETURNING EARLY. (reasons briefly)  2   Personnel failure
                                                     Mechanical     "
8. OTHER INFORMATION, IF IMPORTANT  Nil

9. ADDITION, OF ANY, INFORMATION ON BOMBING RESULTS: Good  Strikes 500
                                                                 yds E
10. ADDITIONAL OBSERVATIONS   1040  4821N-0031E Large column of dust
                                     on road believed to be a long convoy
11. FLAK Target - meagre     1119  4800N-0012W Fires in town
             and inaccurate  1148  4820N-0001W Large fire in wooded area
12. E/A OPPOSITION  Nil            4815N-0034  SE of Mayenne heavy guns
                                               firing from edge of forest
13. BATTLE DAMAGE (ESTIMATED) MAJOR  Nil  MINOR ___ Nil  SALVAGE  Nil

14. WEATHER    Thick clouds and severe icing over England during
               assembly.
               Target 5/10 low clouds. Visibility 15 mi - haze
               No contrails.
```

There were other Bomb Groups having difficulties on the morning of August 12, 1944, and one was incorrectly linked to Charles's crash.

2nd Lt. John D. Ellis of the 577th Squadron 392nd Bomb Group was part of a wing of B-24 bombers, which had taken off from their base at Wendling at 7:45 am for a target in France. There had been unofficial reports over the years that Lt. Ellis had collided with Charles Searl's plane, causing Ellis's ship to crash and explode at Waltham Cross.

This never happened as the evidence[66] clearly reveals: the time of Searl's crash and that of Lt. Ellis is almost 60 minutes later, and the

---

[66] See the report and the eye witness accounts.
https://www.b24.net/MM081244.htm

distance between the two sites is 44 miles. Importantly, several eyewitnesses, including those of Ellis's own squadron, saw his plane either in a spin, or a stall mode. While there was evidence of fire and engines malfunctioning, the manner of his crashed landing by the eyewitnesses said he came down in a swooping motion. In the author's opinion, based on the official and unofficial (diary) reports, heavy icing could have caused this.

Clearly, Lt. Ellis's ship could not have collided with the Searl's plane, because Searl had already crashed on Lude Farm before Lt. Ellis had even taken off.

Major Miller's report made several references about adverse weather and difficulty of assembly, even with changed assembly points. I should point out that the icing was a continuing problem for combat crews in the months ahead. Two examples of that include:

Aircraft 42-97093[67] – Assigned: 568 Squadron 390 Bomb Group – 'Docs Flying Circus' aka 'Girl of my Dreams' aka 'I'll Get By,' piloted by Orman Coffin, experienced severe icing during assembly for Kassel mission on December 12,1944 and went into a spin. Two of the crew, Lyles, and Spector, had bailed out, but it killed both. Pilot Coffin recovered from the spin and returned to the base safely.

Aircraft 42-32026[68] – Assigned 568 Squadron 390 Bomb Group – 'Tis a Mystery' piloted by Duane Sweeny iced up on way to target at Kassel December 30, 1944 and crashed in the North Sea. 9 crew KIA MACR 11247.

Plane Identification

Another anomaly, which has caused much misreporting over the years and added to the mystery of the actual crash, is the identity of the plane that Searl's crew flew on the day it happened. The Group assigned them a plane

---

[67] Courtesy of; https://B-17FlyingFortress.de.en
[68] Courtesy of; https://B-17FlyingFortress.de.en

they had never flown before. This was a ship usually flown by a Lt. Elwood with the serial number 42-107191 and, according to David Hardie, who had interviewed the friend and long-time neighbor of the plane's bombardier the late Mr. George Schatz, after the war, who said it had the nose art nickname of 'Peggy.' Schatz's neighbor had told Hardie they had named it for Lt. Elwood's wife.

Since flak had badly damaged Searl's regularly assigned plane on August 6, 1944, on a mission to Berlin and was still not ready to fly on the 12th, the Operations Officer assigned them 42-107191. The navigator, Lt. Saul Kempner's diary entry for August 6th confirms that heavy flak caused a lot of damage to Searl's plane. This must have been the reason it switched the crew to another ship. Interestingly, Ed Ginther[69], of the 305th Complimentary Squadron ground support group, had flown with Lt. Searl on August 3rd on a check-ride to ensure the ship was airworthy before the August 6th mission to Berlin.

Once I had secured through the Freedom of Information Act the full Declassified Secret Operational Records of the 600th Squadron, I could determine the identity of the planes Searl and his crew flew on all their missions with the Squadron. The plane assigned to them for 19 of their 30 missions had the serial #42-102507, although 2 of those missions were not credited. So, since their ship had no nose art, or nickname, they simply knew it as the "Tomahawk Warrior" and Lt. Kempner, the navigator, always referred to the plane in his diary entries as the "Warrior."

George Schatz, the bombardier of Lt. Elwood's crew, wrote a short memoir of that day, and I reproduce it here, courtesy of the 398th Bomb Group Memorial Association:

---

[69] From Ed Ginther's personal notes 1944.

(Citation)

The fourth bright, shining morning after our crew's final mission, I was hanging some freshly washed socks and handkerchiefs out to dry on a fence railing near our hut, happy and relaxed as a clam. Then some officer walked down towards us, probably from our 398th's Headquarters, and seeing me, came over and told me that the crew that had taken over our plane #191, were all killed when it exploded while it was circling around on its climb up to assembly over England! I have an old small Kodak photo of Charlie Searl and Leo Walsh on which I had written on the back, in pencil: "Played ball with these two boys yesterday; today they are dead! Lost over England in our #191 plane." There were no survivors of that Searl Crew on that morning of August 12, 1944.

None of us still living have yet recovered from that news. It seems needless to relate how often, over these following, fortunate years, the question of what if that abstract formula had chanced to pro-rate us for a 33 mission tour instead of our saving 32? That giant number, 33, will persist in our brains, as in our hearts. All that morning, the four of us pondered the terrible news in our dark Quonset hut, and for days kept speculating if undetected leaking oxygen valves or gasoline tanks were struck on 42- 107191 on our last low mission of August 8th. We'll never know, but those of our Elwood crew who are still living will ever continue to ponder. (End citation)

The Searl crew were popular in their squadron as reflected in another diary kept by T/Sgt. Armand Fugge's Diary, Engineer/Top turret Gunner 600th Squadron and reproduced here courtesy of the 398th Bomb Group Memorial Association:

(Citation)
August 12, 1944

Slept late. The boys hit an airfield southwest of Paris. Lost Searl's crew. Their plane crashed in England before the mission then exploded. They were all killed, so that ended the career of the "Tomahawk Warriors", their combat name. That makes eight crews lost from our squadron so far out of eighteen. Our plane losses, to date, are 11 out of 18. We have seven originals left. Played ball most of the afternoon. My pilot left for the States today. I don't know when I'll be leaving. Don sure has been a swell guy to us all. (End citation)

MISSIONS FLOWN BY SEARL AND ELWOOD 1944
Identifying the plane # Kempner called "Warrior" or "Tomahawk" in his diary

		SEARL		ELWOOD	
PLANE #	MISSION #	TARGET	DATE	MISSION #	PLANE #
			6-May	1	7242
2487	* 1	BERLIN	7-May	2	7114
2507 N	2	BERLIN	8-May		X
X			9-May	3	7218 T
2507 N	* 3	FRANCE	11-May	4	7186 L
X			12-May	5	401
2507 N	** 4	BERLIN	19-May		X
X			20-May	6	73399 H
25536 c	5	VOIPPY FRANCE	23-May		X
X			24-May	7	2519 A
2507 N	6	NANCY FRANCE	**25-May**		X
2600 Z	7	LUDSCHWAFEN GERMANY	27-May		X
X			28-May	8	**7191 K**
X			30-May		X
2596	8	FRANCE	31-May		X
MAY	TOTAL 8	8 MISSIONS	MAY	8 MISSIONS	

2507 N	9	BOULOGNE	2-Jun	9		2487 F
2507 N	10	MANIPEU FRANCE	3-Jun	10		7399 H
2507 N	11	HARIMLOT FRANCE	4-Jun			X
2507 N	12	TROUVILLE FRANCE	5-Jun	11		7191 K
2487 F	13	COURSEILLES D-DAY	6-Jun	12		7191 K
2390 X	14	KIRLEN BATARD	7-Jun	13		7214 V
2507 N	15	LILLE-NORD FRANCE	12-Jun	15		7191 K
2507 N	16	BEAUVAIS	13-Jun	16		7191 K
2507 N	17	BORDEAUX	15-Jun	17		7191 K
2507 N	18	HAMBURG	16-Jun	18		7191 K
2507 N	19	CHERBOURG	19-Jun	19		7191 K
2507 N	20	HAMBURG	20-Jun	20		7191 K
7114 L	21	ILLEGIBLE	21-Jun			X
JUNE	**TOTAL 13**	**13 MISSIONS**		**11 MISSIONS**		**JUNE**
2507 N	22	CAUCHIE D'ECQUES	6-Jul	21		7191 K
7249 N	23	FESNEY-HUNIRES	8-Jul			X
X			13-Jul	22		157
X			16-Jul	23		7191 K
X			20-Jul	24		6157
2507 N	24	MONTREUIL ST MALO	7/24			X
2507 N	25	MONTREUIL ST MALO	7/25	25		7246 T
2536	26	MERESBURG GERMANY	7/28	26		2390 K
2457 J	27	MERESBURG GERMANY	7/29	27		7214 V
JULY	**TOTAL 6**	**6 MISSIONS**		**7 MISSIONS**		

David E. Huntley

X				8/1	28		7214 V
X				8/3	29		7191 K
2507	28		PEENEMUNDE	8/4	30		157 N
2507 N	***29		BRANDENBURG - PLANE DAMAGED	8/6	31		7191 K
7191 K	30		VERSAILLES - CRASHED DURING FORMATION	8/12			X
AUGUST	TOTAL 3		2 MISSIONS PLUS 1 ATTEMPTED		TOTAL 4		AUGUST
ALL	30		30 FLOWN NOT ALL CREDITED		31		ALL

OF THE 30 MISSIONS FLOWN BY SEARL, FROM MAY 7 TO AUGUST 12, 19 WERE FLOWN ON PLANE NUMBER 2507N - B-17 WHICH RETURNED TO THE USA DECEMBER 14, 1945

OF THE 31 MISSIONS FLOWN BY ELWOOD, FROM MAY 7 TO AUGUST 12, 13 WERE FLOWN ON PLANE NUMBER 7191 K

*Not entered in Kempner's diary
** Diary entry refers to O'Neal going down. See Chapter 10 - Mission May 19,1944
*** 2507 N was heavily damaged August 6 & crew had to fly 7191 K on August 12th

SOURCE: Secret Declassified Operational Records of the 600 Squadron 398th Bomb Group USAAC through FOIA.
ARCHIVE UK/ TW/BOOK/PLANE DATA/ MISSIONS BY SEARL

Chart images Copyright of Huntley Associates Dallas, Inc.

Author's note: On Missions May 19, June 3, and August 6, Kempner refers to his plane as the "Warrior" which was plane #2507 N (42-102507)

This is the only known picture of the plane regularly flown by the Tomahawk Warrior Crew.

Courtesy of the 398th Bomb Group Memorial Association website
David Cohen- Mechanic

Searl's Early Life

When I had met Charles's daughter Cheryl, in April 2019, she had given me a wonderful description of her father's early life growing up in Tomahawk. Her grandfather Nile used to tell her about Charles' formative years. He was very proud of his son and both he and Charles's mother, Josephine, were devastated when they learned of his death.

To provide some sense of how Charles had begun his journey from the City of Tomahawk to signing up for duty in WWII, I interviewed Cheryl to get a picture of Charles' early life based on her knowledge of the family history.

Cheryl, do I "understand it right that Charles worked for his dad, Nile Searl, for a while in his sign-writing business, prior to enlisting?"

"That's right, he did. It was interesting because he was an incredible artist and did major signs for various businesses around the City of Tomahawk."

"Where did the family originate from? I know that as America expanded to the West, many people in Wisconsin came from other parts of America?"

"You are right, David. My grandfather, Nile Wesley Searl, had made a detailed study of family history.[70] He discovered that there were three brothers who had come from Warwick in England and landed in Boston in 1634. The three were John, Edward, and Andrew. Our part of the Searl family comes from the progeny of John. My grandfather served and was wounded in the First World War. Previous generations of Searls served in the Revolutionary and Indian wars. So, we had quite a tradition of military service."

"You Americans know more about your English ancestry than I know about my own, and I was born there."

---

[70] A document compiled by Nile Wesley Searl of the complete ancestry of the Searl family since 1610.

"Well, David, it was just that my grandfather Nile had a lifelong interest in the genealogy of the Searl dynasty. As you probably know from your own research into our family, Charles had a sister, Charlotte, who was two years older. Charles also had a cousin, Davis Charles Searl, who was the son of my granddad's brother, Arthur Searl."

(Author's note: Regarding Cheryl's comment about Davis Searl, Cheryl had never had much contact with that side of the family, but it was Kathryn (Kathy) Searl[71], a daughter of Davis Searl, who had contacted me independently, it was she, who told me that Charles considered Davis to be like an older brother and maintained a close contact with him, sharing many experiences together while growing up.)

In continuing my conversation with Cheryl, she said,

"Charles got named after both of his grandfathers.

At the time he was born, the family was living above Jones Grocery Store on Wisconsin Avenue in Tomahawk. His dad, Nile, was a partner with his brother Art in the Flour and Feed business."

"How did Charles do academically at school? He must have been pretty smart to have become a pilot!"

"Oh, well, that's easy. We were a small city, so everyone ended up at the Tomahawk High School."

"Ha Ha David, I don't really know much about that, although his dad Nile always thought he was a smart boy. He competed in the debating and science teams. Nevertheless, he enjoyed football as well. Sadly, I have no written records of these events."

"Are you aware of any extra curricula activities he engaged in while at high school?"

"The only thing I can think of is he had four friends that he used to hang out with and they were called the 'Five Musketeers.' They would goof around together, fishing, and playing ball. All five of them had joined

---

[71] See Chapter 5, Dedication by Kathy and Chuck Searl

the Citizens Military Training Camp in Fort Snelling, Minnesota, even before they had graduated together in 1939."

When I asked Cheryl if she knew the names of these friends, she pulled out an article which was written about them after the war and said,

"Let's see, they were Bob Conant, Dick Gesell, Joe Chvala, and Howard Ball. They were all 17-years-old."

I thanked Cheryl for providing me with some of this family legacy and history.

If I could envisage speaking to Charles again, I am sure he would be delighted to know his friends had all returned home after the war. All four of his friends[72] returned home as WWII heroes, although, like most veterans, they would not like to be given that title. Howard Ball, who became a bombardier in the AAC, got shot down twice and was held in a German POW Camp for two years. Bill Conant graduated from West Point and later, during the war, survived a blast of a land mine. Dick Gesell flew several heroic bombing runs and took paratroopers in to battle. Later, after the war, he taught college aeronautics.

I'm going to devote a separate chapter to Joe Chvala[73] because, in his capacity as a navy pilot, he was engaged in some heroic deeds. But it's what he didn't do that has made him a subject of interest, particularly the connection of the Tomahawk Warrior story to a historic incident in American history.

---

[72] From the archives of Cheryl Surfus in which Jack Chvala, brother of Joe Chvala gave an interview about the five friends.

[73] Chapter 14

The Five Musketeers

L to R Bob Conant – Dick Gesell – Joe Chvala – Chuck Searl – Howard Ball
Courtesy of Cheryl Surfus

Another important date for Charles was on May 6, 1942, when he married his school sweetheart, Arlie Irene Peterson. Arlie was from Irma, a small town 10 miles from Tomahawk. They had met at school and after they graduated, they eventually got married. Their first child, a daughter named Charlene, was born on November 20, 1942.

▲ ▲ ▲ ▲

Enlistment and Officer Pre-Pilot Testing

After Charles had graduated from Tomahawk High School, he applied and was accepted at the University of Wisconsin. He was not there for long before he transferred to DePaul University in Chicago. He spent a couple of years there before war broke out.

Based on Charles's letters and correspondence with his parents during this period, the attack on Pearl Harbor did not surprise him in 1941. The audacity and timing were of course, a surprise to everyone. He and his friends had been training at the Citizens Military training camp, so the threat of war was not unexpected.

Charles did not enlist straight away after Roosevelt made his "Day of Infamy" speech, but did so on February 17, 1942. Not long after that, on March 11, they put him on a train to Texas to undergo formal military training. His thoughts were for his parents and, of course, about his dad who had served in WWI and was wounded in that conflict. That war was supposed to end all wars.

In a letter[74] to his parents, he wrote:

Wasn't sure at first where we were headed. They transferred us to St. Louis at 5:30 pm, then on to Chicago. We were told we were going to Texas. We left Chicago at noon March 12th and came straight through on a Pullman, arriving at Kelly Field,[75] Texas at 5:30 pm. I enjoyed the train ride, and I got $1.33 for food, although one meal cost that much! There were ten of us that came down, but none of us knew anything. There were plenty of others who had been there eight weeks and were still unassigned! Most were pilot washouts.

---

[74] These are extracts from the letters and correspondence between Charles and his parents. Courtesy of Cheryl Surfus.

[75] During World War II almost 7,000 men graduated from the Advanced Flying School at Kelly between 1939 and 1943. In 1943 Kelly Field's primary mission became aircraft maintenance and supply; training functions moved to other fields. As a result, the Kelly site was transformed into a major center for aircraft maintenance, repair and overhaul of aircraft—a legacy that continues. Ref; – https://kellyheritage.org/wwii-era.php#2

From another letter he said:

This place is enormous, and we were all in tents. It's a replacement center. Some people said we may take some tests. There are no uniforms, just coveralls. It just seems slow going and rumor is we may get shipped elsewhere. Other talk is we may get pilot tests for possible future training. It's all confusing because no one knows anything. No two fellows say the same thing. It's all rumors. I hate waiting around.

We eventually got our uniforms and equipment. 2 pairs of pants, flight caps, and blouse. We have everything, all officers, equipment, and clothing. I may be here in Tent City for quite a while, so here is my address: it is A.C.R.D Co C Kelly Field Texas.

We don't have any commissioned officers, and things are a mess. One has to have a pretty passive attitude or one can go nuts, Army style. I found out I was eligible for pilot training as long as I pass all my tests, etc.

The weather here in Texas is hot like summer, even at night, although a bunch of soldiers from Panama swore, they were freezing.

I had no chance yet to take any photos, but I promise I will once I get into active training. Now that I have my uniforms and equipment, I have shipped my suitcase back home and sent the key in a letter. This sure is a big place!

▲ ▲ ▲ ▲

Training, Graduation and Deployment
Sept 2 1942

In his other letter Charles wrote:

By this time several of us had had a serious of tests that kept us in the pilot training squad. I was happy I had not washed out yet. I began training at the Pampa Army Air[76] Field in Texas. Here, I got introduced to my first plane ride, a Stearman PT-17 bi-plane. The instructors really made you learn the rules, or, as they said, the fundamentals. If you failed to follow the rules, they quickly washed you out. I was constantly anxious about doing better on my flights or I would be on my way to becoming a bombardier.

The Stearman PT-17, courtesy of Steve Hayes – AeonAviation Photography

I often felt sick and didn't enjoy flying this plane. It was like a bank clerk trying to balance his books on the running board of a Model T on a country road! The plane pitched and heaved something awful.

We would fly across country to Laredo or Corpus, but it didn't seem much of a trip because we didn't stop. It didn't seem we covered much ground. Meanwhile, we must not get into clouds, as that would fail you immediately. If your fuel gage showed 1/2 full, you had to head home straight away. Watching oil pressure and other instruments was a constant

---

[76] The Army Air Forces Training Command operated the Pampa Army Airfiled from 1942 to 1945. It is situated about ten miles East of the town of Pampa, Texas.

practice. You learned slow rolls and spins, but on no account were you to invert. This was highly disciplined and tight training to ensure you would not be a reckless pilot.

The time sure went fast after the 3rd week and Dead Reckoning only lasted 6 weeks, then we got 9 weeks of celestial. It just didn't seem possible that we were getting so much, a person gets used to the long hours. Everyone, including me, worried about making it. At the time, I thought it would be a miracle. I thought the entire experience was interesting but awfully tedious and exacting, and I'm not neat or exact. I was anxious at this point to get through the next 13 weeks.

Charles, did in fact, get through his pilot training with flying colors, graduating with honors as head of his class.

Here is Charles's graduation certificate from the Pampa Advanced Flying School. Charles had sent this to his close cousin, Davis Searl.

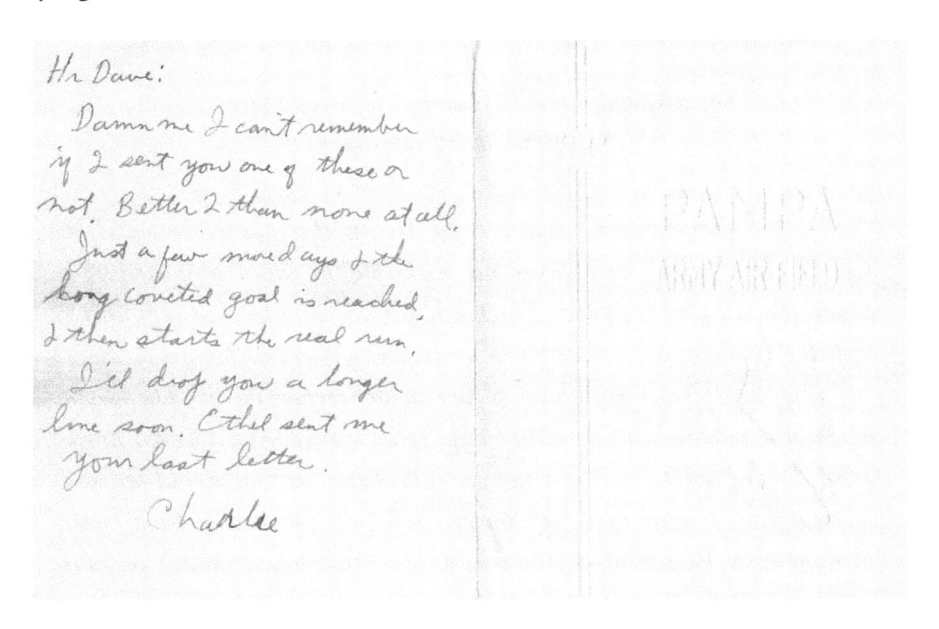

> Hi Dave:
> Damn me I can't remember if I sent you one of these or not. Better 2 than none at all. Just a few more days & the long coveted goal is reached, & then starts the real run. I'll drop you a longer line soon. Ethel sent me your last letter.
> Charlie

This and the documents below courtesy of Kathy Searl

Army Air Forces
Advanced Flying School
of
Pampa, Texas
announces the graduation of
Class 43-H
Monday morning, August thirtieth
nineteen hundred and forty-three
at ten o'clock

Images courtesy of Kathy Searl

I secured, through official sources, Charles's declassified pilot flight logs, which showed that he was transferred to other fields for further training. Each of these fields must have held special or significant memories for him. For instance, after graduation they transferred him to Lockbourne Air Base in Columbus, Ohio, where he began flying twin engine AT-9's and AT-17's.[77]

---

[77] The **Cessna AT-17 Bobcat** was a twin-engined advanced trainer aircraft designed and made in the United States, and used during World War II to bridge the gap between single-engined trainers and twin-engined combat aircraft. The AT-17 was powered by two Jacobs R-755-9 radial piston engines. The commercial version was the **Model T-50**, from which the AT-17 was developed.

Curtiss AT-9 Twin Engine Trainer   Cessna AT-17 BobCat trainer
Images courtesy of the United States Air Force Museum

During his time at Lockbourne, he graduated from the Bobcat trainer to the 4-engined bomber B-17E and a few hours on the F version. He stayed there until November 1943, and then got transferred to Salt Lake City, Utah. Here, he spent a month on B-17s, and some hours were spent night flying as first pilot and as a co-pilot.

The army taught him that while a pilot is in command of the ship and crew, he should ensure his co-pilot can take over command of the plane and crew in the event the pilot is killed or severely wounded in combat. The command pilot is trained to ensure all the crew can perform their respective tasks as one cohesive unit, and with good morale.

After sometime, Charles was transferred to Rapid City, South Dakota and spent the month of December there with more training on a B-17F. He was told he would be assigned to the 398th Bomb Group. Then, in January, his 9-man crew was assembled to join him, and, together, began training to make a cohesive team. They were assigned as a part of the 600th Squadron. He also did some training in a Link simulator[78] which, he noted in his log, was a unique experience for him.

Charles and his crew trained as a full ten-man combat team through

---

[78] All information on training on the various versions of the B-17 bomber at Rapid City, Dakota and final transit to England, is from Lt. Searl's Declassified Individual Flight Record (Log) in the Author's possession.

January, February, and March 1943. On the 12th of March, they were allocated a brand-new B-17G serial #42-97267 which, after some debate, the crew decided they should name it, *The Tomahawk Warrior* after the city where Charles was born and grew up in Wisconsin. He was very honored that the crew voted for this, and it gave him a lot of confidence in his leadership skills in the future, and knowing the crew was so supportive of his command.

From the photo I have included here, it looks like Charles used his sign writing experience with his dad's business to design the nickname on the nose of the plane.

Photo courtesy of the 398th Bomb Group Association

Charles's daughter, Cheryl, told me the style he used for the plane's nickname was typical of him. The **T** looked like a tomahawk because he placed it to act for both words. They flew this plane in combat simulations through the rest of March and to getting the crew all working together.

The Tomahawk Warrior crew, like many in those days, were very young. They ranged in age from 20 to 25. Charles was only 22 and in command. His co-pilot, 2nd Lt. Albert Dion, at 25 was the oldest of the crew. His navigator, 2nd Lt. Saul Kempner, was also older than Charles, aged 24. No matter what their ages, as the skipper on this ship, it was critical that he kept track of everyone's abilities to ensure that each person's skill sets were maintained. They each depended on everyone else's abilities in combat for their lives.

Based on their combat record, Charles must have been thrilled by the way his crew maintained a smooth and efficient working team in difficult situations.

The crew was transferred from Rapid City in Dakota to Grand Island, Nebraska, on April 4th 1943. They flew several night missions and other practice runs, and then assembled for the move to their ultimate destination in England. The flight logs below (transcribed from the original document and edited for brevity), show how the transition happened.

- *April 15th From Grand Island, Nebraska to Bangor Maine, a flight of just under 9 hours.*
- *April 19th From Bangor Maine to Iceland, an uneventful flight of just under 9 hours with a tail wind.*
- *April 20th From Iceland to Belfast, Ireland, this only took just over 5 hours.*
- *April 22nd From Belfast to the final destination Field #131 in England at Nuthampstead."*

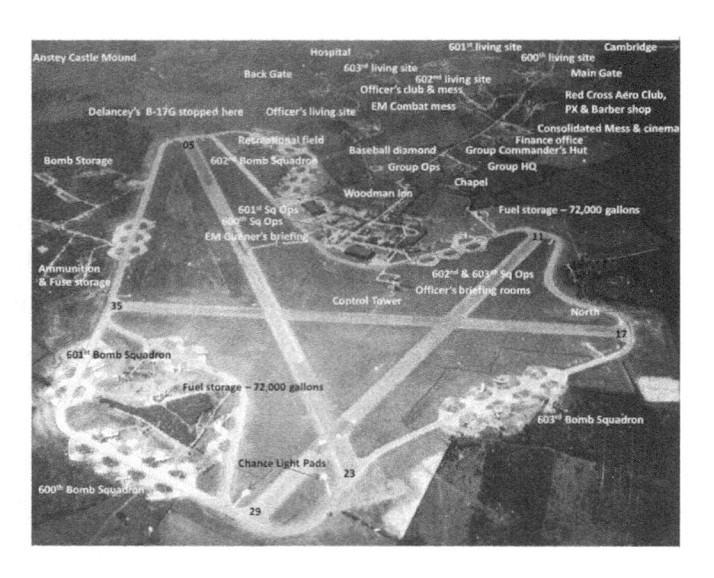

Nuthampstead Field #131 in Hertfordshire, England- Photo courtesy of 398th BGMA

I can envisage Charles and his crew getting a bit of a shock on arrival at Nuthampstead.[79] The first thing was, that their plane was taken from them. It was to be transferred to Ridgewell Air Base to the 535 Bomb Squadron of the 381st Bomb Group. Ridgewell needed the replacement since their 535 Squadron was short of planes. Apparently, The Tomahawk Warrior crew were considered rookies and typically, they could not expect to fly a brand-new plane in combat while there were many crews who had flown scores of missions on beat up and flak ridden ships. The life expectancy of bomber crews was very short and until rookie crews had gone through a baptism of enemy fire, they could not understand what they were up against.

So, the plane with The Tomahawk Warrior painted on the nose, serial #42-97267 was transferred to Ridgewell, but it had an unfortunate life there. One day in 1945, when it was taxiing on the ground, it caught fire, exploded, and was destroyed.

Here are some photos of its time at Ridgewell

1 and 2, 381ˢᵗ Bomb Group at Ridgewell

---

[79] Nuthampstead was the home base for the 600th, 601st, 602nd and 603rd Squadrons of the 398th Bomb Group

3 grounded by fog, courtesy of B-17FlyingFortress.de.en

Later, as they flew their missions, they seemed to be allocated one plane more times than any other and this became their new *Tomahawk Warrior*. Charles never got to paint the nickname on the plane, but everyone knew the crew as the Tomahawk Warriors."

As I have mentioned in Chapter 7, according to the Declassified Secret Operational Records, Charles and his crew flew 19 of 30 missions on the ship which had the serial #42-102507, although 2 of the 30 missions were not credited.

It might have had a different outcome the day of the crash, if they had flown 2507 instead of 7191, which was a plane that Lt. Ellwood's crew had flown regularly,

When Charles left for England, his wife, Arlie, already had one child, Charlene, but he knew there was a second child on the way. It was in July[80] 1944 when he was told that Cheryl had been born in June and he was thrilled, of course, that he had a healthy second child.

Several weeks prior to Cheryl's birth, Charles had written to his wife Arlie in quite an emotional way about how much he loved her. It seemed as if he had a sort of premonition that he might not make it, and might

---

[80] It was mentioned in a letter by Charles (Chuck) L. Searl, the son of Davis Searl

go down in combat. (Although he didn't say that directly, I felt the letter strongly hinted at it).

That was either end of June or the beginning of July, 1944, and they had survived some very heavy flak when bombing the targets on the coast of France-he must have wondered if they would complete all their missions, so he must have been rather contemplatively thinking of his family and the odds of making it.

Here is the letter:[81]

Dearest Arlie

I guess I'm rather morbid, but I figure I should write you one last letter.

There is a chance that I may not come back & if I don't, I'd want to say a few things. Something like if I were there when you receive my few personal belongings.

My happiest days were with you and Charlene. All the beer in the world could never take the hurt out of my heart when you and she are not near me.

I don't feel that any of my sacrifice (sic) are so great as that of being parted from you & Charlene. I have loved you from the first time I met you, I believe, & I still love you even deeper than I ever thought I could love anyone.

Charlene means the world to me & in spite of the pleasure I gain from your companionship & love, I couldn't be any place else, but where I am.

If things seem bad, bear up & the sun will shine. I hope you will never receive this letter, but if you do, realize that I may be back, and if I don't come back, I'll always be with you, & I haven't failed in life completely. Charlene is part of me & part of you.

If I go down it will be for a good cause & I hope your life is happy.

I love you
Charles.

---

[81] Written by Charles while serving his country in England 1944. Courtesy of Mrs Cheryl Surfus, daughter of Charles Searl.

Who could suppress tears reading this good-bye letter?

These were very scary times and those who were married would often think of their wives and children. No one else in Charles's crew was married, but I'm sure his crew also had their own concerns about how their parents were feeling while they endured combat at 28,000 ft at sub-zero temperatures.

▲ ▲ ▲ ▲

CHAPTER EIGHT

THE NAVIGATOR, 2ND LT. SAUL KEMPNER

▲ ▲ ▲ ▲

Saul Kempner History and Basic Training

WHILE THERE IS A LITTLE direct historical data on Saul, his nieces provided me with some correspondence that Saul had with his twin brother. After transcribing it, some interesting facts of his life at the training camp, as well as, other aspects of his personal life emerged.

He started out his basic training in the gunnery class at Santa Ana Army Base in California. His brothers would become pilots, but we don't know if this was Saul's plan as well, or whether he got through the first tests. The wash-outs from any pilot school training became either bombardiers or navigators. From his letters, it appears Saul did some training as a bombardier, but we now know he became a navigator.

In order to give you some idea of Saul's time in training as a navigator in California, I have received permission to include some aspects of the website memoir of Marshall Stelzfreid.[82] Saul would have gone through the same training as Marshall, at the same camp, but one year later. The following is a version of Marshall's experience in navigator training, but edited for brevity,

---

[82] [http://www.stelzriede.com/warstory.htm about his wartime history as B-17 navigator.]

Marshall Stelzdfried: (Citation)

For the aviation cadets who were at Santa Ana in March and April 1942, the most lasting memory had to be of the continuous rain. The feature lacked paved streets, and the base was not complete. It was the only time in my entire term of military service in World War II that I had ever heard of GIs being permitted to enter a mess hall barefooted. In some places on the unpaved streets, the mud reached half way from ankles to knees. The commanding officers were not about to have hundreds of new pairs of shoes ruined simply to meet the niceties of regulations. The pay of a cadet amounted to the pay of a buck private plus 50 percent more for flight pay, or $31.50 per month.

In this new military atmosphere at Santa Ana, they assigned me to Company 20 of Class 42-J. For one month, we were treated to a wide variety of activities designed to teach us the basics of being in the Army. The most interesting segment of the training there was an explanation by civilian pilots of the theory of aerodynamics. They also demonstrated a simulated control system of an airplane and of piloting a plane.

They established personnel records at Santa Ana that would follow us and expand as our careers expanded. The most important accomplishment at Santa Ana was the taking of the qualification tests. The staff of the base determined, based on the educational background, physical examinations, simple intelligence tests, and the preference of each cadet, etc., whether a man should enter training to be a pilot, navigator, or bombardier. When I joined the Air Corps, my initial ambition was to become a navigator, where I felt I could make the best use of my mathematics education. But viewing the enthusiastic preference of most of my fellow cadets for becoming pilots led me to reconsider my preference for navigation. If a pilot was the thing to become, I would try for it. So I opted to become a pilot trainee, and that is what they approved me for.

This initial phase at Santa Ana, as packed as it was with activity, lasted only one month, and now we were ready to proceed into actual flight training.

Author's note: Marshall was washed out of the Advanced Pilot Training although he had performed well previously. He did not like the twin engine Cessna AT-17 and the boring level the flying required. He requested to train as a navigator, and they accepted.

Navigation Ground School — Santa Ana, California

Finally, transfer orders came through on October 1, 1942, and I again boarded a Pullman for Santa Ana to prepare for entry into Navigation School. Since there was no reporting date on the orders, I spent three days in Los Angeles before going to camp. On October 6, I arrived at Santa Ana again. The base was better developed than it was when I first was there, and it was not nearly as muddy as before. They assigned me to standard GI barracks instead of a tent as in my first stay there.

After five weeks at Santa Ana, the log-jam broke and pre-flight navigation ground school actually began. To some extent, these classes were a repetition of those I had taken, along with my pilot training. On that basis, I tried to have this phase of navigation ground school waived, but the effort was unsuccessful. I thoroughly enjoyed the classes, which provided a good foundation for Advanced Navigation School. It was a good chance for me to apply some of the simpler college-level mathematics in which I had majored before Uncle Sam took me.

In the second week of February 1943, our Class 43-8 finished at Santa Ana. But before leaving there, we held our graduation party at the Beverly Hills Hotel, one of the nicest hotels in the Los Angeles area.

Advanced Navigation School — Sacramento, California

On February 14, 1943, we left Santa Ana for Advanced Navigation School at Mather Field, near Sacramento, the capital city of the state of

California. The trip was made, as usual, by train, up through the lush, beautiful San Joaquin Valley. In the mountains, it was interesting to see the train gain altitude to climb over a mountain by making one turn of a spiral over itself.

Sacramento is a good place to spend time in the military. The area is steeped in the history of the great California gold rush of 1849. Sutter's Mill, the site where James Marshall discovered gold [in January, 1848], is located nearby at Coloma, on the American River. Land Park was a good place to play baseball or touch football. The old Senator hotel was a source of wonderful food. On a hitchhiking trip toward South Lake Tahoe one weekend, a buddy and I took a side trip at Placerville along state route 49, the so-called "Route of the 49ers," and visited several quaint gold-mining towns along it. The term "49ers" refers to the gold miners of 1849.

Physical training became fun at Mather Field, because I devoted mainly to playing basketball. My team ranked at the top because we developed a fast break — long before they became commonplace at the college and professional level. We had one player who could throw the ball accurately from one basket to the other and another who could outrun all the others to get there to receive it.

There were two primary purposes for a navigator in the Air Force. He had to determine where the aircraft was at any given time. It was also his job to provide the pilot with the directions to fly from where you are to where you want to go. Navigation, using the procedures practiced in WWII, was an art and not a science. However, during ideal situations, it could be reasonably accurate. The purpose of the Advanced Navigation School was to teach students to navigate accurately under those ideal conditions, and to navigate successfully in non-ideal situations.

The training at Mather field was a combination of ground school, to learn the processes, and air time, to practice what I learned on the ground. In those days, there were basically four methods of navigation: pilotage, dead reckoning, radio, and celestial, and the methods were very mechanical and relatively crude compared with how navigation is performed today, with computers and all.

Pilotage is a method of finding an airplane's location on a map. The ability to perform pilotage requires that the navigator recognize features on the ground and locate them on the map. Continuously following the map over a distance enables him to plot a course that is being followed, and correct the course if necessary. Obviously, this method can is only used when visibility outside the airplane is good.

Dead reckoning is a method of navigation that is performed, whether visibility is good or not. This is normally carried on under all conditions of flight to some extent, as a cross-check of the accuracy of other methods of determining position. It's also a convenient method of maintaining the log sheet. It uses such aircraft instruments as the compass, the airspeed meter, the altimeter, and others.

Radio navigation requires that bearings, or directions, of two or more radio stations of known locations, as determined by a radio compass, be plotted on a map. The crossing point of two bearings, or the center of a triangle with three bearings that don't all cross at the same point, is considered being the location of the airplane. This method is the least accurate of all the methods, because air or thermal conditions, coastlines, or can bend the bearings even deliberately bent magnetically. Once during WWII, the Germans bent the bearing of radio stations that were being used by a squadron of American planes returning to England from a raid and the planes ended up, tragically, over a nest of anti-aircraft guns. They have not probably used radio bearings for wartime navigation since.

Celestial navigation is the most sophisticated of the methods. An instrument called a sextant, or octant, depending on its configuration, is used to determine the angular elevation of a known bright star or stars. The navigator was required to memorize the identity and location in the sky of 50 stars. These could be used for navigation in various parts of the world. The precise locations of the stars in the heavens were tabulated and available to the navigator. To use the elevation readings, the navigator would assume the best location of his position that he knew, apply the location information of the star he observed, and calculate how far he was and in what direction from his assumed point.

Every feature of these navigation processes were taught and drilled in the classroom and practiced in flight applications. We made the flights in Lockheed Hudsons, with four students and an instructor on each plane. In a typical instructional flight, all the students would perform dead reckoning and pilotage for the entire time. They would do this while headed for a destination named by the instructor.

They mainly flew the flights to practice celestial navigation at night, when the students chose the stars each would take shots on. But they gave each a time to shoot the stars, so the instructor could grade the accuracy of positions determined by the students at those times.

On May 28, 1943, Class 42-J, including me, graduated from Advanced Navigation School at Mather Field with the rank of Second Lieutenant and qualified as Air Navigators. They issued all of us orders transferring us to bases where we would join the crews we would fly with on combat missions, and orders that would give us leave time to go home before reporting there. They also issued us the heavy flight clothing and the navigation equipment we would need in the new phase of our Air Corps careers.

Phase Training — Pyote/Dalhart, Texas

With my new commission in hand, they assigned me to the 19th Bomb Group at Pyote, Texas, to prepare for being sent to overseas active duty. With fourteen days leave en route, everyone went home on the way to Pyote. I arrived at Pyote on June 11, 1943, and was assigned to B-17 crew number 19-5-15, as the navigator in a ten-man crew.

Dalhart to Scott Field for New "Flying Fortress"

*On August 14, 1943, the Savoie group transferred to Scott Field, Illinois, with 32 crews. The Air Force assigned us a brand new B-17 there (**# 42-30646**), to deliver to the United Kingdom, and during the eight days we spent at Scott Field, we calibrated its navigation instruments, made several familiarization flights around the area, and got thoroughly briefed on the upcoming flight over the North Atlantic to the United Kingdom.*

The airplane we had flown from the U.S. to Prestwick got taken taken from us there, and ferried to one of the combat bases for instant use, replacing a plane that had been destroyed or badly damaged in combat.

(End of Stelzdfreid citation)

(*Author's Note*: From the official records, the plane **#42-30646,** taken from the Stelzdfreide crew on arrival in England, (just like I had described that happened to Lt. Searl's plane) was assigned to Alconbury, England on Sept 2, 1943. It became MIA (Missing in Action) with the target of Schweinfurt, Germany, October 14, 1943 with the Flemming crew, which crashed at Gerolstein, Germany. 2 KIA (Killed in Action) and 8 POW (Prisoners of war). MACR 745.)

With the above extracts and the contents of Saul Kempner's letters to Irving, one gets a fairly good idea of how Saul spent his time during his training. Saul liked to get mail from his brother and gaily discussed personal matters regarding his girlfriends, etc.

One can tell from his letters, that Saul had a great sense of humor. He had a wonderful talent for radio work before the war, which could have led him to a successful career in that field. His cryptic tone and the tongue-in-cheek comments are evident in his complete combat mission diary, which I publish in later chapters.

Some examples from Saul's correspondence:

David E. Huntley

Sante Fe Army Air base
Santa Ana California
May 10, 1943

Dear Irv,

I had hoped I would receive a letter from you today so that I could answer it as well as write you for what other reasons I have.

We are in our home stretch here as far as school goes. We have a weekend and a half of school left and then do not know what is in store for us as far as travel orders go.

I might as well ask a few questions since I haven't heard from you. What is the situation with athletics at Monroe and what particular uniform regulations do you have? I imagine you are in sun-tans by now, but what about otherwise?

Another thing–you can do me a great favor and give me a pretty good start if–after you are finished–you send me <u>all</u> the dope you can about Celestial Navigation. It is the only subject that should cause me trouble.

Well kid, it looks like I'll need your help after all. This allotment played hell with me this month, but what with a statement of changes and another peculiarity in the payroll, they did not leave me with much dough. So, if you could send me $10.00, you'd sure pull me out of a hole. I have a large amount of .03 to tide me over until my next paycheck. I know it will be $20.00 I owe you, and as soon as any silver shows, I'll get it back to you.

Try to write soon and more often, eh, kid? This pre-flight has finally got me under the skin and it is irritating. I hope I can hang on long enough through this last stretch.

As ever,
Saul.

P.S. I'm enclosing this news shot to find out if you know anything about it. The guy in the center is me or my twin brother, and that's you. I can't seem to recall when it was taken. As you can see, Dad has written that they took it at Victorville, but I'm not sure. Send it back when you are through with it. S.

July 1, 1943

Dear Irv,
Your letter arrived a couple of days ago, but I've been sort of busy this past week and this is my first opportunity for answering.

Yes, my darling brother, I do want a copy of your celestial navigation notes. There is no time like beforehand to study for something you are about to get in school. If there are 40 definitions to learn–I might as well get started on them early. I've done a little reading on it already, but some accurate notes would come in handy.

I imagine that by the time you get this, Mary Tanenbaum will be there with you, so say hello to her for me. They seem to give you guys a pretty wonderful break on the visitors' deal, including a pretty good pass.

It looks pretty much as though my happiness were short-lived–for the prevailing rumors say we go to Mather Field in California for Advanced. That California curse really has me–I can tell you. But who cares now? It's been so beaten into me I accept it as part of my fate now. It just looks as though I'll never have time to get anywhere near close to home before I finish my training.

Look–let's keep our letters clean by not even mentioning Frances in our letters, eh? After all–there's no sense in making the conversation unpleasant.

Don't get fooled by this gunnery training. The minimum requirements are that you must make at least an average of 3% hits on air-to-air firing and 3 hits out of every hundred. The real deal though, is that you must average at least 50% of the class average.

Say, that the class average is 14% for air-to-air firing, in order to pass, all you would need is 7% hits. Catch it? It's damn near impossible to wash (washout) What they do wash you for is chronic air sickness.

I've got 94% average in my schoolwork and dammed if I'm not one of the lowest in my class! It should show you what the work is like.

Look, friend. How about a talk–talk over the L.D. telephone? I will be here for 3 and a half weeks. Why not? If it only means $3.75 person to person after seven o'clock from here to New York–it should be a pretty simple thing on our pennies for us to pow wow for a few minutes. Give me your convenient time and place–and try to make it for the middle of the week sometime.

There must be some place you can get to a phone on your base.

Thanks for building me up with Irene. Did you tell her I belonged to the Royal Order of Bagenhoven? Sure–I am none other than Rasmusan Bagenhoven–Earl of Piffendoffer. Used to own the chief...

Investigate this Milamed babe kinda thoroughly. She's a pretty good friend of Irene's and is supposed to be sort of on the mellow side.

In answer to your question–When I was at Victorville, the circular error allowed was R75 feet. The class following mine had to qualify with R30 feet, but the C.E. has got raised again, as I understand it to be 250 feet.

My personal log book shows I qualified, but according to the photos and estimates–they tell me I didn't. Nothing anyone will ever say or do will even convince me I can't or don't know how to bomb. I will always maintain I got screwed.

That's all for now. Write soon and don't forget to send those notes.

As ever,
Saul

One of the saddest letters I have transcribed was from a Vickie Housiary of Wisconsin. Vickie wrote it to Irving in September 1944, after learning that Saul had died in England. She must have been someone with whom Saul had become very close. She obviously was known to the Kempner family. As an author, I was curious because Vickie was obviously a Catholic. Yet, Saul, being Jewish, seemed to have fallen in love with this girl and was "set on making their dreams come true."

Here is the letter which, once again, reinforces my earlier statements. This book illustrates not just a story of WWII heroes who lost their lives fighting for freedom and democracy, but encompasses so much more in the totality of the human condition.

I transcribed it without editing:

September 15th, 1944

Dear Irving,
I just received your letter and I guess I was just like you, when you first heard it–somehow it seems impossible I can make myself believe that he's not coming back.

In my last (sic In his last letter to me) letter he said even if he was injured seriously, he'd live, he had to come back and make our dreams a reality. He stated that they'd have to kill him outright before they'd get him and it was getting too late in the game to do that.

He was so sure, and I was too, I guess too sure.

I've prayed for him every night and whenever I didn't hear from him for a long time, a certain prayer always brought a letter. Every Sunday in Mass, I received communion for him. God has a funny way of doing things but He knows best.

As you see from my address, I'm in Milwaukee. I've been here since the first, "iffiliating" (affiliating)-sic with a children's hospital. I enjoy the work because I want children in my life. That is another thing Saul, and I had in common. I will be here until I get back to my hospital.

By now, I hope you have heard some more news. I was sure my last letter was written August 19. I guess I was mistaken but I'm (unintelligible) have to have another check. Please let me know if you have any further information or details.

Please forgive me feeling so selfish about Saul. I know the shock must have been heartbreaking to both you and your folks. Saul talked constantly of you and you two seemed like one in your likes and dislikes. He was going to give me some pictures of you two, but he left them at the base. I got an enlargement of their crew picture and several snapshots of Saul alone.

I guess there is not much left but to try and get over it. I shall never forget him or all our plans because they meant everything to me. To me Saul was the only person God even created (I guess I should say two since he was a twin).

There's not much more to say so I shall close hoping to hear from you and your wife soon.

Please give my regards to your folks.

Sincerely,
Vickie.
....
Milwaukee WIS 3

The B-17 Tomahawk Warrior: A WWII Final Honor

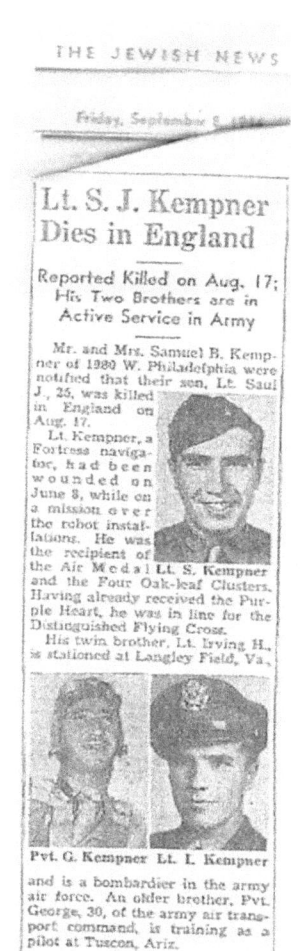

Detroit Jewish News report of Sept 8, 1944 about Saul Kempner's death with the wrong date, and a second report in the Detroit Free Press with several factual errors, date of report unknown. Courtesy of the Kempner family archives

▲ ▲ ▲ ▲

David E. Huntley

Family Efforts To Communicate With The Army After The War

Here is the letter that every parent dreads to receive when their son or daughter serving in the armed forces is reported, Killed in Action.

```
HEADQUARTERS 398TH BOMBARDMENT GROUP (H)
            Office of the Chaplain
            APO 557, Postmaster,
            New York, New York

                                            18 August 1944

Mr. S. B. Kempner
1980 Philadelphia,
Detroit, Michigan

Dear Mr. Kempner:

    Pursuant to the request from the Commanding General, Eighth Air
Force, and on behalf of the Commanding Officer and men of the 398th Bomb
Group, I wish to express our heartfelt sympathy upon the receipt of the
news that your son, Lt. Saul J. Kempner, O-702095, was Killed In Action.

    There are times when words cannot express the full meaning of our
thoughts and this is one of them. The loss of your son and his comrades
was a personal blow to all of us and each member will be missed. Your
son was well liked by all of his friends and I am proud to have been
associated with him. These are times which exact sacrifices and Saul
was ready to give his all. His life was given for that which he loved
best, his home and country.

    You may rest assured that Saul was given a Hebrew burial by a Jewish
chaplain and full military honors were accorded him.

    May God's blessings of comfort and strength be with you in your hour
of sorrow.

                                    Sincerely yours,

                                    James T. Duvall
                                    JAMES T. DUVALL,
                                    Chaplain, Captain.
```

In 1944, after Saul Kempner's parents received news of his death in England, Pearl Biber, a close relative of the Kempners, wrote letters to the Army on behalf of the parents, Samuel and Ida, requesting the return of Saul's personal belongings.

The B-17 Tomahawk Warrior: A WWII Final Honor

```
                                                              9-2
  DOWN TOWN OFFICE                                       UNIVERSITY 3-2246
  2128 NAT. BANK BLDG.
    ? CA. 3173
                           MAX BIBER                     114161
                       ATTORNEY AND COUNSELOR
                         18281 PRAIRIE AVE.
                           DETROIT, MICH.
                                              (600th Bomb Sqdn
                                     Re: Lt Saul J Kempner( 398th Gp.
                                     Home Address: 1380 W. Philadelphia
                                                   Detroit, Michigan
                                     A.P.O - #557, c/o Postmast N.Y.C.
```

Dear Sir:

We have just been informed that Second Lt. Saul J. Kempner, Navigator, of the 600th Bomb. Squadron, 398th Gp., has been killed in action in England - August 12th, 1944.

Both of the boy's parents have been in a state of nervous collapse for the past three days, and it is, therefore, our desire to save them as much further heartbreak as possible. Will you be good enough to arrange to have the boy's personal effects of every kind and nature sent to the following address:

    Mrs. Harold Waldman
    2297 West Buena Vista
    Detroit, Michigan

Mrs. Waldman is the boy's cousin and devoted friend and she will see that they are finally given to the parents, but at a time when they can cope with the tangible reminder of their son's fate.

I am confident you can understand and will be good enough to take all steps necessary to insure this change of address. Please accept our sincere thanks for your kindness.

                Sincerely,

                Pearl Biber
                (Mrs Max Biber)
                first cousin of deceased

ARMY SERVICE FORCES
KANSAS CITY QUARTERMASTER DEPOT

114,161 D

JRM:ER:rt
September 6, 1944

Mrs. Pearl Biber
18251 Prairie Avenue
Detroit, Michigan

Dear Mrs. Biber:

I have your letter of recent date, regarding the personal property of Lieutenant Saul J. Kempner.

As yet the Army Effects Bureau has not received any property belonging to Lieutenant Kempner.

All War Department agencies are under instruction to forward the personal property of military personnel to the Army Effects Bureau for disposition, and it is reasonable to assume that his property ultimately will be received here; however, because of transportation difficulties, considerable time may elapse before the shipment arrives here.

You are assured that upon receipt of any of Lieutenant Kempner's property, Mrs. Harold Waldman will be notified promptly.

Yours very truly,

LESLIE L. KETTERING
Captain Q.M.C.
Assistant

Copies of letters to and from the Army in 1944 (From the author's research recovery under the FOIA)

There were many letters to and from the Army concerning Saul's belongings, which were eventually returned to his father, Samuel.

Through the research process, I secured a large volume of correspondence between the Army and the Kempner family that was dated from 1945 through to the 1970s. I passed all this archival material to the nieces of Saul Kempner. They were quite overwhelmed and grateful to get this material.

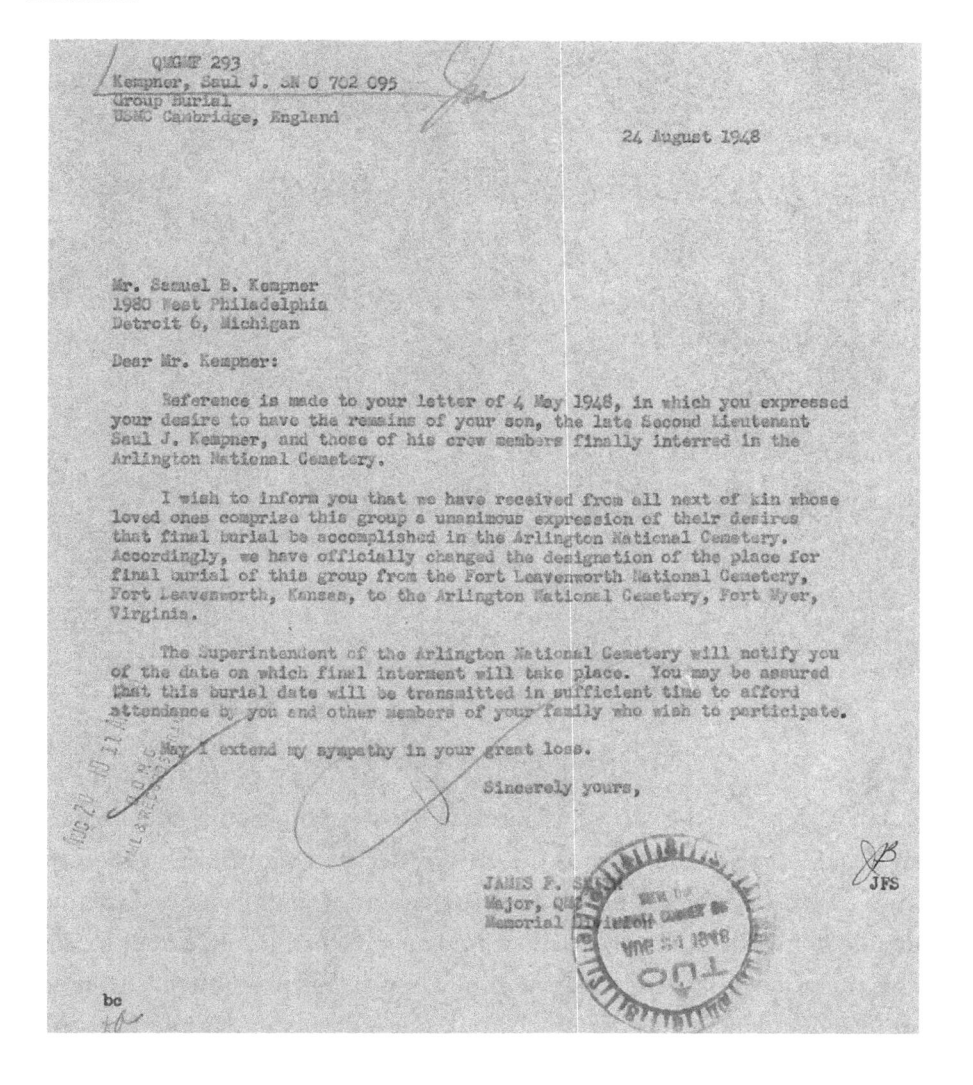

> QMGMF 293
> Kempner, Saul J. SN O 702 095
> Group Burial
> USMC Cambridge, England
>
> 24 August 1948
>
> Mr. Samuel B. Kempner
> 1980 West Philadelphia
> Detroit 6, Michigan
>
> Dear Mr. Kempner:
>
> Reference is made to your letter of 4 May 1948, in which you expressed your desire to have the remains of your son, the late Second Lieutenant Saul J. Kempner, and those of his crew members finally interred in the Arlington National Cemetery.
>
> I wish to inform you that we have received from all next of kin whose loved ones comprise this group a unanimous expression of their desires that final burial be accomplished in the Arlington National Cemetery. Accordingly, we have officially changed the designation of the place for final burial of this group from the Fort Leavenworth National Cemetery, Fort Leavenworth, Kansas, to the Arlington National Cemetery, Fort Myer, Virginia.
>
> The Superintendent of the Arlington National Cemetery will notify you of the date on which final interment will take place. You may be assured that this burial date will be transmitted in sufficient time to afford attendance by you and other members of your family who wish to participate.
>
> May I extend my sympathy in your great loss.
>
> Sincerely yours,
>
> JAMES F. S[...]
> Major, QM[...]
> Memorial [...]
>
> JFS
>
> bc

> DEPARTMENT OF THE ARMY
> OFFICE OF THE QUARTERMASTER GENERAL
> WASHINGTON 25, D. C.
>
> IN REPLY REFER TO QMGMC 293
> Kempner, Saul J.
> SN O-702 095
>
> 29 October 1952
>
> Mr. Samuel B. Kempner
> 1980 West Philadelphia
> Detroit, Michigan
>
> Dear Mr. Kempner:
>
> Reference is made to the interment of your son, the late Second Lieutenant Saul J. Kempner, and his comrades, which was made in Grave 3143, Section 25, Arlington National Cemetery, Fort Myer, Virginia. It is regretted that because of the fact it was impossible to identify individually the remains of your son, you were deprived of the comfort and consolation which you might have been afforded by interring his remains at home.
>
> It is felt that you might like to have the inclosed photographs of the stone which has been placed at the grave.
>
> You are assured that the grave will always be cared for in a manner fully commensurate with the sacrifice your son has made for his country. Any desired information concerning the grave or cemetery will be furnished upon request.
>
> Sincerely yours,
>
> JAS. F. WATT
> Lt. Colonel, QMC
> Memorial Division
>
> 1 Incl
> Photographs

From the author's research recovery

With a letter to the Army on March 26, 1945, Irving, Saul's twin brother, also began corresponding with the authorities in which he requested the return of any documents his brother left behind. Irving described them as valuable family documents. I believe he knew his brother had kept a diary of his missions in England, although he knew it was prohibited. (After all, getting documents was difficult. It took me requests under the Freedom of Information Act, (FOIA), to discover the Secret Declassified bombing missions flown by Saul's 600th squadron).

The Army replied to Irving's letter in May 1945, stating their records of property collected were complete and no further items had been recovered. Irving and the family received several documents, but the diary was not among them. To get it, they approached Senator Homer Fergusson for help in this matter. The Senator wrote a letter to the Army on September 26, 1946, specifically asking the Army to secure this diary, and any other personal effects that may not yet have been recovered.

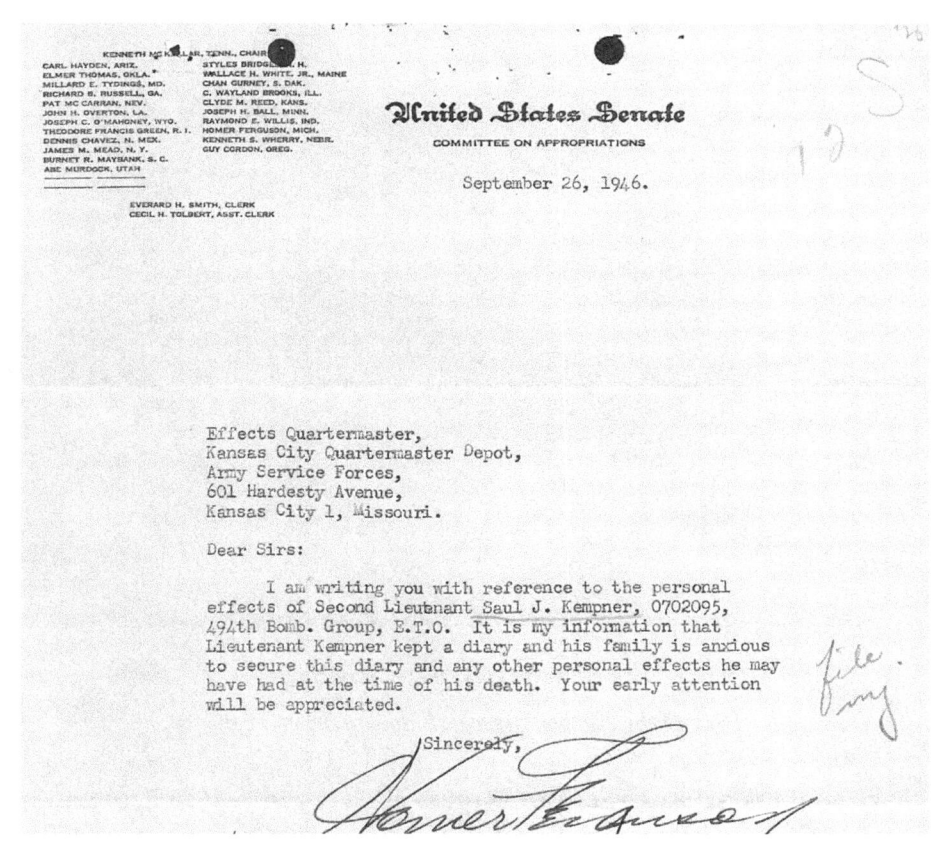

Copy of Senator Fergusson's letter.
Part of the Author's research document recovery

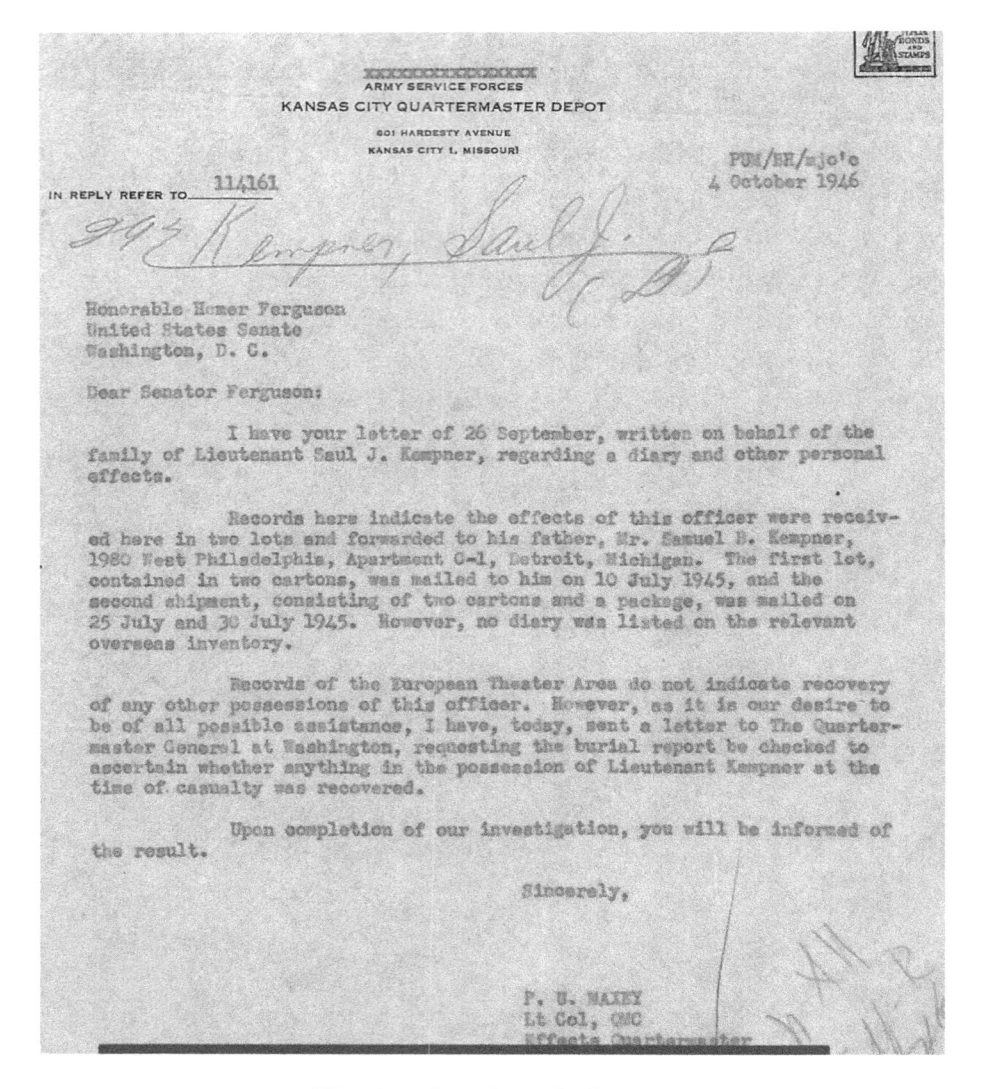

> ARMY SERVICE FORCES
> KANSAS CITY QUARTERMASTER DEPOT
> 601 HARDESTY AVENUE
> KANSAS CITY 1, MISSOURI
>
> IN REPLY REFER TO: 114161
> PUM/RH/mjo'c
> 4 October 1946
>
> Honorable Homer Ferguson
> United States Senate
> Washington, D. C.
>
> Dear Senator Ferguson:
>
> I have your letter of 26 September, written on behalf of the family of Lieutenant Saul J. Kempner, regarding a diary and other personal effects.
>
> Records here indicate the effects of this officer were received here in two lots and forwarded to his father, Mr. Samuel B. Kempner, 1980 West Philadelphia, Apartment C-1, Detroit, Michigan. The first lot, contained in two cartons, was mailed to him on 10 July 1945, and the second shipment, consisting of two cartons and a package, was mailed on 25 July and 30 July 1945. However, no diary was listed on the relevant overseas inventory.
>
> Records of the European Theater Area do not indicate recovery of any other possessions of this officer. However, as it is our desire to be of all possible assistance, I have, today, sent a letter to The Quartermaster General at Washington, requesting the burial report be checked to ascertain whether anything in the possession of Lieutenant Kempner at the time of casualty was recovered.
>
> Upon completion of our investigation, you will be informed of the result.
>
> Sincerely,
>
> P. U. MAXEY
> Lt Col, QMC
> Effects Quartermaster

The Army's reply to the Senator
Part of the Author's research document recovery

From the response to Senator Fergusson's letter in 1946, it became apparent to the family that the diary was lost forever. This had to have been disappointing for Irving, who, more than likely, knew from one of Saul's letters that he was keeping a diary.

Was it an act of Providence that the diary was found? As you already know, I, as a small boy, watched the remains of the Tomahawk Warrior crew being retrieved from the charred wreckage of a field. Wasn't it indeed peculiar that seventy-five years later, the diary came into my hands as I described in Chapter 4? I completed the circle when I arranged for it to be returned to the Kempner family.

Another of the family's concerns pertained to the re-internment of Saul's remains and his fellow crew members from the American Cemetery in Cambridge, England, to the national cemetery in Fort Leavenworth, Kansas.

Saul Kempner's father, Samuel Kempner, in correspondence with the Army, protested vigorously against the proposed location for the re-internment and suggested it should be closer to the Eastern part of the USA and Arlington National Cemetery.

By August 24, 1948, in a letter to Samuel Kempner from the Quartermaster General of the Army, Memorial Division, it states the remains of Saul, and his fellow crew members will be interred together at the Arlington National Cemetery, Fort Myer, Virginia. However, it was not until four years later did the family receive a letter dated October 29, 1952 announcing that the actual internment would take place there with the grave #3143, at section 25.

The champion of the Kempner relatives was again Mrs. Pearl Biber, a close cousin, who protested vehemently about the gravestone for the crew of the Tomahawk Warrior, which was a large engraved stone lying flat on the ground. She strongly advocated for this memorial to be re-positioned as a vertical marker. After extensive correspondence [83]between Mrs. Biber, Senator Phillip A. Hart, and the Army, they made little or no progress to resolve this issue.

The family were happy that the Army eventually honored the crew with a fine vertical gravestone. (It was shown in Chapter Three)

---

[83] From letters in the Kempner family archives dated in the 1970's.

The descendants' relatives of all the crew can today thank the persistence and dedication of Pearl Biber to have a standing commemorative gravestone to pay their respects to their loved ones.

Fortunately, a photo of the flat gravestone was preserved and made available by courtesy of Sue Wales of the Albert Dion family archives

▲ ▲ ▲ ▲

The Return of the Kempner Diary

After discussions between the Kempner nieces, Martin Ginther, his family and myself, we came to an agreement to meet on August 24, 2019, in Detroit. The venue would be determined at a later date. Martin, was to personally hand over the original diary to the Kempners.

Janice Morgan sent out the following Press Release:

The B-17 Tomahawk Warrior: A WWII Final Honor

Press Release:
WWII Hero's Diary Returned to Family after 75 Years.
FOR IMMEDIATE RELEASE
CONTACT: Janice Morgan
Lost diary of a fallen flyer to be returned to a Michigan family
85-year-old who witnessed crash connects the two families

Birmingham, MI- August 16, 2019- After Saul J Kempner 2ND LT US AAF was killed in a plane crash on Lude Farm, England, his family frantically tried to have his detailed personal diary returned. Mr. Kempner was one of the crew of the Tomahawk Warrior, which went down in a rural area of England August 12, 1944. Many letters were exchanged between the war department and Saul's father, cousin and identical twin brother Irving requesting the document be returned to the family but to no avail.

David Huntley was a nine-year-old boy whose family had moved to High Wycombe to escape the London Blitz. He witnessed the incredible destruction at the crash site minutes after the fiery explosion from impact. The plane's pilot knew shortly after takeoff they were in trouble. He fought hard to maneuver the plane away from the village, and the plane and the crew met their demise in a farmer's field. It hurt no one on the ground. Mr. Huntley's immediate sense of gratitude for the crew has remained with him since. Now in his 80s, he is writing a book to honor the soldiers who saved his town.

During Huntley's research, he became aware that Saul Kempner's diary was in the possession of another soldier, Ed Ginther. The Air Force charged Ginther with cleaning out the lockers of the deceased airmen and he found the diary in a wastebasket and took it home with him. It had remained in his possession since 1944. Huntley's research also led him to find the surviving relatives of Kempner. Ed Ginther passed away in May of this year. Before he died, he clarified that he wanted the diary returned to the family. With the coordination of David Huntley, Ed's son, Martin, will come to the Detroit area from Columbus, Ohio to present Lieutenant Kempner's diary to his two nieces, Andrea Blake and Janice Morgan.

The exchange will take place Saturday, August 24. Time and location TBD

Photos available

▲ ▲ ▲ ▲

The eventual venue chosen by the Kempner's for this historic moment in their family history was the Birmingham Historical Museum and Park, Detroit, Michigan. Several friends and family were invited. The event was covered by television news crews and a reporter, Elizabeth Katz, from the Detroit Jewish News Magazine. Ms Katz wrote a wonderful article[84], in which she described the return of the diary and how this made an emotional impact on the Kempner family.

L to R Angie and Martin Ginther- David Huntley – Janice Morgan and Andrea Blake discussing the diary
(Photos © courtesy of The Kempner family)

---

[84] https://thejewishnews.com/2019/09/10/sisters-receive-uncles-diary-from-wwii/

With the meticulous planning by Janice Morgan, the exchange of the diary went off smoothly and everyone enjoyed a celebratory glass of champagne with some light hors d'oeuvres. The Kempners were kind enough to host everyone to an Italian restaurant for dinner that evening.

▲ ▲ ▲ ▲

CHAPTER NINE

The Diary Kept By 2nd Lt. Saul Kempner

▲ ▲ ▲ ▲

SUB-CHAPTER:

MAY 1944 – Missions #1-8

2ND LT. SAUL KEMPNER WAS the navigator and a part of the crew of the "Tomahawk Warrior" assigned to the 600th Squadron of the 398th Bomb Group of the United States Army Air Force. The following are the entries from his diary, together with the extracts he had taken from some news sources he felt relevant to the crew's mission on a particular day.

Additional material and observations, together with footnotes of important information, are provided by the author.

For accuracy, it was necessary to secure through the Freedom of Information Act, (FOIA) the Declassified Secret Operational Records of the 398th Bomb Group and specifically, the 600th Squadron, the assigned home of the "Tomahawk Warrior."

I should note that in his initial diary entry, Lt. Kempner states that it was their first mission on May 8th, 1944: According to the official Operational Records, he was part of the crew that flew on May 7th. Although both missions were to Berlin, so it is possible that in the "fog of war" he confused the number of missions. It appears from the Official records that their ship on May 7th, suffered mechanical failure and returned to the base. It is still a part of the total missions record, and so I will record both even though one was not completed or possibly credited[85]. We just don't know why, but he misses another one[86] from his diary, which I will explain later.

Kempner records each mission number in his diary but, for informational purposes, I have added the official number in parenthesis. In the final analysis, this will clarify the total number of missions listed in Operational Records. All flown operations could be recorded either as completed or not completed and not credited.

Based on Operational Records, I specify in each of his diary entries the serial number of the plane the crew flew for each mission. This will help to identify what Kempner refers to occasionally in his diary, as the 'Tomahawk' or the 'Warrior.' A photograph of this 'substitute' 'Tomahawk Warrior' plane appears in Chapter 7. (You may remember that their original plane had been taken from them on their arrival in England).

Since they flew one particular plane more than any other during their period of service in England, they became attached to it as if it were the original "Tomahawk Warrior." In fact, other crew members of their 600th squadron and in the 601st squadron, knew the crew as the "Tomahawk Warriors."

The Diary of 2nd Lt. Saul Kempner- B-17 Navigator of the 600th Squadron 398th Bombardment Group, United States 8th Air Force

---

[85] According to the 398th BG Historian, Lee-Anne Bradley; The Searl crew aborted the mission of May 7th *on the way* to the target due to mechanical problems, it was not counted as a sortie. *"Over Belgium one aircraft aborted due to engine trouble"* Kempner did not make an entry for this mission because it was not credited for the crew

[86] Major Lucky Luckadoo a 101-year-old veteran of the 100 Bomb Group informed me that a mission was not counted as a "combat mission" unless the crew encountered the enemy – either by being fired upon by anti-aircraft guns and/or attacked by fighters. This rule applied even though the crew may have formed up in formation and flown over enemy territory, but not been engaged by the enemy.

FOREWORD[87]

The "Tomahawk Warrior" and its crew were attached to the 600th Bombardment Squadron of the 398th Heavy Bombardment Group of the U.S. Eighth Air Force.

Their plane was the B-17G, the latest of the Flying Fortress Models and saw plenty of action. This good ship earned the loyalty of the crew.

The crew arbitrarily named the 'Tomahawk Warrior' after its pilot's hometown in Wisconsin because it represented a good fighting spirit.

(Author's Note)

The first mission the crew were assigned to, according to the Official records, was to Berlin on May 7th 1944. Those records list 2nd Lt. Searl as the pilot, 2nd Lt. Dion as the co-pilot, 2nd Lt. Kempner as the Navigator, and 2nd Lt. Walsh, the Bombardier. They were assigned the aircraft B-17 serial #2487-F and were supposed to take the Lower Group in the 22-ship formation, with Baker as the lead.

It appears Searl experienced mechanical problems and was forced to return to base and the Formation Chart showed he was not (ot) over target.

▲ ▲ ▲ ▲

---

[87] It should be noted that this Foreword was entered by Lt. Kempner at an unknown date prior to his death and the rest of the crew. Also, they did not die in the plane he refers to as the "Tomahawk" or as the "Warrior" in other of his diary entries and this is explained in a different Chapter.

Diary Entry May 8, 1944

First Mission[88] (2nd) and a Bronze Star!
Plane Flown B-17 – 42-102507 N
Target – Berlin Germany

In spite of how this reads it was a very easy mission. No fighters attacked our group, and the flak was never close to us at all. None of the 398th's ships had so much as a flak hole in it. All of <u>our</u> ships came back.

We had a cloud cover under us, which kept us well hidden.

News Reports[89] for May 8th, 1944

Damage Mounts In Ravaged Capital

American heavy bombers carried the Allied pre-invasion air offensive to the heart of Germany again yesterday, battering Berlin for the second day in a row and striking Brunswick for good measure.

Nearly 1,000 heavies were engaged in the double attack. They again heaped explosives on the German capital which, in the words of Nazi commentators, has been "condemned to death by the Allies."

While Fortresses were giving Berlin its ninth American blow of the war, Liberators attacked the fighter-production city of Brunswick, 125 miles to the southwest.

---

[88] The Author wishes to point out that this in fact was their second mission to bomb Berlin. According to official records, Lt. Kempner was the navigator on the plane number ending in 2487 on May 7th, 1944. It was likely not credited to their mission total.

[89] I believe Kempner may have taken these Newspaper reports from the, "Stars & Stripes," a publication common in 1944 but I have no confirmation of this.

An equal number of P38s, P47s, and P51s of both Eighth and Ninth Air Force escorted the heavies.

Thirty-six heavy bombers and 13 fighters were lost. Bomber crews claimed 60 German fighters destroyed and the escort pilots 59.

Although declaring that complete cloud cover protected the U.S. planes, German radio reported widespread aerial combat over central Germany, and some returning crewmen told of the fiercest dogfights they had ever seen.

Several German fighters, unable to break through the tight Fort formations, attempted to ram the bombers in suicide attacks, U.S. flyers reported.

The Brunswick raiders, too, were heavily attacked. Some Liberator crews reported that over 100 ME109s and FW190s rose through solid cloud seeking combat. Other airmen reported seeing 200 fighters.

So fierce and reckless were Berlin's defenders that "fighter and Forts were colliding all over the sky," according to 2/Lt. L. Houston, of Helena, Mont., pilot of the Stars and Stripes.[90]

Other fliers said that the fighters attacked in wave after wave, zooming through the bomber formations 25 at a time.

Another unnamed newspaper termed this the war's most effective attack on Berlin – spoke of the city as doomed.

"Houses in ruins, reduced to a pile of rubble, bomb craters in the streets, curb stones hurled hundreds of yards away, houses with their fronts shaved off" was the description of the city given by a Berlin correspondent of the Scandinavian Telegraph Bureau.

The Stockholm Morgontidningen reported that thousands killed in Sunday's massive raid and that "fires broke out in many places, particularly in the western part of the city."

Differing sharply from yesterday's bitter German assaults on the heavies was the absolute lack of combat reported Sunday by crews taking part

---

[90] Lt. Frank L. Houston became a significant benefactor of the Air Flight Museum in Seattle Washington after the war. https://www.museumofflight.org/

in the attacks on Berlin and the Munster-Osnabruck area. In those assaults, eight bombers and five U.S. fighters were lost.

At both Berlin and Brunswick yesterday, some crewmen reported the flak was the heaviest they had ever seen in one area.

▲ ▲ ▲ ▲

(Author's Note)
According to Official Declassified records, the Searl crew were assigned to a mission to Sarreguemines, France on May 11, 1944, as part of a 14-ship formation of the 600th Squadron. I have no explanation why Lt. Kempner missed this mission entry in his diary. Regrettably, I have no Official Formation, De-Briefing or Formation Records that would explain why he missed this entry. However, the Operational Records[91] clearly show he was the Navigator on that mission. So, once again, I have corrected the Mission number in parentheses on May 19th to reflect the additional bombing flight undertaken for May 11, 1944.

The following diary entry by Lt. Kempner mentions the loss of the 1st plane of the 398th Bomb Group. I have included some debriefing interrogation reports, as well as witness reports, from the 398th BGMA, which provides a stark image of what these valiant crews had to endure.

Diary Entry May 19, 1944
2nd (4th) Mission
Plane Flown B-17 – 42-102507 N
Target – Berlin, Germany

We did it again. It seems our crew gets only the long jobs. 11 hrs of flying time on this one. This was the Group's 8th mission, and we lost our 1st ship

---

[91] According to the 398th BG, the records show that only 1 of the 14 ships were shown on the combat report. The fact that Kempner did not record this mission in his diary lends credence to the fact that he and 12 other shps did not take off that day.

[92] *by our own doing. They were not killed – only forced down in enemy territory – Denmark.*

I nearly caught it on this mission: two pieces of flak tore through the top of the nose not six inches from my head. I wasn't wearing my flak helmet.

Our ships were well hit by flak and the "Warrior" had 5 holes plus several dents. Flak was only moderate but <u>very</u> accurate and was on our ships all the time we were over Berlin.

None going in, none going out. Good fighter support. Didn't see a single enemy fighter.

Why O'Neal went down on Mission to Berlin

Notwithstanding the comment in Lt. Kempner's diary, his pilot Lt. Searl had a much better view of what happened to Lt. O'Neal in plane 42-7339 Y who went down and described in the following transcript of the De-Briefing Record and Interrogation Report:

Official Reports (CONFIDENTIAL)
Report of an eyewitness of Missing Aircraft B-17G 42-97339 on Berlin Mission of May 19, 1944.

While flying directly opposite Lt. O'Neal on May 19th, 1944, a few minutes after 1355, I saw his ship hit by most of the 100lb incendiary bombs from the ship directly above him. The bombs were dropped in salvo and hit from the cockpit back to the radio hatch. Some bouncing off and several hitting the wing. I saw a pinkish flame, possibly a bomb exploding and I could see the wing was badly torn. Lt. O'Neal then dropped behind and I lost sight of him.

Charles J. Searl
2nd Lt. Air Corps 0-691204
Pilot, B-17G 42-102507

---

[92] Lt.. O'Neal in plane 42-7339Y went down.

A further Report of an eyewitness:

I was riding as left waist gunner in the lead plane of the high group. Lt.. O'Neal was flying number #50 of the lead group and Lt. Nelson was flying on our left wing. About two or three minutes after other planes had dropped their bombs, I saw the bombs appear to fall in salvo from Lt. Nelson's plane directly on Lt. O'Neal. Most of them hit over the cockpit, top turret and front radio hatch. One bomb hit #3 engine and flamed up, but the fire went out. The plane went out in a nice sweep as though out of control and then came back into position for a few minutes and then went down under us and out of my vision. All the bombs hit flat as they did not have enough time to turn. The lieutenant was not in position when the accident happened.

C.A. Bennet, 3154527
S. Sgt, L. Waist Gnr B-17G 42-102390

George Gramm provided a further report after the war in 1945. Both he, as the Radio Operator and Lt. Baer, the Navigator, bailed out and were captured and became POWs until they were liberated. Gramm said in a report that he saw an empty parachute and harness floating down beside him, which he was sure was Lt. O'Neal's. He stated that Lt. Baer had told him he saw the copilot killed in the plane. He saw Bob Jenkins, the tail gunner, complete with a parachute on the ground. Gramm also stated he saw Barsano, Cone, Farren and Lt. Duel in the waist with no chance to bail out because of the force of gravity on them.

With the permission of the 398th BGMA, I include here an excerpt from the diary of Howard F. Baer, Navigator, with the O'Neal Crew, 600th Squadron. Howard died in 1993, but not before he had recorded his version of those dramatic moments high in the skies over Berlin on May 19, 1944.

We were flying in the No. 2 position of the lead "slot" element, off the wing of deputy leader Bill Markley. As we approached the target, direct flak burst in the nose and hit us. It struck me in the forehead and the concussion opened a big hole in the plane's nose. I was not stunned, but I was bleeding. Almost simultaneously, the plane lurched to the right and seconds later bombs from a plane above us fell through the cockpit, top turret and radio room. The plane started into a spin and the bailout alarm bell sounded. I saw blood coming down from the cockpit. Then O'Neal came down and said the co-pilot (Roger Comer) had been hit and that the bombardier (Merritt Deull) and I should get out now. I pulled myself up from the navigator's seat. Then Merritt motioned me to rub my face as I was getting frostbite. I went out the hole in the nose. After I jumped and pulled the ripcord, I wondered why I was sitting so low in the harness. It had been my practice to unsnap the parachute harness while navigating, then I realized that the leg straps were unbuckled. I never saw Merritt or Ira alive again. I landed within 400 yards of George Graham and started towards him. A German took several pistol shots in my direction, so I stopped. One of the Germans approached me and said in very good English, "For you, the war is over." An hour later, I saw the rest of the crew. They were in a cart. All eight were dead.

(Printed in *Flak News*[93] Volume 10, Number 2, Page(s) 7, April 1995)

Again, with the permission of the 398th Bomb Group Memorial Association, I am including a further report by Allen Ostrom:
O'Neal Crew Was 1st Loss For 398th By Allen Ostrom

Mission No. 8 for the newly arrived 398th Bomb Group to the 8th Air Force Theater of operations was to Berlin. It would be the fourth such trip to the German capital in May 1944. The total would be nine before the war ended. Planes from all four squadrons took part in the May 19 raid, but it scattered them in two formations. Jean Miller led "A" Group and Judson

---

[93] *Flak News* is a publication of the 398th Bomb Group Memorial Association.

(Fred) Gray the "B" Group. They would remember the mission as the day the 398th lost its first plane and crew in combat. Ira O'Neil and his men were on their fifth mission, and it was their second time around for Berlin. It was a long haul out over the North Sea, across the neck of Denmark, then straight southeast to Berlin. A wide pass out of the city and then back home on somewhat the same route. The mission narrative described the flak over the target as "heavy and accurate" on the bomb run. Indeed, it was, as at least one 88 made a direct hit in the nose of the O'Neil aircraft as it was on the wing of deputy leader Bill Markley. The plane immediately drifted to the right. At the same moment, the lead bombardier, Gil Goldman, in the nose of Miller's lead B-17, unloaded his rack of 100-pound incendiaries. Keith Anderson, a regular copilot on the Miller/Gene Douglas lead crew, observed the following drama from his observer's position in the tail turret: When we dropped our bombs, I looked down and saw several bombs drop right on the O'Neil plane. He had drifted directly under Bob Nelson's plane in the high element and apparently no one saw it in time to hold up the bomb release." George Graham, the radio operator and one of the two survivors of the mishap, along with navigator Howard Baer, corroborate this view in the accompanying articles. When Graham and Baer met at a reunion many years later, the two remember seeing another parachute descending. They saw just the chute and harness. Nobody was in it. O'Neil had jumped . . .but had fallen out of his chute. Others who perished on the ill-fated O'Neil B-17 were Roger Comer, copilot; Merritt Deull, bombardier; Dale Schaupp, engineer-gunner; Joe Barzano, ball turret; Gerald Farren and Frederick Cone, waist; and Robert Jenkins, tail gunner. Printed in *Flak News* Volume 10, Number 2, Page(s) 7, April 1995.

The following is a Mission report from Captain Alan A. Arlin's Diary
Arlin Mission No. 1 Date-May 19, 1944 Assigned Target – Berlin, Germany Targets Attacked – Berlin, Germany Results – Good. Aircraft

Number – 7203-Z Bomb Load – 42 – 100 lb. Incendiary Position in formation – Lead of low element of low sqdn., of low group. Time – 10 hrs. 15 min. Altitude over Target – 24,000 ft. Casualties – None Damage – One flak hole in waist Losses – None

Loading list Pilot – 1st Lt. Arlin, Alan A. Co-P – 2nd Lt. Stallings, Harold O. Bomb. – 1st Lt. Baxter, Morris V. Nav. – 2nd Lt. Walkup, Charles A. Eng. – T/Sgt. Chmielewski, Raymond J. Radio – T/Sgt. Buchsbaum, Louis Gun. – Pvt. McCort, Joseph J. Gun. – S/Sgt. Wilson, William C. Gun. – S/Sgt. Carter, Charlie M. Gun. – Pvt. Hoffman, Arnold W. Losses Ship No. 7339-H Lt. O'Neil and Crew

Arlin Mission No. 1 Date-May 19, 1944

They scrubbed both missions at the last minute because of weather. Today the weather was much better, so we could get our first mission out of the way. The C.Q. [Charge of Quarters] woke us at the 0200 this morning, all later than usual. By 0330, we had finished breakfast and were at the briefing room.

Briefing started with a roll call. When everyone was present, Major Jones, the group S-2 Officer [from the Intelligence Section], began his part of the briefing by rolling up the screen that covers the wall map. Our routes were shown along with the primary and secondary targets. Our target today was the Wilhelm-Strasse Railroad Station in the center of Berlin. Our routes in and out were to be the same. Across Holland into Germany between Bremen and Hanover and straight on in to Berlin. After going over the routes and the targets in detail, he lowered the screen and projected detailed and enlarged pictures, maps and R.A.F night charts of the target area showing the exact size and shape and location of the target and discussed the best method of picking up in identifying it. He also pointed out the M.P.I [which is the mean point of impact, or center of desired bomb pattern on target]. After this, he discussed the flak chart showing the disposition of the 450 flak guns protecting this target. In closing, he said we could expect heavy fighter opposition and intense flak in the target area.

S-2 finished, the Operations Officer, Major. Miller gave us part of his poop. Times for engines, taxi and take-off, our position in the division, fighter support, targets being hit by other divisions, gas load, bomb loads, etc.

The weather officer, Lieutenant Held, showed us the weather to be expected from the base to the target and return. He also gave us the temperature, pressure and winds up to 30,000 ft. When he finished, the Bombardiers and Navigators were dismissed to attend their special briefing.

After the room had quieted down, operations gave us the information on the assembly, buncher, base altitude, bombing altitude, assembly altitude, flares, take-off runway, taxi instructions and other information needed by the pilots.

The Communications Officer, Capt. Cameron gave us instructions regarding radio procedures and discipline. Named the ships guarding B and C channels, fighter call signs, instructions for releasing chaff, and all other data concerning communications. We held a discussion to clear up questions before we were dismissed.

We had our equipment out at the ship with time to spare. The crew installed the guns, checked the ammunition, gas, bombs, flak suits, radio in the ship. Engines time came up, and we were ready to go. The engines started and warmed up; we taxied out to takeoff position. While waiting to take off, the engines were checked and run up. One last check and we taxied out and took off on time at 0805.

We climbed out and arrived at the Debden Buncher on time at 6,000 feet to find some of the other ships already there forming. After 20 minutes, the ships were all in formation and it was time to depart.

We flew a jagged course over England, climbing and getting into proper position with the division. By the time we departed the English coast, our wing was in the division formation and we were climbing out over the channel towards Holland.

A few isolated flak guns greeted us as we crossed the enemy coast for the first time. We climbed on up to 24,000 feet, our bombing altitude, and proceeded in to the I.P. [initial point], skirting flak areas and keeping our eyes peeled for Jerry. Up to the I.P. we encountered no opposition, other than occasional light flak. P-51s, P-47s and P-38s in large numbers were continually under, over and all around us going and coming.

As we turn off the I.P. toward the target, a huge black smudge in the sky showed us where we were going. Everything seemed to happen at once. First, we could see dog fights between our escort and the Jerries in his F.W. 190's and M.E. 109's. Then ships bearing black crosses could be seen flashing past as they bored through our formation. I couldn't get a good look at them because I was so busy. About this time, flak began bursting all around us and for what seemed like hours. They filled the sky with exploding shells. A B-17 off on our left and a little ahead received a direct hit and his right wing disappeared in a cloud of smoke and flame. He exploded a few seconds after being hit. Another ship went down in flames behind us. That was Lieutenant O'Neill. I saw his crew to bail out OK.

For a time, it filled the sky with smoke, exploding shells and burning ships, fighters and bombers alike were going down. Then bombs away. Ours didn't release immediately, so the late release threw them out into the edge of the city. The flak was still intense as we made a turn away from the city. As we left the flak area, Jerry was there waiting. He gave us a little trouble for a short way before he left us and took on another group behind. Some other groups suffered severe losses to Jerry.

As we left the target area and headed home, still escorted by fighters, we could look back and see the battle still going on as other wings behind us were still dropping their bombs. Over Berlin was a huge black cloud of exploding and spent flak. Out of this cloud hung many black ribbons, each marking the end of some ship. Approaching and leaving this cloud hundreds of ships could be seen. Off, to one side where our fighters had tangled with the enemy fighters, was what appeared to be swarms of bees milling around and around with smoke trails falling out of the bottom of each swarm, showing that someone else had got it. We were too far away to distinguish whether they were friends or enemy. Below it all we could see an occasional chute of someone who had been able to bailout.

The return was uneventful. We were too high and there were too many clouds for us to see much of the country. Again, as going in, we could skirt the flak areas and fighters did not attack us. After crossing Germany and Holland, a few flak bursts came up. It seems like they have to have those few parting bursts. We let down crossing the channel and came home and landed in formation.

After parking and cutting the engines, we crawled out fully expecting to find the ship riddled, but found only one flak in the waist. Some of the other ships were pretty well shot up, but most like ourselves got off pretty easily. Interrogation and chow over with, we find ourselves exhausted and let down. The best thing for that is a good shower and many hours in the sack.

Notes:

- First Lieutenant Alan A. Arlin of the 601st Squadron was the pilot of Rapid City original crew No. 31. On many of his missions, 1st Lieutenant and later Captain Alan A. Arlin was a lead pilot for his squadron or for the group.
- The above transcription provided by Dave Jordan.
- This transcription is a careful reproduction of the original except for occasional spelling and punctuation changes. In some circumstances, based on relevancy, some material may not have been transcribed.
- Clarification of acronyms or special words, or guesses of certain words, are shown in brackets [ ].

Here is George Graham's version of the O'Neal incident printed in the *Flak News*:

A B-17 Out of the Blue

By George Graham Radio Operator, O'Neal Crew 600th Squadron
"Eternity is forever." It happened in just a few minutes and yet it seemed forever. They hit our plane. I knew it to be so because it threw me to the floor of my radio compartment and I was hurting. Am I bleeding? I asked the ball turret gunner. No, there was no evidence of blood. The radio hatch had slammed into my back and the movement was excruciatingly painful and almost impossible. I kept thinking, I must move, must get out of this situation. What will my mother think if I don't come home?

With help from one of my fellow crew members, I could get to my knees. I dragged myself to the window. I could see flames shooting into the sky. No. 3 engine was on fire! My body might have given up, but my mind wouldn't let it. I crawled, with great pain, to the waist door by pulling myself along the ribs of the airplane. At the doorway, I reached up and yanked the emergency handle, releasing the door, which blew off. It was at this same time that I realized that the tail of the ship had broken off and I was now crosswise in the doorway, entangled in the cables which led to that broken-off tail, and I was totally incapable of pushing myself out.

The plane was spiraling down now, going faster and faster. Suddenly there was a wrenching jolt that set me free from the maze of wires and I was catapulted out into space. I reached for my parachute ring and yanked. The ring came off in my hand. My parachute had not opened! I had no sensation of movement as I fell. Frantic now, I began tearing at the elastic bands that held the chute, and finally the lifesaving silk responded to my urgent tugging and I floated to earth.

As I neared the ground, more trouble awaited me. This time in the form of German civilians who had witnessed my descent and were firing at me. Fortunately, they were not excellent marksmen and as I lay flattened on their territory, they captured me and they took me to a German Military Hospital in Berlin. I spent one month in the hospital with a severe back injury before being released and moved on to an interrogation center in Frankfurt.

At the Frankfurt center, they confined me to a room, and the questioning began. The questions were precise and persistent. I refused to answer and eventually, and to my total amazement, they knew all about me and they told me so. The year I had graduated from high school; when I had entered the service; when I was sent overseas; my Squadron and my Group.

After the questioning was complete, they sent me to a German Air Force prison camp, Stalag Luft IV, near Stettin. They assigned a room to me in the barracks. The room was approximately 15x15 and housed eight prisoners. I was allowed to keep the clothing I had been captured in and given a few personal items, shaving equipment, toothbrush, and a comb.

Each day began with a German guard awakening us with a loud shout and roll call was taken. Shortly after, we prepared for the day. A central kitchen that dispensed all the food provided for breakfast. A typical breakfast comprised hard German brown bread and whatever rations we had in our Red Cross care package. This package should have been one per person per week, but because of a shortage, two prisoners shared one parcel per week. Sometimes no Red Cross package arrived. Then we reduced our food intake to extend whatever food was on hand. Lunch and dinner usually comprised soup and always there was hard bread, palatable enough when you're hungry, but not recommended for a daily diet!

The buildings forming the prison camp surrounded a compound. During the summer, almost everyone gathered in this area to exchange stories and participate in athletics. Baseball was a favorite. A walk around the perimeter of the compound provided our daily exercise. This was repeated every single day that the weather permitted. During the rainy season, I washed my clothes by using a scrub brush and soap that the Red Cross had provided. Wet clothes were hung in the barracks or left outdoors hoping the sun would eventually do the job. There were guard towers at the four corners of the compound to discourage any attempt to escape. Two or three guards manned each tower, and they were highly visible. These efforts to keep us in control were effective. NO ONE EVER TRIED TO ESCAPE.

The highlight of the week was when there would be a new arrival of prisoners at the entryway to the camp. My inquiry was always the same. 'Was anyone from my bomber group?' One day I came across someone from the 398th Bomb Group and asked which squadron he had been in. He replied the 600th. I didn't remember him and, upon further questioning, learned he was a replacement crew member. I further asked which crew he had replaced and he said "O'Neal's crew." He had replaced MY crew, and now he also was down. There was limited access to what was happening in the war. We had no papers, no books, and no radio. The days were long and the nights endless. We conjectured much when the war would end. We were never mistreated. Perhaps we were lucky in that the head of our camp was a German captain who had been educated in the United States and had returned to his homeland in 1937.

We were often hungry; cold in the ill-heated barracks in the winter; and they limited supplies for personal hygiene to whatever we got from the Red Cross. One day in December, our captors announced we were abandoning this camp because the Russians were approaching. What a revelation that was! We were marched to a railroad siding and loaded onto what was commonly known as a 40-or-8, either 40 soldiers or 8 horses. In our case, they crowded approximately 80 to 100 inside. For eight days, this was our home on wheels as we railed down to Nurnberg (Author: Nuremberg?). One day was spent in the marshalling yards of Berlin. Berlin was under siege by day by the American bombers, and at night, by the British. It was our good fortune not to be affected by this bombardment, although we stood on the periphery of it. We eventually reached Nurnberg, where we spent the next three months. It was during these three months, January, February, and March 1945, that Nurnberg was under heavy attack by the Allied Forces.

I witnessed several B-17's leaving their formation and ultimately being destroyed. At night, it was an eerie feeling to see the British drop huge flares that lit up Nurnberg (which was about 10 miles from our camp) and to hear the tremendous explosion of the 4,000-lb. blockbuster bombs, which must have done heavy damage. To see British bombers and/or German fighters on fire and hurtling through the sky was a sight, which I shall never forget! As the three-month stay at this camp neared an end, we knew that the war must be about to end because they informed us that we were being marched to a camp farther into the interior of Germany. This march lasted approximately seven days, and what a sight it was to see the American fighter planes zoom down and strafe targets of opportunity such as trains, buildings, and convoys. I witnessed all this from our position on the ground.

We finally reached a camp in Moosburg, which was a hodgepodge of people, and not very well organized. We were there only a short while when, on May 8, 1945, we heard rifle fire. From that point on, we saw no other German soldiers. The Americans had entered our camp. Twenty-six months after entering the Service, I celebrated my 21st birthday on May 11, 1945. Happy to be alive and free again! Printed in *Flak News* Volume 10, Number 2, Page(s) 6, April 1995.

In accordance with protocol at the time, the Germans sent their report about the Internment of members of enemy crew Refer to: Shot-down of a Boeing B-17 near, Alt-Ruednitz. 9 km north-east of Bad Freienwalde on 19 May 1944 at 1358, but identifies O'Neal's plane on 19th may 1944. The report continues to state the names of the dead as 1.Barzano, 2. O'Neal, 3. Comer, 4. Schnup, 5. Farren, 6. Cone, 7. Jenkins, 8. Deul. They further report that the men were buried at the cemetery of Alt-Ruednitz on 23rd May 1944 for the men 1 to 7, and on the 27th of May 1944 for No 8 in the South east corner. (This is not clear and was difficult to read)[94]

It appears, the plane crash-landed and there is also a German "Report of

---

[94] If any descendant relatives would like copies of these official reports they may contact the author.

Captured Aircraft" at Airbase Headquarters Airfield Command Strausberg 19th May 1944 at 1358 hrs. It describes the equipment of the plane and the following comment:

"Every above types are US Construction. Engines broken off by crash. Fuselage pushed together. Wings deformed. Plane is lying in marshy county of Oderbruch."

> Signature illegible
> Major & Officer in Charge.

News Reports for May 19th, 1944

Berlin Blasted

Brunswick Also Hit; Heavy Battles with Luftwaffe Indicated.

Germans Tell Of Fierce Aerial Fighting: Early Reports Hint U.S. Planes Took Big Toll Of Nazis

Strong forces of Fortresses and Liberators, striking a double-barreled blow to renew the Allied air offensive on Hitler's Europe, bombed the Berlin and Brunswick areas in broad daylight yesterday.

The bombers, escorted by swarms of fighters, met fierce opposition according to German radio. Preliminary reports here showed the Luftwaffe was dealt a heavy blow.

In their first mission in four days and their first major operation since last Saturday, the heavies stormed over Berlin to give the capital, last hit by Tuesday night by Mosquitoes, its tenth American raid.

Announcing violent battles over its achtung alarm system, German radio said "three separate" forces of the USAAF and Luftwaffe were engaged in combat over Berlin at the same time.

Particularly fierce engagements were reported over Osnabruck, vital rail center in northwest Germany, which was battered by heavies on Saturday,

Although at a late hour last night there was no official U.S. announcement on results of the operations, preliminary reports suggested that escorting P47s, P38s, and P51s of the Eighth and Ninth Air Force and the bombers themselves had chalked up a big score in German aircraft destroyed.

Returning B24 returning crews reported intense flak and fighter opposition in the Brunswick area. "Between 150 and 200 fighters attacked us," Sgt. Howard S. Murphy, of Dorchester, Mass., gunner on the B24, Little Shepherd, reported. "Plenty of those got shot down, though," he added.

S/Sgt John C. Pershing, of Uxbridge Mass, said, "Flak came up constantly while were in the target area and fighter attacks against our Liberator formations were ferocious. Our bombers and fighters shot down quite a few German fighters."

One interesting report came from Capt. Harold W. Flaton, of Portland, Ala.

"I saw four P47s strafe 35 Me109s," Flaton said. "We had wonderful protection from our fighters, although I saw one bomber in another formation blow up."

As Germany was being warned of approaching raiders, the Allied Expeditionary Air Force[95] sent small formations of Mosquitoes and Typhoon fighter-bombers over northern France.

---

[95] The **Allied Expeditionary Air Force** (AEAF) (also known as the **Allied Armies' Expeditionary Air Force**, AAEAF) was a component of the Supreme Headquarters Allied Expeditionary Force (SHAEF) which controlled the tactical air power of the Allied forces during Operation Overlord.

Its effectiveness was less than optimal on two counts. It did not function as the controlling headquarters for all Allied air forces, with the strategic forces of RAF Bomber Command and the US Eighth Air Forcebeing retained by their national command authorities until pressure from U.S. General Dwight D. Eisenhower resulted in them being placed directly under SHAEF instead of AEAF. Its commander was also not universally liked. Sir Trafford Leigh-Mallory was regarded by some as being too inept for his place in the high command.

The Alarm that Luxumbourg radio gave shortly after, Munster radio reported the bombers crossing the Reich border. Just after 2 PM, the raiders were located over Berlin. It was not until 4:30 PM that Luxumbourg radio gave the all clear.

At 7:30 last night, Vichy radio faded from the air, showing that Allied aircraft might still be sweeping over the Continent.

German radio again gave signs of breaking down under the strain of the raids. At 3:30 PM German News Agency was still sending out the previous day's messages, breaking off each one after a few sentences, then starting all over again. Several weeks ago, after a heavy daylight raid, the agency exhibited the same erratic behavior.

In the only operation from Britain on Thursday, the Second Tactical Air Force swept roads in north France and Belgium. One Allied plane was lost as Typhoons, Mustangs and Spitfires strafed trucks and also hit rail sidings in Folligny, junction of the Granville-Paris and Avranches-Cherbourg railways.

▲ ▲ ▲ ▲

Diary Entry May 23rd, 1944

3rd (5th) Mission
Plane Flown B-17 – 42-102536 C

This was a pipe. Had to take the secondary target – the RR Marshalling yards at Saarbrücken. Plastered it with 1,000 pounders.

It had two major components, the RAF Second Tactical Air Force and the USAAF Ninth Air Force. Each supported their own nation's Army Group. It also had operational control of the Air Defence of Great Britain, but with that organisation not being under the control of SHAEF.

AEAF was dissolved after Leigh Mallory was reassigned to command RAF forces in the far east, later being killed in an air crash. Source Wikipedia

No fighter opposition and only about 36 shots of flak during the whole fracas. All of our ships came back – not so much as a hole in any of them.

We had more fighters with us on this one than I ever thought existed. They were all over the place – P38's, P-51's, P-47's. What a show!

News Reports for May 23rd, 1944

Luftwaffe's Nests Hit by U.S. Fleets

Heavies, Fighters Sweep Europe Looking for a Scrap, but Nazis Refuse

Three thousand American and Allied warplanes stretched an aerial dragnet across the skies of western Europe yesterday, hunting down the German air strength Hitler is saving for invasion day.

From the edges of the Biscay provinces eastward to the Reich itself over 1,000 American Fighter craft – greatest fighter force ever sent up on a single mission – escorted some 600 Fortresses and Liberators to six of the Nazis key air bases, to two rail yards around which centers European transport hinges, and to other unspecified targets within western Germany.

The big air fleet, which pounded out from British bases at dawn's first light, split into task forces across western Europe as it carried into its fourth day the newest phase of the pre-invasion offensive aimed at destroying the Luftwaffe and neutralizing the German capacity to shift men and material to meet the Allied D-Day.

1,000 Bomber RAF Raids

Nazi sirens had barely quieted after a night in which the RAF, working on the same plan of widespread attack, had dispatched over 1,000 heavy bombers to six targets in Germany and the occupied countries.

But where the RAF had flown into bitter combats with night fighters, the big fleet of U.S. daylight heavies and their escorts found almost no resistance, and bomber crews and fighter pilots alike came home with stories of Luftwaffe interceptors which refused to give battle and left their bases to be destroyed without interference.

As the daylight force sought to combat, the Forts and Libs made virtually unopposed runs over the railway junctions of Epinal and Chaumont, in southeastern France near the Swiss border, and over six of the main German airfields just behind the first-line coastal defenses: Caen, Avord, Orleans-Bricy, Bourges, Chateau d'Un and Etamps-Mondesir, all within a 120-mile arc south and southwest of Paris.

More than 1,000 Eighth and ninth Air Force Thunderbolts, Lightnings and long range Mustangs flew with the bombers, and when it became obvious the Luftwaffe would not fight went down to earth and strafed locomotives, military trains airfield hangars and gun emplacements.

Only one bomber group reported interception attempts, and these were beaten off by escorts, who reported that everywhere the German fighters fled from combat.

▲ ▲ ▲ ▲

Diary Entry May 25th, 1944

4th (6th) Mission
Plane Flown B-17 – 42-102507 N

This was truly a "milk run." We ran into flak in two places – no more than a dozen shots in either place. But the first batch caught one bomber in another Group. I saw it go down with No. 3 & No. 4 engines afire and it slowly began to spin. I saw three parachutes before we were too far past it.

Our wing hit the airfield at Nancy and really plastered it. What a sight! No one in our Group was hurt and none of our ships were even hit.

All our ships got back. We met no fighter opposition – but had plenty of fighter support.

News Reports for May 25th, 1944

North-South Blitz Rips Anti-Invasion Rail Links
Over 1,500 American bombers yesterday struck from two sides of Europe at the network of railways, reinforcing Hitler's defense against invasion through the conquered lands of the west.

One thousand Flying Fortresses and Liberators flew out from Britain to bomb nine railway junctions and four airfields in France and Belgium, while from the Mediterranean other heavies flew northward to batter the railways funneling into Lyon and Toulon, in the south of France.

As the ETO (European Theater of Operations) bomber forces ranged up and down the eastern border of France they saw only a scant handful of German fighters, not a one of which got through the covering escort of some 750 Eighth and Ninth Air Force P47s, 38s, and 51s.

Crews reported intense flak over some targets, however, and the day's losses were reported as four heavy bombers and 12 fighters. We destroyed nine enemy aircraft in the air, U.S. pilots reported, and an unspecified number on the ground.

Fighters Again Strafe

While the bombers were hammering Hitler's railway network in the wake of a shattering RAF night raid on the rail junction of Aachen, the motor-assembly works at Antwerp and other targets, American fighters supplemented the heavies' attacks with another day of deck-level strafing of locomotives, troop trains, radio stations and army trucks all across the occupied countries.

First reports told of at least 36 locomotives shot up, and four Lightning pilots caught a loaded troop train, blasted it to a stop and then systematically gunned down German soldiers scrambling vainly for shelter in fields along the right of way.

Other fighter guns were trained on barges and tugs in the canal system of northern France and Belgium and on military installations all up and down the Atlantic Wall.

Chief targets for the bombers were the rail yards at Mulhouse, Belfort, Sarreguemines, Metz, Thionville, Charleroi and Blainville, all eastern or northeastern France and at Brussels and Liege in Belgium.

The Nazi airfields at Nancy-Essey and Bretigny in France also got hit by the heavies, and they carried smaller attacks out on airfields near Brussels and Antwerp.

▲ ▲ ▲ ▲

Diary Entry May 27th, 1944

5th (7th) Mission
Plane Flown B-17 – 42-1026

This one started out like a milk run. We encountered absolutely no opposition on the way over and thought it would be like the last one.

Our target was Ludwigshafen – The Railroad Marshalling yards, and we blasted the hell out of it. The weather was beautifully clear and we could see everything. Only two or three bombs fell into the town. I saw an oil car go up with a terrific blast of flame.

The "milk run" developed into a Broken-Fist business when we hit the target area. They didn't aim the flak at us, they knew what we were after. They threw it straight up over the target with the idea in mind that we <u>had</u> to pass through that spot. *Fortunately for us, their gunnery was poor. We lost no ships from our Group and our ship had two holes in it. One in each wing.*

We had no fighter opposition on this one, but our own fighter support was magnificent. What a pleasure the sight of the "Buzz-Boys" is!

News Reports for May 27th, 1944

40 Hrs. See Blitz Reach Record Pace.

1,200 U.S. Fighters Escort 1,000 Bombers Over Reich, France.

The air offensive which for 40 weekend hours saw five tons of bombs a minute dumped on Hitler's Atlantic Wall and the defense points behind it last night echoed the thunder of pre-invasion intensity as Allied air fleets rounded out their biggest day-and-night attacks of the war.

One thousand American heavy bombers, covered by over 1,200 U.S. fighters-the biggest escort force of the war-yesterday carried the fair weather blitz through its second day with a cascade of explosives and incendiaries on targets in central and southwestern Germany, bringing to approximately 11,500 the RAF and U.S. bomb tonnage for the 40 hours from dawn Saturday.

While over 1,000 U.S. and Allied medium and light bombers, fighter – and dive-bombers were carrying out more attacks on the concrete fortifications guarding Europe's northwestern perimeter, the heavy bombers and their escorts were sweeping far inland on their second day in a row of 1,000-bomber strength. From Saturday morning, a survey showed at least 7,500 sorties had been flown by Allied warplanes based in Britain.

At a cost of 24 bombers and 7 fighters, the formations hit targets in Ludwigshafen, Saarbruken, Konz Karthaus, Mannheim, Neunkirchen, and Karlrushe, in Germany, and engine-repair plants at Strasbourg and Metz, as well as the railway bridge leading from France to Germany at Strasbourg.

Other heavy bomber units lent a major weight to the attacks on military installations along the coast of France.

Weather over the Continent was ideal Saturday, crews reported, and for the first time in days they stung the Luftwaffe into putting up resistance.

As usual, some Groups made their bombing runs over rail yards and bridges with only flak to oppose them, but at other targets the Nazis threw in groups of 100 fighters, and the U.S. fighter pilots reported 36 enemy craft destroyed in combat, while bomber gunners claimed 13 more.

▲ ▲ ▲ ▲

Diary Entry May 31st, 1944

6th (8th) Mission
Plane Flown B-17 – 42-102596
Awarded Air Medal

This one was almost no mission – but it turned out o.k. So now we have an Air-Medal!

Our original target was the Marshalling yards at Mulhouse in France. However, when we got across the Channel, we found nearly the entire continent covered with towering cumulus clouds. It would have been suicidal to get through. So 572 bombers went scouting around for a target.

We finally found a hole in the clouds about 20 miles across right over the airfield at Florennes in France. So we circled and looked at it. I must laugh when I think of it. It was a very unorthodox procedure. Then – we backed off and flew down the run and blasted the revetments and hangars to hell. We then circled back to see our results!

No fighters at all, no flak. We had a tremendous escort all the time. For a target of opportunity – it was very opportune. And we did get in a mission. To say the least, it was a laughable affair.

News Reports for May 31st, 1944

Rail Yards In Germany Are Blasted.

Ploesti Bombed; Lines Feeding West Wall Hit; Wall Itself Plastered

Freight yards in Germany which feed the Wehrmacht in France

And 250 to 500 Britain-based Fortresses and Liberators pounded the Low Countries yesterday, while the great Ploesti oilfields in Rumania were dealt another heavy blow by American heavies based in Italy.

The actual drubbing of the Germans' first line anti-invasion defenses in northern France went on, meanwhile, unabated.

The Eighth Air Force heavies, winging into Germany for the fifth straight day beneath a protecting umbrella of over 1,200 fighter planes, stabbed at the crowded rail yards of Hamm, Osnabruck, Schwerte (10 miles southeast of Dortmund) and Soest (15 miles southeast of Hamm).

All funnel supplies to German forces in the occupied countries along the coast, and Hamm is probably the largest distributing point for rail traffic from the Reich to the coast. In addition, an air base at Luxeuil, 70 miles west of Mulhouse in France, got pounded.

The giant escort of Eighth and Ninth Air Force Thunderbolts, Lightnings and Mustangs found very few enemy aircraft in the skies and, for a change, moderate flak, according to returning airmen. They said great cloud banks necessitated the use of the scientific bombing-through-the-cloud methods in some places.

From Italy, Libs and Forts, escorted by P38s and P51s, scored hits on at least one major refinery at Ploesti, and crews reported large columns of smoke visible for miles, obscuring the target and preventing observation of other results. Intense ack-ack and some enemy fighters were encountered.

Ploesti, 30 miles north of Bucharest, capital of Rumania, got bombed four times in April and twice previously in May.

▲ ▲ ▲ ▲

SUB-CHAPTER:

JUNE 1944

Diary Entry June 2nd, 1944

7th (9th) Mission
Plane Flown B-17 – 42-102507 N

Well – I thought we had had milk-runs until this one – but this took the prize.

Our target was some gun emplacements about 4 miles inside the coast of France. It was like our operational training days. No flak, no fighters.

It was just a mad scuffle. We kept meeting Groups who had already dropped their eggs and were on their way home. Didn't even bother to test fire my guns on this one.

Our target was just a little north of Pas de Calais, about 10 miles south of Boulogne. We had to bomb PFF[96] which is bombing through clouds.

---

[96] A leading bomb group Path Finder Force would identify the target through the

News Reports for June 2nd, 1944

Calais Gets Its Biggest Blow Of War.

1,000 Heavies From U.K. Rip Coast; Force from Italy Hits Hungary.

Huge fleets of American heavy bombers yesterday thundered over France's Channel coast to give the Pas de Calais its heaviest single pounding of the war, while at the same time, Italy-based U.S. heavies raided rail yards in eastern Hungary and Transylvania.

After a night in which the RAF struck at targets from Denmark to the Balkans, a force approaching 1,750 USSTAF[97] bombers launched another north-south offensive to hit the so-called invasion coast of France and five Balkan rail junctions.

Possible 3,000 tons of explosives were heaped on Germany's West Wall defenses by nearly 1,000 Britain-based Fortresses and Liberators. Not one enemy fighter was encountered as the heavies, shepherded by about 500 Eighth Air force P47s, P38s, and P51s, dropped their bombs through the cloud. Not one aircraft was lost.

The Return To Calais

The raid marked the return of U.S. heavies in strength to the battered Pas de Calais after nearly two weeks in which major blows from Britain had been directed at strategic targets deep behind the coast and in the

---

clouds and drop smoke flares to guide the following bombers on to the target. It was not very accurate and smoke flares would drift from the target area due to winds etc.

[97] United States Strategic Air Force Europe

Reich itself, although minor attacks in the Calais area have been kept up.

Almost simultaneously, in another sharp attack on German rail lines in the Balkans, MAAF[98] U.S. heavy bombers plastered railroad yards at Miskolcz, 100 miles northeast of Budapest; Szolnok, 55 miles southwest of Budapest; Szeged, 5 miles from the junction of the Jugoslav, Rumanian and Hungarian borders, and the Cluj and Simeria, in Transylvania.

For the Szolnok area, through which the Germans funnel supplies to their Eastern Front, it was the second attack in hours by Mediterranean-based aircraft. Preceding the daylight assault was a blow struck by RAF medium and heavy bombers through thick haze.

Shortly after midnight yesterday, a small force of RAF bombers swept over Saumur in the second attack in as many nights on the French rail center 150 miles southwest of Paris.

At the same time, an unidentified military objective near the coast of France was raided and Mosquitoes pelted a target in Denmark. No planes were lost.

Operations of the Allied Expeditionary Air Force Thursday were confined to an evening attack by Ninth Air Force Marauders on military targets in northern France.

Meanwhile, USSTAF headquarters announced that American heavy bombers had rained over 63,000 tons of bombs on German Europe in May from battered Pas de Calais to the Balkans.

▲ ▲ ▲ ▲

---

[98] **Mediterranean Allied Air Forces** (MAAF) was the major Allied air force command organization in the Mediterranean theater from mid-December 1943 until the end of the Second World War.

Diary Entry June 3rd, 1944

8th (10)th Mission
Plane Flown B-17 – 42-102507 N

This one was almost identical to our last one, but for the fact that we ran into some flak today.

Otherwise, there was nothing to it. We are beginning to feel like aerial milkmen.

Again, our target was more gun emplacements just south of Boulogne, France. We did it this time. We bombed on PFF, but we could see the bomb strike.

Ho Hum!

No ships lost. No one hurt, no battle damage to the "Warrior."[99]

News Reports for June 3rd, 1944

Boulogne Is Hit 4 Times In Two Days.

Libs, Forts, Other Craft Lash West Wall in Big Pre-Invasion Blitz.

The French Channel port of Boulogne got pounded by American heavy bombers for the fourth time in two days yesterday as Allied aircraft swarmed over the French coast and the West Wall in never-ending streams to round out the heaviest weekend of the pre-invasion air bombardment.

Hit twice by the B-17s and B24s, Boulogne, only about 30 miles from the English coast, was raided in the morning and again later in the day as the heavies carried out their third double mission in three days.

At the same time, the invasion-tense French coast, which was hit

---

[99] Notice Kempner calls his ship "Warrior"

again and again in a series of crushing weekend blows, felt the weight of American bombs along a 200-mile stretch.

Over 250 Marauders and Havocs pelted military objectives along the Channel-washed beaches of France and smashed at a vehicular bridge at Courcelles-sur-Seine, 40 miles north of Paris. All the bombers, which were escorted by Ninth Air Force P51s and P47s, returned.

Joining in the mounting assault on the German front-line defenses, planes of the Second Tactical Air Force and the Air Defence of Great Britain swept over the strip of France closest to Britain, dropping their explosives on enemy radio installations.

▲ ▲ ▲ ▲

Diary Entry June 4th, 1944

9th (11th) Mission
Plane Flown B-17 – 42-102507 N

This is beginning to get monotonous. For the third time in three straight mornings – we were over there, south of Boulogne, pounding away at more gun emplacements and installations.

No flak, no fighter. We didn't even have an escort. Milkmen – that's us! Somehow, I smell Invasion!

No battle damage – no wounded– All our ships returned.

News Reports for June 4th, 1944

French Coast Gets Non-Stop Pounding By Heavies.

Fortresses and Liberators In Heavy Action.

Fortresses and Liberators twice blasted Pas de Calais and the Boulogne area without losing a bomber. In the morning the heavies were escorted by Eighth Air Force P47s and P38s, a force which was augmented in the afternoon by P51s. Only one fighter did not return.

Meanwhile, over 400 Mustangs, Lightnings and Thunderbolt fighter-bombers carried out a series of strafing, dive-bombing attacks on France. Their targets included canal and river barges, factories, railroad bridges, locomotives, grounded airplanes, an airfield, rail yards, motor convoys, oil storage tanks, troop-carrying trucks, warehouses, flak tower, railroad facilities sheds, and radio installations.

No enemy aircraft were encountered, but they reported flak barrages in some of the target areas to be heavy and intense. Two P47s and one P51 were lost.

Even as the Air Ministry revealed that the Germans were trying desperately to patch the communications which the Allied Expeditionary Air Force had cut over the Seine and the Meuse rivers, Ninth Air Force Marauders and Havocs, escorted by P47s, struck at a bridge over the Seine near Paris late Saturday evening. Marauders and Havocs also bombed an airfield near Chartres and fighter-bombers and rocket-carrying Typhoons attacked a wide variety of targets in north France.

Three AEAF bombers and four fighters were lost.

The weekend blows at the so-called invasion coast of France followed the very heavy attack made by Forts and Liberators Friday on their first mission. In their second operation of the day, the heavies hit a variety of military targets west and southwest of Paris.

▲ ▲ ▲ ▲

Diary Entry June 5th, 1944

10th (12th) Mission
Plane Flown B-17 – 42-102507 N

I am puzzling over this "milk run" business. There must be something at the back of it.

Today was like the previous three-days bombing. We hit a gun emplacement across a bay from Le Havre in the Pas de Calais. It was a beautiful bomb-strike.

No fighters – no flak. Just a milk run.

We lost no one – none of our ships were missing.

Not a bad way to chalk up the missions.

News Reports for June 5th, 1944

Forts, Libs Hit Calais Boulogne.

Blows Come After U.S. Heavies' First Triple Mission In A Day.

American heavy bombers for the fourth consecutive day concentrated yesterday on France's Channel coast, blasting German installations in the Boulogne and Calais area.

The heavies, striking at the Continent's so-called invasion coast for the sixth time in four days, flew out only hours after a history-making force of Forts and Liberators late Sunday had completed their third mission in one day.

Up to 750 B-17s and B24s, escorted by about 500 Eighth Air Force P47s and P51s, yesterday dropped an estimated 2,200 tons of explosives on the Nazi-fortified coast, which was lashed during the night by aircraft of RAF's Bomber Command.

The new American blow raised the tonnage dropped on the stretch of Europe closest to England since late Friday to around 15,000 tons. Other targets in northern France were factories at Conflans and Juziers and a radio station at Louviers,

Forts and Liberators yesterday smashed all records for heavy bomber operations by flying their eighth mission in four days. The previous record for the number of operations by British-based American heavies was five raids in three days and seven in five.

The softening-up offensive on Europe reaches a new peak Sunday when U.S. heavy bombers, after twice pounding the Channel port of Boulogne, mounted a third mission, thundering inland to heap destruction on targets in the Paris area. From all the operations, four bombers and three escorting fighters were lost.

Hit in the historic third attack were a railway junction at Massy-Palaiseau, an aerodrome at Bertigny, a locomotive depot at Versailles-Matelets, a railway at Villeneuve-St, George, all in the Paris area, and several aerodromes south-west of the city.

▲ ▲ ▲ ▲

Diary Entry D-Day June 6th, 1944

11th (13th) Mission
Plane Flown B-17 – 42-102487 F

*This was **it**! What a surprise to go to the briefing and be told this was D-Day.*

We had gun emplacements at Le Havre, our target – and went in in six ship formations. The air was full of ships and bombs.

While we had to bomb PFF, we could see the invasion forces in the channel – what a sight!

Again, we met no opposition – no fighters – no flak. This is history of a momentous sort.

I am proud and happy to have been a part of it.

David E. Huntley

News Reports for D-Day June 6th, 1944

Greatest Umbrella For Landing.

Armadas Of Allied Planes Hammer Nazi Targets. This Was The Invasion.

Unleashing the full fury of Anglo-American air power, Allied aircraft yesterday bombed and strafed mile after mile of French beaches, seizing undisputed mastery of the air and heaping record-breaking tons of explosives on Nazi coastal installations in providing the greatest umbrella in history for the invasion forces.

Between midnight and 8 AM yesterday alone, 10,000 tons of steel went cascading down on German targets on the coast of Normandy. In the same period, over 31,000 airmen, not including airborne troops, dominated the sky over France.

It was estimated that in a final recapitulation, the number of sorties flown yesterday would soar to over 20,000.

Luftwaffe Stays Down

So sparse was the Luftwaffe opposition that many airmen did not encounter a single German fighter. Few of the 1,750 fighter planes, which it is estimated the Nazis can muster to oppose the invasion, put in an appearance.

High ranking officers of Supreme Headquarters emphasized. There was no reason to believe the Luftwaffe had been defeated.

"Fighting of the greatest severity is in store before the Luftwaffe is wiped out," according to one officer.

Bombing, strafing and patrolling fighter aircraft of the Ninth Air Force were in the air continuously yesterday from 4:30 AM, covering the movement of the Allied Expeditionary Force over sea and on to the beaches, and probing ahead of the landing parties for tactical objectives beyond the operations zone.

The first ten waves of Ninth Air Force fighter-bombers to go into action reported no serious opposition anywhere over the Channel or the beachheads.

Between 11:30 PM Monday and sunrise yesterday, more than 1,000 RAF heavy bombers, divided into ten task forces, battered the French coast to clear the way for the ground troops.

Taking up the attack where the RAF left off over 350 Marauders swept across the Channel t pound enemy coastal guns in a sharp three-hour raid.

Almost simultaneously, over 1,000 Fortresses and Liberators rocked German fortifications in France's coastal area.

As the Allied craft filled the sky over France, strafing German troops and smashing at enemy transportation and communication lines, only 50 German planes were counted.

▲ ▲ ▲ ▲

Diary Entry June 7th, 1944

12th (14th) Mission
Plane Flown B-17 – 42-102390 X
Substitute Co-pilot today was Lt. G. Pappas
Today we were awarded Oak Leaf Cluster to our Air medal

What a nightmare this one was!

Our target was originally an airfield southwest of Lorient, France, but we had a little difficulty in forming up – so we dropped into Ridgwell's 381'st Bomb Group[100] formation.

There was flak, and it was accurate. It rattled off our ship like hail on a tin roof. So, what do they do – but turn about over the ocean and fly back over the

---

[100] Ridgewell was the Air Force's #167 Airbase in England during WWII

target to see what they had done! We saw a terrific number of fires and bomb strikes – what a sight!

We had had about 35 minutes in which to brief and take off again. Strictly a hurry-up job, and we went a-bombing another airfield just east of Brest, France, on the Peninsula.

Then, to top things off, the Group got lost over the Channel. By the time we got back to the U.K. it was dusk and the rat-race began. With rain and darkness, and low clouds, we really had a handful.[101] *What a job we had dodging other ships up there. But we landed at our own field.*

We lost no ships and there was no fighter opposition.

News Reports for June 7th, 1944

Allied Craft Keep Skies Free Of Foe.

Allied aircraft, maintaining their 200-to-one air superiority over invasion beach-heads, dominated the skies over France again yesterday as they hammered German troop concentrations and smashed enemy lines of communication almost without challenge from the Luftwaffe.

After a record day in which the Allied air forces, flying the staggering total of 13,000 sorties, rocked the French coast with 22,500 tons of explosives at a cost of but 31 aircraft, U.S. planes roared out from their bases at dawn and on through the day to blast everything German.

Although enemy aerial activity picked up slightly yesterday, at 5 PM the Allies had lost only 70 planes since the first landings in Europe, most of them presumably to flak.

---

[101] A masterful & calm handling of critical situations demonstrated Pilot Searl's flying skills.

Heavies Bomb Near Caen

Eighth Air Force heavy bombers continued their support of ground troops yesterday afternoon by attacking several road intersections near towns south of Caen to block off possible German reinforcements.

Besides escort duty, Eighth fighters strafed and bombed over a 50-50 mile arc in advance of Allied ground forces.

Up to early afternoon, only two formations of 12 enemy aircraft approached the beaches and had no chance of attacking Allied troops. They destroyed a total of 20 German fighters for the loss of five Allied aircraft.

Every type of aircraft in the Ninth Air Force -mediums, light and fighter bombers -gave close support to ground troops, strafing German forces and pounding enemy supply and communication lines in a belt 30 miles inland from the French coast.

Fighter bombers shuttled between Britain and France throughout the day. By noon, over 500 P47 fighter-bombers had flown over 17 separate missions over the Cherbourg Peninsula. In the only reported engagement with the enemy, one Me4120 (sic Me 410) was shot down by a P47 12 feet above the ground. By late afternoon only 12 fighter-bombers had been lost, all of them to ack ack fire.

Concentrating mainly on the Cherbourg Peninsula, the tactical aircraft struck at the rear of the battle line, hitting troop concentrations and all German targets sighted.

Marauders, flying as low as 1,000 feet, for the first time strafed German troops, vehicles and supply convoys. Havocs hit a German headquarters behind the line on one of the beachheads.

Planes of the RAF's Second Tactical Air Force flew from dawn to early evening over the beaches and deep into France. Twenty-three enemy planes got destroyed in missions on which the RAF also lost 23.

Preceding the assault by Forts and Liberators, medium bombers hit Rennes, Le Mans and Laval, three principal railway centers on the east-west railroad line leading into Brest peninsula, just west of the Cherbourg peninsula.

Rounding out the greatest day of air activity of the war, the RAF on Tuesday night struck another 5000-ton blow, battering roads and railways from 15 to 40 miles behind the bridgeheads. Thirteen aircraft were lost.

They announced yesterday that the Allied air forces, hammering rail centers before D-Day, flew the stupendous total of 71,000 sorties in the first six days of June.

So effective was the offensive. SHAEF said that before the landings, 25 railroad bridges and nine highway bridges across the Seine got destroyed.

▲ ▲ ▲ ▲

Diary Entry June 12th, 1944

13th (15th) Mission
Plane Flown B-17 – 42-102507 N
Substitute Co-pilot again today was Lt. G. Pappas

With our target at Lille-Nord – an airfield, we went bombing PFF. Don't think we hit much on this one – but we raked up another one, anyway.

Flak was very light – and we met no fighter opposition. This is the first time in the last five missions in which I've seen our own fighters at all.

We lost no ships – none even damaged considering the fact we put up a complete combat wing – 3 groups of 18 ships each. That's pretty good!

News Reports for June 12th, 1944

Heavies' Attack Cracks Record.

Nazi's Put Up Strongest Resistance Since D-Day; 1,400 Bombers Out.

The Luftwaffe put up its strongest resistance since D-Day yesterday as every type of American aircraft ranged over and beyond combat zones and the Eighth Air Force dispatched the greatest number of bombers ever sent on a single mission.

As aerial combat flared over the skies of France, scores of enemy planes were encountered by Eighth Air Force fighters and by 4 PM the pursuits had reported the destruction of 17 Nazi aircraft.

In three operations alone, Ninth Air Force Thunderbolts took a toll of 22 of the Luftwaffe's precious hoard, while P51s destroyed 17 on the ground.

Despite the Luftwaffe's appearance in force, the Allies dominated the air above France, and preliminary reports showed the record of 13,000 sorties in D-Day would be surpassed.

After a night in which RAF Lancasters and Halifaxes battered rail junctions and a rail bridge in a wide arc behind the Normandy battle zone and Mosquitoes for the third night pelted Berlin, American bombers roared out on their greatest mission of the war.

More than 1,400 Fortresses and Liberators, escorted by about 750 P47s, P38s and P51s of the Eighth Air Force, dropped their bombs visually on 16 German airfields and six bridges in France.

Seven Bomber Lost

The fighters, besides their escort duties, strafed and bombed 11 locomotives, 63 railway cars, 102 trucks and 11 other vehicles, three radio and flak towers, one tank, several marshaling yards and rail junctions. Fourteen fighters did not return.

Among the targets hit by the heavy bombers were the airfields at Lille-Nord, Montdidier, Evreux-Fauville, Vitry en Artois and Beauvais – Tille, all in the north of France.

▲ ▲ ▲ ▲

David E. Huntley

Diary Entry June 13th, 1944

14th (16th) Mission
Plane Flown B-17 – 42-102507 N
Co-pilot Lt.. A.L. Dion back on board today.

We pulled this one in late afternoon. The bombs our group dropped were the only ones that hit the target. The bomb strikes before ours landed right in the middle of the airfield.

Our target was at Le Bourget – and we could have done better for it.

We lost no ships. Some got hit by flak and one gunner got wounded.

No fighters – and we had a little support. We are slowly eliminating a lot of potential trouble for our foot soldiers over on the continent.

News Reports for June 13th, 1944

Greatest Bomber Force Ever Sent Out On Strikes From The U.K.

By Joe Flemming[102]
Stars and Stripes Staff Writer

A force of Fortresses and Liberators 1,500 strong, the greatest task force of heavy bombers ever dispatched, yesterday plastered targets in France, Belgium, Holland and Germany itself as the Allied aerial campaign to knock out Luftwaffe bases and Von Rundstedt's supply lines soared to a new peak.

As the heavies roared across the Channel on their record-shattering mission, Ninth Air Force Marauders, Havoc, fighter-bombers and aircraft of the RAF's Second Tactical Air Force rained their explosives on Nazi

---

[102] This report is credited to the Stars and Stripes Newspaper as it was in the Kempner diary.

targets rocked by over 44,000 tons of steel in the first seven days of the Normandy campaign.

And while the air war to support advancing ground troops on the Continent was pressed with increasing intensity, Italy-based U.S. heavies made another attack on strategic enemy installations, battering oil refineries in Hungary.

Among the targets lashed by the Eighth Air Force armada, which topped by about 100 planes the force of 1,400 bombers dispatched Monday, were an oil refinery at Emmerich, northwest of the Ruhr, and French airfields at Le Bourget and Creil, at Paris. Outlying Etampes-Mondesir and Chateaudun. Luftwaffe bases in Brussels-Melsbroek, in Belgium, and Eindoven, in Holland, were also pounded.

15 Bombers, 8 Fighters Lost

Several sharp but brief dogfights were reported by pilots of the escorting Eighth P47s, P38s and P51s, which, besides shepherding the heavies, scoured the countryside for German targets in the air and on the ground.

Two enemy aircraft were shot out of the air by the pursuits and preliminary reports indicated that 16 locomotives, 44 railroad cars, three trucks and eight flak towers were destroyed or damaged. Cost of the historic blow was 15 bombers and 8 fighters.

Late Tuesday evening, in their second mission of the day, Forts and Liberators struck two airfields north of Paris and several airfields in Normandy and Britany, south and southwest of the bridgehead. Two bombers and four fighters were lost in the day's operations.

Eighth fighters destroyed six German planes and destroyed or damaged six locomotives, 40 railroad cars, 30 trucks, five armored vehicles and a staff car. Five bridges were damaged.

Eleven skytrains[103] and eleven gliders of Ninth Troop Carrier

---

[103] A Douglas C47 transport aircraft used extensively in WWII and other wars since.

Command landed on the American-held sector of the Normandy beachhead late Tuesday evening with supplies, rations and other materials.

Landing on an advanced Ninth Air Force landing strip, all the skytrains returned to England safely.

▲ ▲ ▲ ▲

Diary Entry June 15th, 1944

15th (17th) Mission
Plane Flown B-17 – 42-102507 N

This one was just like "old times." No milk run – this. Our target was the airfield at Bordeaux and what a shellacking we gave it!

Today's bombing was the most magnificent I've ever seen. Visual bombing – and such destruction!

Although we lost no ships – there was just enough flak to make it interesting. No fighters – and our own support was swell.

I liked this one. The weather was CAVU[104] and we could see the ground forces at work. Our Naval units were out in strength shelling the hell out of something – and it was fascinating to see the tremendous flashes their guns made.

One ship down there looked like the U.S.S. Dakota.

News Reports for June 15th, 1944

Targets In France, Reich battered; 9th's planes Aid Ground Troops.

---

[104] Ceiling and Visibility Unlimited" A military term indicating perfect flying weather.

The B-17 Tomahawk Warrior: A WWII Final Honor

By Joe Flemming
Stars and Stripes Staff Writer

Another huge force of American heavy bombers dumped lethal explosives on enemy targets in France and Germany yesterday and Ninth Air Force warplanes joined in the fierce struggle raging for the Normandy town of Villier-Bocage after a night in which the RAF smashed at Le Havre's E-boat pens with 12,000 pound blockbusters.

Over 1,300 Eighth Air Force Fortresses and Liberators, mounting their third huge attack in four days, at a cost of only three bombers flew 300 miles south of the battle in the deepest penetration of France since the European landings to hit an airfield at Bordeaux, French rail junctions, rail bridges, airfields and aircraft assembly plants and unspecified objectives in the Reich.

German radio reported that the great industrial city of Hanover was bombed.

No Luftwaffe opposition was encountered by most of the heavies, but one Liberator combat wing drove off two sharp assaults near Tours by 50 German fighters-the largest number seen by the bombers since the start of the Continental campaign,

Twelve enemy planes were shot down, seven by the B-17s and B26s and five by escorting P51s, P38s and P47s. In addition, the Eighth pursuits carried out low level strafing attacks on transport, shooting up two locomotives, four freight cars, six flak towers, five trucks and other ground targets. Three fighters were lost. Carrying tactical support to within a very short distance of the American lines.

▲ ▲ ▲ ▲

Diary Entry June 18th, 1944

16th (18th) Mission
Plane Flown B-17 – 42-102507 N

This was a holy terror! Old times are really back!

Our target was an oil refinery and dock installations at Hamburg. It turned out to be as bad – if not worse than Berlin. The flak was the deadliest I've seen yet. It was good enough to knock out our Squadron C.O. who was deputy Group C.O. I don't think he got out – I saw the ship blow up about 2000 feet below us. It was a terrible sight.[105]

We lost one other ship out of the group – but no fighters attacked us. This was really a rough one. But really plastered the target. Our ship had its share of flak holes.

News Reports for June 18th, 1944

'Robots' Coast Battered Anew.

Pas de Calais Is Hit 6th time In 3 Days; 1,300 Heavies Bomb Reich.

By Joe Flemming

Launching the sixth Allied air attack in three days on France's robot plane coast[106], up to 250 Liberators yesterday afternoon pounded the Pas de Calais after a morning mission in which the Eighth Air Force, switching from operations in support of ground troops on the Continent, dispatched over 1,300 B-17s and B24s to bomb oil plants at Hamburg and other targets in northwest Germany. It was the largest force of U.S. heavies ever sent against strategic objectives.

---

[105] 398th Historian says the SQ CO he is referring to is Maj. John G. Weibel, KIA

[106] Lt.. Kempner is referring to the German V1 rocket installations on the French coast.

The record American assault on the Reich combined with RAF's shattering weekend blows to press home to Germany the Allied air forces' determination to smash enemy industry and beachhead communications and pilotless plane installations.

No enemy fighter opposition was encountered by the bombers, but 11 were hit, presumably by flak, as the Germans, instead of interceptors, threw up one of the greatest ack-ack barrages of the war.

Although the Forts and Liberators outnumbered their escorting fighters more than two to one, not one German aircraft was seen.

▲ ▲ ▲ ▲

Diary Entry June 19th, 1944

17th (19th) Mission
Plane Flown B-17 – 42-102507 N

The Cherbourg peninsula is really taking a beating – I can tell you.

We went back down to Bordeaux to one airfield 35 miles south of the city and plastered the hell out of it.

We passed the other airfields that the other outfits had left in smoking and burning ruins. They did a complete job, but then so did we.

We really had some more of that "Pickle Barrel" bombing. I have never seen such fires since we started.

No fighter opposition – but plenty of flak. We caught about five pieces in the ship. This was hardly a milk run. They were out to get us. We lost no ships but we all got hit.

News Reports for June 19th, 1944

'Robots' Coast Battered Anew

Pas de Calais Is Hit 6th time In 3 Days; 1,300 Heavies Bomb Reich.

By Joe Flemming

American heavy bombers yesterday made two sharp attacks on the Pas de Calais and for the first time it was officially announced that the targets of the raiders were "German pilot-less-plane launching platforms."[107]

Rocked in the morning by an aerial task force of between 250 and 500 Fortresses and Liberators, the bomb-cratered of France was battered again late in the afternoon by about 250 B-17s, and B24s in an assault which the Eighth Air Force said was directed against the winged bombs' launching ramps.

Meanwhile, Lt.. Gen, Lewis H. Brereton, Ninth Air Force commander, revealed that Thunderbolt fighter-bombers now were permanently based in France. The P47s became the first element of any U.S. air force to establish permanent stations there.*

The French bases eliminate the long Channel flight for the P47s and enable Ninth Air Force to step up the offensive to support Allied ground troops that have virtually driven the Luftwaffe from bridgehead skies and badly disrupted enemy communication and supply lines.

Although it had been announced previously that U.S. aircraft were landing on French strips to refuel and rearm, yesterday's announcement was the first disclosure that American airmen had taken up permanent stations in France.

Besides hitting the Pas de Calais, heavy bombers yesterday morning raided four German airfields in the Bordeaux region of southwestern France. Struck were aerodromes at Bordeaux Merignac, Casaux, Corme

---

[107] These were the V1 rocket planes nick-named by British public as, "Buzz Bombs, or Doodle-Bugs!

Ecluse and Landers Bussac. Seven bombers and 16 escorting fighters were lost.

Weather deteriorated over the Continent yesterday and air operations to support ground troops did not equal Sunday's great activity. On Sunday, Ninth Air Force planes attacked hundreds of moving targets on the Cherbourg peninsula. Over 800 retreating Germans were killed or wounded when P47 fighter-bombers dive-bombed and strafed a convoy.

During the night, the RAF, maintaining the fierce tempo of the air war, sent Mosquito bombers out in strength behind the combat zone. Road and rail transport, bridges, junctions and rail yards were pounded, as well as ammunition stores and other military targets.

*Author's Note: On my website, I describe the interviews[108] I had in post-war years with several pilots of a P47 squadron and the tar paper airfields they flew from in France. In particular, there was an airfield in Picauville, which was carved out of an apple orchard. Several of these P47 pilots became friends of mine. During the war, my late wife Sophie had lived close to a similar aerodrome near Coulommiers in the Seine et Marne region. The field had been occupied by German bombers, which were used in attacks on England. The Americans captured it later and flew P38s from there. Years later, I asked Sophie, jokingly, of course, why she did not join the resistance and sabotage the airfield to stop them bombing me in London? She replied, "How could I? I was only nine years old.

▲ ▲ ▲ ▲

---

[108] https://deathwatchbeetle.net/veterans_ww2.html. One of these pilots, Arlie Blood was shot down and fought with the Maquis.

David E. Huntley

Diary Entry June 20th, 1944

18th (20th) Mission
Plane Flown B-17 – 42-102507 N
Oak Leaf Cluster N0 2

What a routine! Bordeaux, Hamburg, Bordeaux, and today, Hamburg again.

Again, we ran into a holocaust.[109] *The flak was terrific, but there were no fighters.*

Our target was the docks and oil installations in Hamburg and with visual bombing, well, we really pasted it. We started what were possibly the biggest fires in history. What a wonderful sight. This particular target has been eliminated.

We were luckier this time – we lost no ships and had a couple of boys wounded. But every ship came back with holes. Our own ship had better than ten – one piece smacked through the Plexiglas nose and got stopped by Leo Walsh's flak-suit. It hit him in right the chest – a small piece – but deadly enough. I got sprayed with the Plexiglass.

Things are getting rough!

---

[109] It's interesting to note how Saul, himself a Jew, used the word holocaust before this word had entered into the US lexicon of usage.
https://newrepublic.com ' article › 121807 › when-holocaust-became-holocaust.

In Hebrew, the calamity quickly became known as "Shoah," which means "the catastrophe." But it wasn't until the 1960s that scholars and writers began using the term "Holocaust,"

And after Word War II, the "Final Solution" was often called a holocaust. By the 1960s, according to the Jewish Magazine, it became common to refer to the Nazi genocide of Jews as "The Holocaust."

The Oxford dictionary describes it as 'whole burnt-offering'; 'wholesale sacrifice' or 'destruction'

News Reports for June 20th, 1944

Calais, Reich Hit In Record Aerial.

Over 1,000 U.S. heavies Out; Robot Runways, Nazi Factories Pasted.

The Eighth Air Force yesterday struck the greatest blow of the war against German strategic targets, explosives from a record force of Fortresses and Liberators raining down on the Reich as almost every type of Allied warplane joined with the heavies in the drive to shatter the runways from which the Nazi robot planes have been hurled at southern England in the last week.

More than 1,500 B-17s and B24s were out in today's operations, possibly the largest number of bombers ever sent on one mission. Over two 200 hundred of them showered steel on the Pas de Calais, while more than 1,300 roared into Germany to pound several oil refineries and plants producing war materials.

Dogfights were thick over the skies of France and Germany as the Luftwaffe fought desperately to stave off the huge assault. Thirty-five enemy aircraft were destroyed in the air and 12 on the ground by strong forces – possibly 1,500 or more -escorting P47s, P38s and P51s of both the Eighth and Ninth Air Forces. One Liberator formation was attacked from the enemy coast to Politz and back again by from 60 to 75 enemy fighters.

German radio claimed 31 American planes were shot down and the Swedish government announced 21 bombers made forced landings on Swedish territory.

For the first time, the Eighth, Ninth and RAF joined in the attack on the robot plane bases, heavy, medium and dive bombers whipping across the Channel in a steady stream.

Over 200 Marauders and Havocs flew through intense flak to bomb several launching platforms, running roughly in a line from 30 miles south of Calais to seven miles north of Abbeville. Ninth Air Force said most of the targets were well hidden only a short distance inland from the coast.

Mustangs, meanwhile, pursued the craft[110] as they cleared the French coast and cut some of them off over the Channel.

No enemy aircraft were seen over Calais. All of the raiders returned.

Other runways for the lethal missiles were pounded to rubble in the mornings by bomb-carrying Mustangs of the RAF's Second Tactical Air Force. They scored several direct hits on catapults hidden in a forest in the Pas de Calais.

Yesterday's offensive followed an evening mission by a force of RAF Lancasters on Monday. Flying in formation with Spitfire escort, the heavies attacked while it was still light and waited 20 minutes for the thick cloud over the secret weapon coast to clear.

Ninth Air Force P47 and P38 fighter-bombers at daybreak attacked rail yards, tracks, bridges, rolling stock and military trucks in France yesterday. Five FW190s were shot down at the cost of three Lightnings.

Targets of the American heavies yesterday included oil plants at Hamburg, Hanover, Magdeburg and Politz, an aircraft factory in the Brunswick area and an ordinance tank depot at Konigsburg.

▲ ▲ ▲ ▲

Diary Entry June 21st, 1944

19th (21st) Mission
Plane Flown B-17 – 42-107114 L

Well – this one was a dilly. Our target was Berlin – no installations – just Berlin.

---

[110] There is no report of how these V1s were intercepted and "cut off over the Channel"

We pulled a retaliatory raid for their sending over their pilotless planes[111]. *Berlin really caught it, but so did we.*

We lost another C.O. This time the C.O. of the whole 601st[112] *Squadron. He was flying lead in the PFF ship, which wasn't even needed. Evidently flak got them. The PFF crew was one of our squadron's favorites. "Rip" Rohrer went down.* *

We caught everything that day. We saw the wing ahead of us get hit by fighters. I saw four of our ships go down and saw two enemy fighters explode from hits by our own guns.

One B-17 had a dogfight with an Me-110 right below us until a P-38 chimed in and the Me-110 went down. But the Me-110 had taken a shot at a parachute first. **DIRTY POOL!**

Our one compensating thought is that Berlin is now a little flatter than it was.

Our tail gunner nearly caught it by way of a piece of flak about 5 inches long and an inch around, went right by his knee and struck his gun mount.

Whew! They're after us!

Story of Lt. Rohrer & crew shot down
*Author's Note:

In his diary entry above, Lt. Kempner noted that, 1st Lt. R.L. Rohrer was Commanding Officer of the 601st (Author: he was of the 600th) Squadron and was shot down. Some of Rohrer's crew managed to bail out but were captured. By publishing extracts from their post-war diaries, I felt it would provide a significant measure of the courage and fortitude shown by these airmen in WWII,

Can you imagine flying into hostile enemy territory at 27,000 ft in subzero temperatures all the time hoping not to be hit by flak of varying intensity? And, at the same time, you are fighting off the Luftwaffe first on the way in, and then on the way out from the bombing run on the target. Suddenly, your

---

[111] V1s or buzzbombs, doodlebugs.

[112] Author note-I believe Kempner meant 600th Squadron as records show.

ship is hit with flak, and you must bail out directly over the target you have just bombed. This is a taste of the war these men fought on each mission.

You are floating earthward glad to have exited the plane which is now spiraling to the ground, and hoping your fellow crew members got out too. Now, as you land among the angry hostile civilians on where near you just dropped your bombs, your life is in as much danger on the ground as if you were in the air. At least until a police officer or military come to pick you up in time.

Of the 350,000 men assigned to the Eighth Air Force in World War II, 50,000[113] airmen paid the ultimate sacrifice and an additional 28,000 became prisoners of war.

The following extract is from the Recollections of Phil Jones, as well as accounts by other members of "Rip" Rohrer's crew, Harvey Kramer, and Clarence Franks, by courtesy of the 398th.org website.

Accounts of Downing of Rohrer Crew
Phil Jones WWII Recollections
by Philip H. Jones Tail Gunner, Rohrer Crew—600th Squadron

1ST PILOT _____ 1ST LT. R.L. ROHRER CO-PILOT _____
2ND LT. A. SISTEK NAVIGATOR _____
2ND LT. H.B. KRAMER BOMBARDIER _____ 2ND LT. C. FRANKS
ENGINEER _____ SGT. D. CHISNELL
RADIO OP _____ SGT. H. COOPER
ASST ENG _____ SGT. R. GREEN
WAIST GUNNER _____ SGT. _____ . MONTGOMERY
BALL TURRET _____ SGT. F. HENNING
TAIL GUNNER _____ SGT. P. JONES
SUB KEY _____ 2ND LT. T. CANTRELL

---

[113] https://www.afa.org/publications-news/news/2019-10-03/afa-statement-on-loss-of-historic-b-17—painful-reminder-of-the-

Philip Jones, tail gunner, relates the story of "Rip" Rohrer going down.

Combat Experiences

My first mission was a target in France in May 1944… air field? I flew in 10 missions. The first 5 missions were not too stressful.

The 6th mission was on 'D' Day. We bombed behind the beaches.

The 7, 8, 9 and 10th missions were not without their fears of the outcomes. Since they assigned us to a Pathfinder Bomber, we flew Lead Plane of the Wing, or Deputy Lead.

On our 10th mission over Berlin, June 21, we were the Lead. No. 3 engine was hit by flak burst and pilot "Rip" Rohrer could not feather the prop. He rang the bailout buzzer, a signal to be ready for the bailout. He rang it again. I bailed over the center of Berlin and was captured immediately. I was a POW in Stalag Luft IV from July 1st, 1944 to Feb. 6, 1945.

On Feb. 6th, 1945, we were marched out of camp westward for 2-1/2 months. On April 18th, I was liberated by a British Armored Division in a small country village. Sent to a British hospital in Brussels and then transferred to a U.S. hospital in Great Britain. Flown back to U.S. on May 30th to a hospital near Pittsburgh.

I received the Air Medal, European Combat Medal and, of course, the P.O.W. Medal.

Then follows two separate accounts of the downing of their B-17 over Berlin, first by Lt. Kramer, the navigator, and the second by Lt. Clarence Franks, Jr., the bombardier, who apparently ended up in the same prison camp.

By Lt. Harvey B. Kramer:

"At approximately 10:20 A.M. on June 21, 1944, we made our turn off the I.P. [Initial Point–the beginning of the bomb run] on to the Bomb Run for another assault on Berlin. (The crew had been flying almost daily bombing missions over Berlin since May 7, 1944.) With the visibility unlimited, they set us for a perfect pattern in the heart of the city.

"Ours being a lead ship with Major Killen in command, there were three of us in the nose, creating rather cramped conditions. Going in on the target, our positions were Lt. Franks in the bombardier's chair, Lt. Waramer was perched on the foremost edge of the navigator's table, and I was seated on an ammo box in front of the 'G' set."

"About 1-1/2 minutes before 'Bombs Away', I was tossed off my impromptu seat by a terrific jar. We immediately knew that they had hit the ship, but how badly–we in the nose, did not know. The nose compartment was filled with powder smoke of almost blinding intensity."

"A matter of seconds after it hit us, Lt. Rohrer (the pilot) called over the interphone to prepare for bailing out, and to do so upon the sounding of the emergency bell. Upon his order, we immediately shed our flak suits and hooked up our chest packs, noticing in the meantime that our oxygen supply had mysteriously vanished."

"Also during this brief interval, Lt. Franks (the bombardier) had dropped his bombs, and I discovered I had received a gash in the head which was bleeding rather profusely."

"At this time, the 'bail out' signal was given by Lt. Rohrer, and we left the ship thru the nose hatch after having destroyed as much secret matter (log, radio code, maps, etc.) as was possible. We were directly over the target when we bailed out, and consequently I didn't resort to an extensive delayed jump, and popped my chute at about 12,000 feet, hoping the wind would cause me to drift out of the target area. During my descent, I observed several wings of bombers drop their bombs, and also saw our target was one mass of smoke."

"I landed in a back yard several blocks west of the target, and was greeted by a civilian wielding a sledge-hammer. Fortunately, I rolled with the fall so much that his stroke – instead of crushing my already aching and bleeding head–simply glanced off the back of my skull-bone."

"Before he could recover for another swing of his hammer, I had freed myself of my (parachute) harness, and had grabbed him by the throat. Just at this time, the Police arrived and separated us."

"By this time, the blood from the wound I had received in the air had covered my eyes and face so that I had to use a strip of my chute to stop the flow."

"The Police conducted me on a 'forced march' thru the streets of Berlin via the kicking and pummeling method to a Police Station. This was interrupted by a meeting with two members of the Gestapo, who dragged me into an alley, where we had a veritable one-sided free-for-all.

"At the Police Station, I was relieved of all my possessions, and kept in solitary confinement without food or water until the following afternoon when I was taken to an airport on the outskirts of Berlin, where I joined up with Major Killen and Lt. Rohrer. Here also, a piece of flak was removed from the wound in my forehead."

"During my walk thru the city, I observed widespread ruins and devastation, and the attitude of the populace was extremely hostile. I had received no food or medical attention for two days."

"We left Berlin on the 23rd for the Interrogation Center near Frankfurt. Here, I was placed in solitary for seven days and interrogated four times. We were moved from here to the transient camp and thence to Sagan, where we arrived on July 5, 1944."

(Author's Note: Lt. Kramer states the nose area was cramped. I assume because of additional personnel of Major Killen and Lt. Waramar performing lead flight duties).

By Lt. Clarence Franks, Jr., Bombardier:

"Our target for June 21, 1944, was a (identity of target is erased) in the center of Berlin. Our bombing altitude was 27,000 feet, and I was flying in the wing lead position. We approached our target on P.D. 1 and bombed in wing formation. Our ship was the (erased) plane [possibly 'Mickey' or 'lead' plane), but due to clear weather, we bombed visually."

"At 10:20 A.M., one minute before I cleared our bombs, our ship was hit by a direct burst of flak. The burst tore off the #3 engine propeller dome and sent streams of oil over the right wing and fuselage. The entire right side of the nose section was badly perforated, and the Bombardier–Co-Pilot's oxygen system was shot out. Flak also broke the Plexiglas nose left of the bombsight and struck me in the left groin, knocking me backwards over my chair and turret. The #3 engine immediately began running away, so the pilot, Lt. R.L. Rohrer, gave the signal to stand by to bail out, and a few seconds later, ordered the crew to jump."

"I resumed my original station at the bomb-sight and continued synchronizing on my target. At 1001, I released my bombs, and after seeing the deputy leader drop his bombs on my signal, I jumped from the ship, which was out of control and losing altitude rapidly."

"I made a delayed jump to approximately 10,000 feet, falling directly over our target, and saw our target smoking furiously. On my way down, three wings of bombers dropped their bombs on Berlin."

"I landed in the heart of the city, and my chute caught on the roof of a seven-story building. I stayed there, hanging for one hour until the entire raid was over, during which quite a number of additional bombers came and dropped their bombs on Berlin."

"Police and civilians finally pulled me up by my chute shrouds to the roof, and I descended by way of a roof door to the 7th floor landing. There I was roughly searched, especially for firearms. After reaching the street, the police marched me 7-1/2 blocks to the police station. On the way, I was continually verbally assaulted by the civilians, and on one occasion was kicked by two Wehrmacht soldiers."

"At the police station, I was thoroughly searched and deprived of all my possessions. While sitting there, I received two blows to my chin by a police officer and a soldier. I was later taken to a cell, and three hours later taken to an airport on the outskirts of the city."

"By this time, my groin was causing me great pain, and I tried to encounter a doctor, but with no success. At the airport, I was again searched, and spent the night on a wet concrete basement room floor. At 5 p.m., June 22, 1944, I was taken to one of the Berlin railroad stations, left Berlin, and arrived at Oberursel at 5 a.m. June 23, 1944, at the Interrogation Center."

"I was placed in solitary confinement for 11 days, and after being interrogated two times, was taken on July 2 to the transit camp at Wetzlar. Left there on July 3, and arrived at Sagan, Stalag Luft III on July 5, 1944."

News Reports for June 21st, 1944

2,000 U.S. Planes Strike Record Blow.[114]

Over 2,000 American warplanes, the mightiest air armada ever to hit Berlin, slashed through European skies yesterday to give the German capital its first heavy attack since the Continental landings

The raid also was sharp proof that savage assaults on the heart of Hitlerdom would continue hand-in-hand with blows against the Nazi robot-plane coast and overwhelming cover for advancing ground troops.

Shepherded by an estimated force of more than 1,000 P47s, P51s and P38s of both Eighth and Ninth Air Force, over 1,000 Fortresses and Liberators showered explosives on targets in Berlin and outlying Basdorf.

The record raid-the first by heavy bombers since D-Day and the 12th of the war for the USAAF – marked the first time P47s had taken part in a mission to Berlin, Eighth Air Force announced. It was the longest trip the Thunderbolts ever made.

Maintaining the non-stop offensive against the launching area for pilotless planes, which continued to fall in southern England yesterday, 125

---

[114] 384th BG Sortie report by Lt. Col George Koehne

Marauder, escorted by Thunderbolts, swept across the Channel yesterday morning to heap 200 tons of steel on five ramps between Calais and Amiens.

The new attack raised the tonnage dropped by the Ninth AF bombers on the concrete platforms in the last six months to close to 13,000 tons and followed the previous day's endless assaults by contingents of Marauders, Havocs, Fortresses, Liberators, Mitchells, Bostons, Typhoons and Spitfires.

Eighth Air Force heavies flew two missions against the winged-bomb emplacements Tuesday and the RAF's Second Air Force struck ten of the bases.

Berlin's defenders yesterday threw up an extremely heavy flak barrage and spread a smoke screen over the city in a fruitless attempt to ward off the precision raid. The Luftwaffe, however, failed to appear in force, although some individual dogfights were reported, and 60 Nazi aircraft attacked one Liberator formation.

Cost of the giant blow was 43 bombers and seven fighters. Twenty one enemy aircraft were shot down by the pursuits and from 15 to 30 by the heavies.

Besides escorting the bombers, the fighters strafed aerodromes and communication targets.

American air activity over France Tuesday continued from dawn to dusk. Marauders, mounting their third mission of the day late in the evening, attacked a German gun battery at Houlgate, a coastal town on the left flank of the Allied beach positions and Ninth P47, P51 and P38 fighter-bombers as darkness fell moved over France in more than a dozen formations, attacking freight yards, military traffic. Flak towers and highway bridges.

The evening's extensive fighter-bomber operations increased the Ninth Air Force's total individual attacks to over 1,500. The widespread assaults cost six fighter-bombers. No bombers were lost and 17 enemy aircraft were destroyed in the air and one on the ground.

Revised figures on Tuesday morning's record heavy bomber raid on strategic German targets boosted the number of Nazi aircraft destroyed to 78. Twelve were shot down by the Forts and Liberators, 48 were shot out of the air by Eighth and Ninth fighters and 18 more were destroyed on the ground by the pursuits.

In Tuesday morning's strafing attacks, Eighth fighters reported destroying or damaging 28 locomotives, 110 railroad cars, 31 trucks, five other vehicles, ten barges and a radio station.

▲ ▲ ▲ ▲

SUB-CHAPTER:

JULY 1944

Diary Entry July 6th, 1944

20th Mission
Plane Flown B-17 – 42-102507 N

This one started out like a milk run but ended up free for all.

We were roused rather early. The group was for a mission to Bremen. I was on duty as navigator and had been up all night.

While dressing for the flight – it was scrubbed so I went back and made out the flight plan for the mission we flew. It was to attack P-Bomb installations on the French coast in the Pas de Calais.

Well, the lead navigator of our Group couldn't find the target so we flew around with open bomb-bays for twenty-five minutes! Not only that, but the Jerries have moved an awful lot of flak guns into the area.

The lead navigator took us nearly through three flak areas. For ten minutes, we took a pounding and finally dropped our loads on some airfields over there.

Again, the bombardier's flak-suit saved his life. Another hunk came through the nose and hit him in the chest. It came from the first four shells. They really hit us. No fighters – but the ships were really hit.

Author's Note: Lt. Searl got promoted from 2nd Lieutenant to 1st Lieutenant on this day.

News Reports for July 6th, 1944

1,000 Heavies Batter Calais.

American heavies yesterday gave the Pas de Calais its heaviest battering of the war, 1,000 Fortresses and Liberators bombing 18 German flying bomb sites.

In the mounting campaign against the robot installations, which Prime Minister Churchill yesterday credited having destroyed 100 ramps and retarding the Nazi terror campaign for perhaps six months, the heavies flew out in good weather on their 14th sharp assault on Pas de Calais since D-Day. It was the sixth Allied blow against the buzz-bomb nests in less that 48 hours.

Ninth Air Force Marauded and Havocs mounted one of their heaviest front-line raids since the Normandy landings, and a contingent of up to 250 Liberators hit the German naval base at Kiel.

Fighters' Field Day

With clear weather over Europe after a week of cloud and rain, the Allies flung the full fury of their air power against the Continent, and preliminary reports indicated that it was one of the heaviest 24 hours of air activity since D-Day.

U.S. fighters had a field day, ranging over France in countless attacks on targets of opportunity. In addition to escorting bombers, Eighth pursuits shot down 17 German planes.

Wednesday evening, Marauders and Havocs dropped over 150 tons of explosives on four Pas de Calais military objectives, presumably buzz-bomb sites. No bombers were lost. P47s escorted the A20s, which flew in greater strengths than the B26s.

▲ ▲ ▲ ▲

Diary Entry July 8th, 1944

21st Mission
Plane Flown B-17 – 42-107249 P

Purple Heart

Well – I've had it. We discovered that this was not a milk run. Our target was a buzz-bomb launching site south of Amiens in France – but the lead navigator fouled up and led us through a mass of flak.

Well, as it turned out, we got separated from the Group and couldn't find them again. So we went after a target on our own with no sight on the (sic lead?) ship. We were the only ones to drop our bombs. They hit a railroad and a good sized road junction.

While on the bomb run, though, we were plastered by flak. The first burst of four shells took care of our number one engine. It was feathered[115] *and the second burst was on us, too. A piece of flak came through the floor of the nose and mangled the small toe of my right foot. They amputated it today!*

---

[115] Feathering: A term to describe a method of changing the pitch of a crippled engine's propeller to minimize drag and to prevent it from spinning out of control which could cause serious damage.

Something I was certainly not looking for. That flak sure was deadly.

We staggered home alone finally. There was no ill effect of the wound. It hurt very little throughout. I didn't want to fall behind.

News Reports for July 8th, 1944

Calais Battering Stings Germans.
Luftwaffe Finally Comes Up Over Area as Heavies Hit at Robot Sites.

Stung by the damage done to German robot nests by almost continuous Allied attacks, the Luftwaffe rose over the Pas de Calais yesterday afternoon for the first time in weeks to oppose a force of up to 250 escorted Liberators and Fortresses.

Thunderbolts and Mustangs shot five interceptors down in a region noted for its lack of Nazi fighters. One Liberator formation reported several savage assaults by FW190s, Me410 and Me109s.

In sharp contrast, no enemy fighter action was encountered earlier in the day when B-17s and B24's bombed bridges in the Tours area of France and an aerodrome at Chateaudun, 65 miles southwest of Paris. Cost of the day's operations was four bombers and three pursuits.

Ninth Air Force warplanes, too, reported a dearth of German resistance. P47-escorted Havocs suffered but one lost as they attacked a fuel dump near Rennes, one the main Nazi rear supply bases. The lone A20 fell to flak

A small force of Marauders hit the highway bridge south of Orleans.

Escorting Thunderbolts strafed German gun positions near Rennes and St. Malo, to the north.

Eighth Lightnings and Mustangs, which escorted the heavies on their morning mission, strafed 55 locomotives, 388 freight cars and 68 trucks and motor vehicles. One P38 shot down and Ju290, a four-engine bomber.

Photos showed yesterday that three up to 500 escorted Fortresses and Liberators had put flying-bomb launching sites out of action in Saturday's raid on the Pas de Calais. At least two more were possibly knocked out.

The heavies also scored direct hits on three bridges and cut approaches to three others crossing the Seine River and its tributaries between Le Havre and Paris. Ten bombers and one fighter were lost in the widespread assault, which also included attacks on airfields and rail points.

Escorting Eighth fighters also dive-bombed and strafed enemy airfields and rail targets. Twenty-one German planes were destroyed on the ground, 20 of them by a P51 group commanded by William J. Cummings of Lawrence, Kansas.[116]

The American blow against the robot nest came after a night in which Lancasters made a heavy attack on a large flying-bomb depot hidden in vast limestone caves 30 miles northeast of Paris.

Flying until nearly midnight Saturday, Thunderbolt and Lightning fighter-bombers of the Ninth Air Force destroyed 160 railroad cars, probably destroyed five and damaged 88 more.

Ninth Air Force p47s and P38s joined with Marauders and Havocs in the persistent campaign to isolate the Normandy battleground in the south and east, attacking communications from the Loire River to the Channel and from Orleans westward to Nantes.

▲ ▲ ▲ ▲

---

[116] From his obituary; Col. William James Cummings, Jr., USAF (Ret), born in Lawrence, Kansas on June 30, 1911, passed away November 25, 2007. A decorated fighter pilot in WWII, serving in the South Pacific, Corrigadore, he followed with an assignment at Steeple Morden, England. After retiring from Lackland AFB in 1961, his post military career was as a corporate pilot for Holt Machinery Co. and Osborn Heirs Corp.

David E. Huntley

Diary Entry July 24th, 1944

22nd (24th) Mission
Plane Flown B-17 – 42-2507 I

This was the first mission the crew has flown since I got hurt.

Having been on a 7 day leave, the crew encountered bad weather for another week which kept them on the ground for a while.

However, since I'm in the hospital at the base now, I wasn't on this milk run.

The mission was a tactical go in direct support of the ground forces. They dropped their bombs 1500 yards in front of our troops near St. Malo in Normandy. The kind of mission I go for. No ships lost-but one man hit by flak.

News Reports for July 24th, 1944

Eighth and RAF Blast Germany.

American fighter planes ranged south-west Germany yesterday after a night in which the RAF hurled close to 3,000 tons of explosives on Kiel on the first major British attack since D-Day on a great enemy industrial area and Mosquitoes dropped 4,000-pound block-busters on Berlin.

While Eighth Air Force warplanes swept without opposition over the Reich, nearly 500 escorted American heavy bombers flew from Italian bases in a widespread attack on enemy aerodromes and a harbor in southern France and other objectives in northern Italy and southern Yugoslavia.

Bag 15 Nazi Planes

Attacking German airfields and strafing transportation and communication facilities, Eighth pursuits destroyed more than a dozen planes on the ground and shot three observation craft out of the air.

At Russian bases of USSTAF's Eastern Command meanwhile, 15th Air Force warplanes were being groomed for fresh attacks after the first all-fighter flight from Italy to Russia. Escorted by P51's, Lightnings landed on Soviet territory after strafing Nazi airfields at Bazau and Silistea, in Rumania.

Sending bombs cascading down on Kiel at the rate of 150 tons a minute, RAF heavies Sunday night gave the home of German naval headquarters one of its heaviest attacks of the war.

▲ ▲ ▲ ▲

Diary Entry July 25th, 1944

23rd (25th) Mission
Plane Flown B-17 – 42-2507 I

Another job just like yesterday. I just left the base hospital today – so consequently I wasn't on this one either.

My foot is still tender.

However, from the S-2 reports, I gather that absolutely they met no opposition. No flak – no fighters. Jeeps! What I am missing out on!

We sent out 52 ships today as we did yesterday.

News Reports for July 25th, 1944

Aerial Armada Blasts Path for U.S. Advance.

1,500 heavies, Plus Fleets Of Other Planes, Strike At Nazis in France.

Over 3,000 American bombers and fighters, including the largest contingent of heavies ever dispatched on a single mission battered German front-line positions for 2 1/2 hours yesterday morning to support the U.S. First Army's thrust against the enemy's line at the western end of Normandy front.

In an overwhelming display of both tactical support and Allied air supremacy, the Eighth and Ninth Air Force armadas dropped thousands of fragmentation bombs and 100 pound bombs just ahead of advancing Yank ground troops without meeting a single interceptor.

The Eighth Air Force opened the offensive at 10 o'clock by sending in the first of 1,500 Fortresses and Liberators. Only five of the 1,500 bombers and three of an escorting force of about 500 fighters were lost.

Then wave after wave of Marauders, Havocs and Ninth fighter-bombers pounded machine-gun nests, pillboxes, gun emplacements and enemy troop concentrations to pave the way for the American drive.

All of the bombing, which was carried out visually, was completed by 12.30.

Although more aircraft took part in the assault, it was understood that it dropped a smaller tonnage yesterday than in last Tuesday's attacks to support the British advance southeast of Caen. Instead of dropping ground-cratering high explosives, American warplanes yesterday unloosed small and fragmentation bombs.

▲ ▲ ▲ ▲

Diary Entry July 28th, 1944

24th (26th) Mission
Plane Flown B-17 – 42-2536
Oak Leaf Cluster!!! Air medal

This mission proved to be a good one, like our first Bordeaux raid.

Our target was the synthetic oil plant at Merseburg, Germany, and the only thing that really spoiled it was the fact that we bombed PFF. We had no way of telling whether we did the job right.

Merseburg is 15 miles west of Leipzig, so we were well prepared for the four FW-190's that came along. The FWs didn't even scratch us. They hit the wing ahead of us and the wing behind us, but left us alone. Our formation was beautiful to see.[117] *There were no newcomers flying today.*

Flak was entirely absent all the way except for the target itself – where it was moderate to heavy. Our chaff[118] *kept it 2-3 thousand feet below us until we were about 5 miles past the target, where there was a large break in the clouds. One of our ships was badly crippled – but he limped home all right.*

It sure was good to get back into action even if it was against doctor's orders.[119]

News Reports for July 28th, 1944

Twin Blow At Reich's Oil Struck.

Germany Is Hit by Eighth AF Heavies; Ploesti Raided By Force From Italy.

The Wehrmacht's seriously depleted oil stocks were battered anew yesterday by over 2,000 American warplanes in simultaneous thrusts from Britain and Italy.

---

[117] The more perfect formation they fly, the better the group's protection from fighters. Thus his comment, "No Newcomers flying today" which meant no inexperienced pilots who could mess up a formation.

[118] Chaff was made of thin strips of aluminum foil that was dropped by British and American bombers as a counter measure against enemy radar.

[119] He was supposed to take sick leave to heal his amputated toe.

Returning to Germany for the first time in a week, Eighth Air Force bombers and fighters raided the synthetic oil plant at Merseburg and other objectives in Central Germany, while a 15th Air Force armada gave the Rumanian's oil center of Ploesti its third battering in two days.

From Britain meanwhile, Ninth Air Force planes, striking after a night in which Mosquitoes pasted Stuttgart and Lancasters and Sterlings hit robot-launching sites, pounded rail targets in France to impede the movement of German troops and supplies to the front.

Seven Heavies Lost

Only moderate Luftwaffe opposition was encountered over Germany by a force of up to 1,000 Fortresses and an equal number of escorting fighters. The fighters knocked four interceptors down and one by the B-17s. Eighth losses were seven heavies and two pursuits.

On Thursday Ninth fighter-bombers flew over 1,000 sorties, many of them in support of tank thrusts.

Each tank column heading toward the sea in the Coutances area, according to a Ninth Air Force spokesman, had at least one flight of fighter-bombers convoying it.

In the 48-hour period ending Thursday night, the fighter-bombers were reported to have probably destroyed or damaged 179 enemy tanks and over 300 vehicles

▲ ▲ ▲ ▲

Diary Entry July 29th, 1944

25th (27th) Mission
Plane Flown B-17 – 42-2467 J

While I traveled to Scotland [120]- *the boys went out and took another crack at the oil plant at Merseburg. From what I hear it was visual bombing, so goodbye oil plant. It must have been a dilly of a mission.*

I wish I could have been on it.

However, I am enjoying a good time on my leave.

News Reports for July 29th, 1944

Planes batter Nazis in Aid of Ground Drives.

500 Heavies From Italy Pound Hungary and Jugoslavia.

While some 500 Italian-based American heavy bombers hit strategic targets in Hungary and Jugoslavia yesterday, Allied aircraft from bases in Britain and France blackened the skies over Normandy in support of drives by U.S. and British troops.

Sweeping in immediately behind an RAF assault by Lancasters and Halifaxes, waves of Marauders and Havocs rained fragmentation bombs on German infantry and field gun positions in the Caumont area as the British Second Army began its push.

Covered by Allied fighters, Ninth Air Force medium and Light bombers penetrated heavy clouds to drop their explosives by pathfinder technique. Early reports listed on B26 missing.

The 15th Air Force sent heavy-bomber fleets to pound an aircraft factory, an aerodrome, an oilfield and rail yards in Hungary and Jugoslavia. Among the targets was Budapest's Duna aircraft works, part of the factory system manufacturing Ms110s and Me410s.

---

[120] Although he managed to get on the last mission, Lt.. Kempner was probably given a direct order to take some leave to help heal his previous wound.

Yesterday's activity followed blows against Germany Saturday by over 2000 Allied heavy bombers.

The Eighth Air Force alone dispatched more than 1,100 heavies against the Leuna synthetic oil refinery at Merseburg, battered for the second day, as well as other objectives near Bremen. Thirty-five interceptors were shot down over the Reich. American losses were 17 bombers and six fighters.

Only hours before the U.S. offensive, over 1,000 British bombers attacked Stuttgart and Hamburg, Mosquitoes pelted Frankfurt and a force of Halifaxes raided a supply depot near Watten, which is believed to be connected with the threatened use of long-range rockets. Sixty-two RAF aircraft were lost.

A recapitulation of intelligence reports revealed yesterday that Ninth Air Force fighter-bombers Saturday destroyed 186 enemy armored vehicles, including tanks, half-tracks and armored cars. In addition, Thunderbolts damaged 123 armored vehicles. Twelve enemy aircraft were destroyed for the loss of eight fighter-bombers.

Other P47 formations dropped leaflets over France. It was the first time in the ETQ that fighters were used in psychological warfare, Ninth Air Force headquarters announced.

▲ ▲ ▲ ▲

SUB-CHAPTER:

AUGUST 1944

Diary Entry August 4th[121], 1944

26th (28th) Mission
Plane Flown B-17 – 42-2507 I

---

[121] Although Lt. Kempner dated his diary the 5th August, declassified Operational

I returned from Scotland to find my boys up in the air.

They were after Peenemunde, and from the reports did right well.

One ship, a new crew, failed to return. It blew into very fine pieces[122] *as the result of a direct hit by flak.* *

News Reports for August 4th, 1944

Peenemunde Hit By Forts, Libs.

1,200 Attack Experimental Station, Targets at Kiel, Hamburg and Bremen.

In the first full day of aerial activity in a week, over 1,200 Flying Fortresses and Liberators of the Eighth Air Force ranged over Germany yesterday in heavy assaults upon a variety of military targets, including the Peenemunde experimental stations and oil refineries at Hamburg and Bremen.

The bombers and their fighter escorts encountered little enemy opposition except over Hamburg, where swarms of enemy aircraft, including Me109s, were intercepted.

Among the targets were a fighter component plant and an airfield at Anklam, which was last attacked in October of last year. Major. John B. Carroway, of Raleigh N.C.,[123] a squadron commander who led the initial raid

---

* Records show it was actually the 4th August. Kempner was not on this mission as he had just returned from leave.

[122] Read the authors note on Mission number 27 about the force of this explosion

[123] There is a photo on https://www.americanairmuseum.com/media/12410 of Major John B. Carroway posing in front of a B-17 bomber "Duchess" with Clark Gable the Hollywood actor.

on the field, said, "Today was very different from the last time. We didn't see a single Jerry on the whole long mission. There were 200 of them last year."

Kiel, Rostock Also Hit

Other installations plastered by the Eighth bombers were on an aircraft assembly plant at Rostock, port installations at Kiel and an oil refinery at Hamburg. They also bombarded flying bomb sites and coastal batteries in the Pas de Calais.

The two-way aerial sweep over Hitler's Europe continued throughout Thursday and yesterday as Allied bombers pounded German supply routes in northern and southern France and fighter-bombers operated in close support of Allied ground forces on the Normandy battle-front.

Lightning fighter-bombers of the Ninth Air Force carried out further closely coordinated raids against enemy communications in France, principally in the Loire valley, where railway bridges were bombed and strafed. Thunderbolts maintained their support of American troops advancing into Brittany, while British Mosquitoes battered rail targets from Dreux to Le Mans and barges on the Seine.

Italian-based heavies hammered railway yards at Immenstadt, 34 miles east of Friedrichshafen in southern Germany, and yards at Portes les -Valence in southern France. Eighteen German planes were reported shot down.

*Read the author's note on Mission #27 about the force of this explosion and of the explosion of Mission #28.

▲ ▲ ▲ ▲

Diary Entry August 6th, 1944

27th (29th) & Penultimate Mission (Author's Title Description)
Plane Flown B-17 – 42-102507

What a mess this one was! Our target was Brandenburg, Germany, and it was a visual all the way- so we took a pasting and as well as the target.

The first thing was bad lead navigation. We were constantly off course and 10 minutes ahead of time. We were led right over Helgoland and were shot up and then flew right over Wilhelmshaven where we caught hell.

One of the crew that went down was in our hut. They had to bail out – but they did so over Germany. May God protect them!

On arriving at the target -being ten minutes early – we had to go on our run along with another division! What a sweet mess!

They plastered our ships – but we lost none. The target is now "finis le guerre"

There was a lot of fighter activity – but we had such great cover that they didn't bother us. We saw plenty of dogfights. What a show!

Our "Warrior"[124] *was a mass of holes when we got back.*

Well, I'm in harness again.

News Reports for August 6th, 1944

Berlin Bombed By U.S. Heavies.

Allied bombs can now do 50 percent more damage – without the addition of a single plane or pilot – using a new explosive called RDX, it was announced yesterday as American heavy bombers raided Berlin and targets in the Hamburg and Kiel regions of Germany.

Now in use in Europe, RDX is much more powerful than TNT and detonates with such force that the fragments produced can cut through reinforced concrete fortifications and the blast effect can be almost fatal to

---

[124] Once again Kempner called their plane, "our Warrior" and it's why other crews called the Searl crew the Tomahawk Warrior crew.

the enemy troops as the bomb fragments, Col. I.A. Inke, of the Ordinance Department, announced in Washington.

Declaring that the new explosive gave the Allied air forces the destructive power of an air force 50 percent larger, Inke said that RDX's tremendous blast effect makes a smaller bomb do as much damage as a much larger one filled with another type of explosive.*

After Saturday's attacks – one of the best days for precision bombing – in which the Eighth Air Force raiders severely battered ten major priority targets in Germany and scored damaging hits on two others, over 1,000 British-based Fortresses and Liberators yesterday pounded manufacturing plants, oil refineries and port installations in the Reich and robot installations in the Pas de Calais.

Fighters escorting the heavies to Germany met strong Luftwaffe opposition and 33 interceptors were shot down.

Objectives hit by the Eighth heavies yesterday included a Diesel motor plant at Berlin, an aircraft engine plant at Genshagen, an armament works and bomber assembly plant at Brandenburg and an aircraft engine plant at Marienfelde, all in the Berlin area, four oil refineries at Hamburg, the Salzwedel aerodrome near Marienburg and the port of Kiel.

There was no immediate announcement of American losses.

From Italy, meanwhile, 15th Air Force B-17s and B24s struck rail communications and oil storage areas in the Rhone Valley and submarine pens at Toulon.

Marauders, which were out after dark Saturday in assaults on seven French rail bridges and a nest of camouflaged flak barges in St. Malo harbor, yesterday fired two French fuel dumps. All the escorted Ninth Air Force Bombers returned.

On Friday's flight from Italy to Russia by Lightnings and Mustangs, 24 Nazi aircraft were destroyed, it was announced yesterday. Six of the U.S. warplanes were lost in the assault on the Focşani aerodrome in Rumania.

Thirteen of a force of over 1,100 Eighth Air Force heavies were lost on Saturday as the USSTAF struck a damaging blow to German tank, fighter plane, flying bomb, aero-engine and oil production.

Twenty-nine interceptors were shot down and four Nazi craft were destroyed on the ground for the loss of six of a force of more than 500 escorting fighters.

*Author's Note: See the following and final 28th mission report about the crash and explosion of the Tomahawk Warrior's plane.

▲ ▲ ▲ ▲

The Last and Final Mission of the Tomahawk Warrior Crew August 12th, 1944

Target Berlin

Sadly, the navigator, Lt. Kempner, was unable to make a diary entry. If he hadn't perished in the crash that day, he would record this in his diary as the 28th Mission and my correction would be to state it as the 30th mission.

If any of Searl's crew had served on every single mission allocated by Operations Control, he would have been credited with 28 completed missions. (See the chart in Chapter 7.

The crash was described in preceding chapters.

When I described in my Prologue, how massive the explosion was that day, I thought my research would show it was RDX explosive munitions, but I finally discovered it was something different. The official records I have indicate Searl's plane was carrying 38 100 lb GP bombs (General Purpose), not RDX. But 38 100 pounders would *still* cause a huge explosion on high-speed impact, especially with a full load of fuel. 3,800 lbs is almost the equivalent of a British 'Cookie' or Blockbuster bomb used by the R.A.F. Here is the Armorer's Report for August 12, 1944.

TO : Commanding Officer, 398th Bombardment Group (H), AAF,
APO 557, Station 131.

1. Target – Bus Airfield at Versailles, France the primary target was bombed as briefed. Length of bomb run was 1 minute on a magnetic heading of 16°; IAS 150 mph; indicated altitude 25,500 ft; bombs dropped on Group Leader at 1056.
2. Main Bombfall: 11 A/C in the 398th High Group dropped 416 x 100 lb M30 GP bombs. One (1) A/C crashed over England before reaching target, 38 x 100 lb M30 GP bombs. Fuse setting: no nose, 1/40 tail.
3. Anderson, C.J., 1st Lt., was the lead bombardier for the High Group. On bombing run there was no flak and no fighters. The C-1 pilot was not used as there was a malfunction. AP was slightly difficult to identify due to the similar appearance of the surrounding terrain. The turn at the IP was about 90° and we led all the down bomb run. The primary target was bombed and the run was manual.

TABULAR SUMMARY:

	A/C on Target	Bombing	Number of Bombs
Main Bombfall	11	11	416 x 100 lb M30 GP no nose, 1/40 tail
Other Attacks	0	0	0
Total on Target	11	11	416 x 100 lb M30 GP no nose, 1/40 tail
Bombs Returned			0
Other Expended			38 x 100 lb M30 GP no nose, 1/40 tail
Total (Loaded on A/C at T.O.)			454 x 100 lb M30 GP no nose, 1/40 tail

CARL J. STRICKROTT,
Capt., Air Corps,
Group Bombardier.

Credit courtesy of the 398th BGMA

This photo of the crash site at Lude Farm was taken from a P38. Courtesy of the 398th.org.

It was reported that General Doolittle, the Commander of Bomber Command, based in nearby High Wycombe, visited the crash site. Courtesy of the 398th BGMA

The B-17 Tomahawk Warrior: A WWII Final Honor

Crash site of B-17 " 42-107191", seen as of December 2016.

Impact crater is the depression in the ground seen below hedgeline, slightly left of centre. Lude Farm is just over hedgeline at top right of picture.

View taken looking South-southwest.

Photo, courtesy of David Hardie

The official accident report.

DESCRIPTION OF ACCIDENT

(Brief narrative of accident. Include statement of responsibility and recommendations for action to prevent repetition)

NARRATIVE:

Aircraft crashed into ground and bombs exploded on impact. No witnesses to the crash.

RESPONSIBILITY:

Unknown.

RECOMMENDATIONS:

None.

Signature _____
NORMAN H. SCOTT,
Captain, AC.
Investigating Officer.

Date 18 August 1944.

SECRET

SECRET.
G. 8th A.F.
Date 28 AUG 1944 E-I-4

360.33   1st Wrapper Ind.
Hq, Eighth Air Force, APO 634, c/o Postmaster, New York, N.Y.   28 AUG 1944

TO: Chief, Flying Safety, AAF, Winston Salem 1, N.C.

    1. Transmitted herewith WDAAF Forms No. 14 and allied papers on the following aircraft accidents:-

        a. 1st Lt. Charles J. Searl, B-17G number 42-107191.
        b. 1st Lt. Jesse D. Long, B-24J number 44-40295.

    2. Concur.

        For the Commanding General:

                              BURNIS ARCHER,
                              Major, A.G.D.,
                              Asst. Adjutant General.

2 Incls:
    As above.

- 1 -

SECRET   AC# 20 - 1170

SECRET   1 SEP 1944   SECRET   BY AUTHORITY OF

The B-17 Tomahawk Warrior: A WWII Final Honor

SECRET

1 SEP 1944 SECRET
BY AUTHORITY OF
C.O. CCRC No. 1
INITIALS
DATE

HEADQUARTERS
FIRST COMBAT CREW REPLACEMENT CENTER GROUP
AAF STA 112

E-A-2

APO 639
20 AUG 1944

SUBJECT: Letter of Transmittal.

TO: Military Intelligence Service, G-2, War Department General Staff. (THRU- Director of Intelligence, Eighth Air Force Service Command, APO 636, U. S. Army)

1. In compliance with AAF Reg 62-14 and Eighth Air Force Memo 60-1, Transmitted herewith is form 14 and associated papers on aircraft accident of B-17G number 42-107191, which occurred on 12 August 1944 at Lude and Parsonage Farms, White Horse Lane, High Wycombe, Bucks., England.

For the Commanding Officer:

24251

RECEIVED
21 AUG 1944
HQ. VIII AFSC

Capt. Air Corps
Adjutant

2 Incls:
Incl 1 - Form 14.
Incl 2 - Set of Photographs.

311.5   1st Ind.   D-B-wy
HQ VIII AFSC AAF STA 506, APO 636, U.S. Army, 21 Aug 1944.

To: Military Intelligence Service, G-2, War Department General Staff. (Thru - A. C. of S., A-2, Eighth Air Force, AAF Sta 101, APO 634, U.S. Army).

Forwarded.

WILLIAM KOCH,
Captain, A.C.,
Intelligence Officer.

2 Incls: n/c

The documents above are from the author's declassified research material.

235

CHAPTER TEN

TRACING CREW DESCENDANTS AND THE 'SNYDER MYSTERY'

▲ ▲ ▲ ▲

SUB-CHAPTER:

CREW'S DESCENDANTS FOUND & SNYDER REVEALED

THE CO-PILOT 2ND LT. ALBERT L. DION

IN MARCH 2021, A KEVIN Ducharme contacted me through Facebook to tell me that his father, Albert Ducharme, had been named after Lt. Albert Dion from the Tomahawk Warrior. After speaking with Kevin's father, I learned that Noella Dion, the wife of Lt. Albert Dions' brother, Henry, was still alive and living in Michigan. I also learned that Noella has a daughter, Suzanne (Sue) Wales who is Lt. Albert Dion's niece.

I contacted Sue Wales, who graciously became my major source of information about the history of Lt. Dion and who put me in contact with her mother, Noella. In 2022, at the time of writing this chapter, she was 104 years old. She was deaf and used a captioned telephone with through which we communicated.

She said that Albert Dion attended the Holy Name Grade School in Worcester, Mass and, possibly the Assumption High School in Worcester. After high school, he moved to New York for a short time to find a job. Shortly after the move – the War broke out – Albert came back home and enlisted in the Army Air Corps as it was known then. (Author's Note: Albert trained at Mira Loma[125] Academy in Oxnard, California).

Noella dated Albert briefly before eventually marrying his brother, Henry. Henry passed away in 2012. When I mentioned Albert was a co-pilot on an American plane bombing Germany during the war, she did not remember him saying anything about Germany. She said he could not come home too often after he went into the Air Force. (Well, certainly not from England). "He rarely shared where he was." she told me.

Another younger relative, Robyn, of the Ducharme branch of the family, did share with me an anecdote about her late grandmother, Yvonne Noella Dion Ducharme. Yvonne was Lt Albert Dion's elder sister. Robyn's family told her it was hard for her grandmother to talk about her brother, because his passing hurt her so much. So, the family didn't even tell her when her own son got posted to Vietnam so as not to cause more pain for her.

Robyn also mentioned that the City of Worcester, Mass, had installed a Memorial Plaque for Lt. Albert Dion.

---

[125] History of Mira Loma can be found here http://www.militarymuseum.org/NAASVenturaCounty.html

David E. Huntley

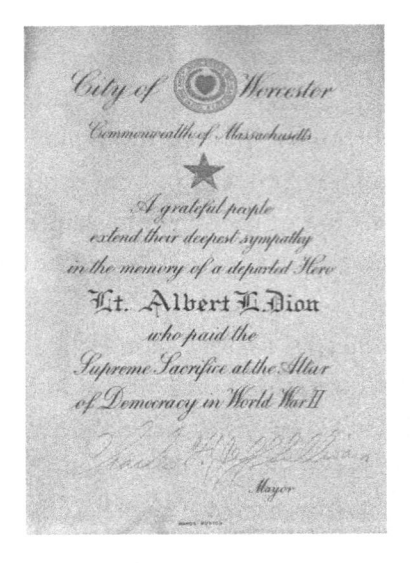

Photos courtesy of Sue Wales   *Lt. Albert Dion*

*Training at Oxnard, CA Lt Dion #3 L-R front row.
In the background is the Stearman PT-17 bi-plane*

238

*Albert Dion's certification as a pilot from Mira Loma
Academy at Oxnard California March 9, 1943*

In 2022, I sent to Suzanne Wales one of the nine Scrolls of Honour[126] the British Authorities had awarded to the crew posthumously in 2019.

▲ ▲ ▲ ▲

ALBERT W. KNIGHT – WAIST GUNNER

---

[126] See Chapter 12. The Scrolls of Honour.

In 2022, I was fortunate to meet Ms. Debbie Duay, the Florida State Regent for the Daughters of the American Revolution. Ms. Duay was also the organization's national genealogist. I mentioned the story of the Tomahawk Warrior to her and that I was almost at the end of my six years of research in trying to find relatives of the crew.

Debbie asked me for the names of the missing airmen. In a couple of weeks, she had found some obituaries that she thought might lead somewhere. One of them was a Glenn Knight, who was Albert Knight's brother.

By that time, I already knew about Glenn Knight from my friend in England, David Hardie, who had told me he had spoken to Glenn a few years ago. However, when I had tried to call him, he had not answered my phone messages, and the lead went cold. On my trying again about a year later, I discovered he had passed away, but his obituary did not yield any discoverable information about his brother Albert.

Debbie Duay, however, had delved deeper and provided me with the name of Glenn's daughter, a Diane Plogger. Taking over from there, in May 2022, I left a message on her phone. I didn't leave much detail because I didn't know if the phone was valid. I left another message in early November, but, again, without a result. As I was writing the very last chapters of this book, I gave it one more try to make contact with her. I resolved to just give up on Glenn Knight in case I failed again.

After calling Diane Plogger's number and while leaving a detailed message; I mentioned the Tomahawk Warrior. This got the same reaction I had received when contacting the nieces of the Lt. Saul Kempner-Diane interrupted me to say how pleased she was that I had persisted because she thought initially, it was just another telephone sales pitch or scam.

Once Diane was satisfied with my credentials, she started sending me copies of some correspondence, copies of newspaper articles, and archival material in the form of images.

The following is a profile of Albert (Bert) W. Knight, which I have compiled from this material, including a touching story concerning his love for the Cleveland Indians baseball team. I am referring to him as Bert, as they commonly knew him in the family.

Bert was born in 1924, one of six children of Albert A. Knight and his wife Pearl Marie Knight. There were four sons and two daughters. Bert was engaged but not married and, therefore, had no surviving progeny.

Diane, his niece, told me when I interviewed her that her father, Glenn, the youngest of the four boys, said that Bert was quite the charmer, a very outgoing, friendly guy. He spent several teenage summers at the Knight family farm in Knox, PA. Her dad said that when his other two brothers would get a little too rambunctious, Bert would be the one to calm everything back down. He rarely picked on his younger brother.

Diane did not have any letters from Bert, but she had some from others who knew him. Remarkably, one of those letters which I have transcribed, and was written by the mysterious missing airman who was not on the fatal flight that killed his nine crew mates. The letter was from Frank A. Snyder, and addressed to Bert's father, dated March 9, 1945. He discussed the accident, but did not know of the cause. Many have wondered what had happened to Frank Snyder and I write about this in another section of this chapter. It was only when writing this chapter on Bert Knight did, I discover Snyder's historical information and where he had ended up. I saw this letter in Bert's archives almost on the same day and time. It was simply another one of those strange coincidences that seems to have guided me with an unseen hand throughout my endeavor to honor the Tomahawk Warriors.

Diane said she remembers her father telling her that Bert had been eligible to go home on leave prior to his fateful mission, but had stayed on a couple more weeks before going home to see Carolyn McFarlin with whom he was engaged.

(Author's note: It appears from the official Operations Records that

Bert had leave from June 20th until his next mission on July 6th 1944. Frank Snyder's letter to Bert's father after the war verified this. See the letter further on in this section).

Bert's obituary reads, "Knight was a graduate of Marshall High School and employed by New York Central System before entering the army in Feb 1943. Three brothers, Orvil, Floyd and Glenn, survive him."

Here is my verbatim transcription of the letter written by Frank A. Snyder, the tail gunner of the Tomahawk Warrior crew who did not fly on the fateful mission which killed his crew mates. He wrote this letter to Albert Knight, Bert's father.

9th March 1945

First of all, you can certainly call me Frank, as Bert would certainly get a kick out of you wondering about being too informal in addressing me – after some things we used to call each other.

I am always very glad to hear from any of you, and especially anything relevant to the accident.

The story that the plane exploded in mid-air was the first one I received, but I was quickly told differently. Now, I don't know if someone was trying to be easy on me or not, but from then on, I could not get much definite information concerning it. Shortly thereafter (the next day) the crew chief and some of the engineering officers went to see the wreckage. I felt so terribly upset that I could not think of asking to see it too.

We were flying another plane that morning and its crew chief was the old crew chief we had in the States who flew over with the boys. He was a very good friend of the crew, and especially of Bert. He felt nearly as bad as me, so I did not think it prudent to ask him questions about the cause etc. (for fear he would get the impression I thought it negligence on his part). If it had been any other crew chief on the field other than him, I am afraid I may have had serious doubts.

Yes, the crew did go to Southend[127] the week of June 20*th* for a rest. I went to attend the Oxford University during this time. I had always planned to go up to Scotland with them again when we finished. I think Bert went to visit Jeanne during this week. In fact, I think that's when he met her.

I hope this hasn't (inelligble) you, but I know how eager we all are to gather any information we can.

Enclosed, you will find a card that you prepared as a result of many questions from you (sic) parents. If you wish any additional information, please ask for it. I hope your Easter is a very fine one, and that someday I will have the pleasure of meeting you. (Bert always said I'd like you very much). Write when you've time and I shall do likewise.

Very Sincerely,
Frank Snyder
P.S. I'll take your typewriter any day-mine has been taken. F.A.S.

I told Diane, "Do not take too much to heart about Frank's comments concerning the crew chief. Maybe he was worried that he did not supervise the safety of the bomb load or something else. I have within a 90% certainty, determined with supporting evidence and documentation, the real reason why this plane crashed on that day. It was not negligence on anyone's part or mechanical failure, nor pilot error. Lt. Searl was one of the more skilled pilots in that squadron. I revealed the evidence within the chapters of this book."

Frank refers to Bert taking leave on June 20th. The operational records show the crew flew on another mission on the 21st without Bert.

---

[127] Southend is the closest seaside holiday town to London on England's South coast.

Their break from combat ended when they all re-commenced bombing missions again on July 6th.

A poignant story about Albert during his wartime in England was when he had been bragging about his favorite baseball team, the Cleveland Indians, as they were called in those days. I have transcribed an extract from the newspaper interview with Albert, conducted by the Cleveland Plain Dealer newspaper's War Correspondent, Roelif Loveland;

LONDON, May 29 1944 – (Via Press Wireless) – **LOVELAND MEETS CLEVELANDERS. Plain Dealer War Correspondent Roelif Loveland sends home word today from these Cleveland soldiers in England.*

Sergt. Albert Knight of the United States Army Air Forces and of .... Cleveland made a bad mistake, but not an unusual one. He began bragging about the Cleveland Indians a couple of months ago.

'They let me down,' he said this afternoon, with distaste covering his youthful face.

Now, wherever I go around the barracks, the guys holler:

'Yah, here's the guy from Cleveland. You know, the guy that thought the Cleveland Indians were going to win the pennant?'

'Hey, Joe, did you ever hear of Cleveland? Do you suppose it is in the United States? Or do the Indians still run wild on the ranges?'

Sergt. Knight took another sip of beer and allowed that he would never brag again.

It was a pleasant little conversation the three of us had in the pub just across from the Red Cross Rainbow Corner. (Author's Note: The pub was the American Red Cross Club near Piccadilly Circus in London). *In addition, there was Staff Sergt. Frank Zeleznikar, also of Cleveland, who agreed that Cleveland, Ohio, was a hell of a long distance away.*

Frank wondered if it would be possible to be remembered to his mother and to Miss Ethel Biro, and Al Knight wished to have his compliments relayed to his mother and Miss Carolyn McFarlin. I should hate to turn the young woman's head, but when I asked Al whether Miss McFarlin was pretty, he replied: 'Oh, boy, I'll say.' I am not surprised. Al is a sort of glamor boy, with about a year in the service.

But Frank is a nice lad himself, and plenty smart, as you see from the fact that his family has subscribed to the *Plain Dealer* for many years. But up to now there has never been a picture of Frank in the *Plain Dealer*, a condition which I hope some of the willing lads back home can correct. After all, a guy who has been in this man's army for two years rates something, and it is no easy job to serve with the ground units of the air forces.

Al flies. He has been on six missions already, three over Berlin, and he is just one more of the lads who maintain that Jerry really knows how to shoot, at least in that geographical area.

Approve Mothers' Victuals.

Frank, studious and of an inquiring mind, never bragged about the Indians and consequently never got into any trouble.

'It will be funny,' he said, 'to get home and to see the lights at night.'

The mothers of both boys will be glad to know that they consider their mothers' victuals tops.

'Chicken every Sunday.'

'There is nothing wrong with that,' said Sergt. Knight.

Rainbow Corner also produced First Sergt. Daniel H. Metcalf of Atlantic City, who has done a bit of thinking about the war and what it takes to fight a war. A few paragraphs of his views might fit in well with the day, because tomorrow my friend Chester J. Koch ought to be leading the Memorial Day parade down Euclid Avenue and people ought to be thinking of what it takes to keep a nation great and strong. It seems too bad it can't be done with lofty sentiment alone, but experience seems to prove it can't.

'I'd go through living hell,' said Sergt. Metcalf, 'to see my wife and my small daughter again. But if it is in the cards that I won't go back, well, they were worth fighting for. I wouldn't want my daughter brought up in a country like Germany under Hitler. I wouldn't care to live in a world where it was considered a mark *of weakness to be kind and considerate. If a man wants peace and gentleness, and a well-ordered life as badly as I want them, he is willing to fight like hell to get them.'*

'Our boys want to get this thing wound up and go home, and they're willing to fight like the devil to do just that. They realize that some of them won't go home. But they don't think about that. I've been in the army for three years. It's a long time, but I don't regret it. But, golly, I'll be glad when the job is done.'

Into our little discussion group drifted Second Lieut. Franklin James of Yakima Wash., an air officer with plenty of experience and a delightful gift of expression.

'I know what it is to feel like a piece of toast,' he said, 'when there is flame below you and your kite is on fire. I thought, first of all, well, this is it. Then something said to me; 'My friend, you wanted wings. Well, you got 'em. But we got out of that without bailing out.'

The Red Cross worker at Rainbow Corner said that of all the hospitality listed on the sign at the hospitality department's desk, 'No 6 was the most popular.' Even more popular, fancy, than an opportunity to visit Windsor Castle or Stratford-On-Avon, No 6 reads, 'Want a date to dine or dance or go to a movie?'

About a month after Loveland's article was published, Chester J. Koch, the city co-coordinator of patriotic activities and a faithful follower of Loveland's articles from abroad, that told the story about Sergt. Albert Knight's ribbing by his pals touched his heart.

Koch thought that the Cleveland Indians winning the pennant would bolster the Sergt's morale but, until that happens, a baseball signed by the whole team would be the best substitute.

The team agreed and felt that a signed ball would be the evidence they were behind him in the biggest game of all. Sergt. Knight wrote to Koch that the ball should be given to his parents to be kept until he returned home.

Diane told me she had noticed that in the newspaper article, "the reporter kept referring to him as Al. The family called him Bert. His father's name was also Albert (but he is not a Jr.), which is probably why I never heard him referred to as Albert."

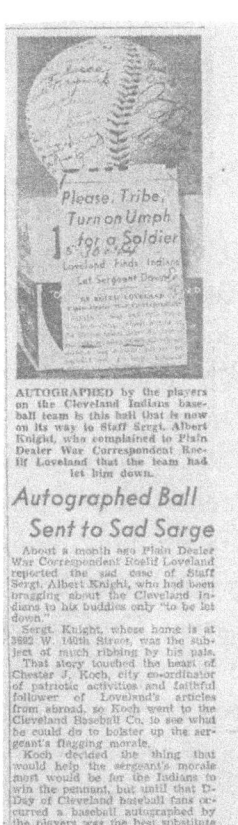

Please, Tribe, Turn on Umph for a Soldier

Loveland Finds Indians Let Sergeant Down

BY ROELIF LOVELAND
Plain Dealer War Correspondent

LONDON, May 29 — (Via Press Wireless)—Sergt. Albert Knight of the United States Army Air Forces and 3692 W. 140th Street, Cleveland, made a bad mistake, but not an unusual one. He began bragging about the Cleveland Indians a couple of months ago.

"They let me down," he said this afternoon, with distaste covering his youthful face.

"Now, wherever I go around the barracks the guys holler:

"'Yuh, here's the guy from Cleveland. You know, the guy that thought the Cleveland Indians were going to win the pennant.'

"Hey, Joe, did you ever hear of Cleveland? Do you suppose it is in the United States? Or do the Indians still run wild on the ranges?'"

Sergt. Knight took another sip of beer and allowed that he would never brag again.

(Continued on Page 6, Column 4)

Autographed Ball Sent to Sad Sarge

AUTOGRAPHED by the players on the Cleveland Indians baseball team is this ball that is now on its way to Staff Sergt. Albert Knight, who complained to Plain Dealer War Correspondent Roelif Loveland that the team had let him down.

About a month ago Plain Dealer War Correspondent Roelif Loveland reported the sad case of Staff Sergt. Albert Knight, who had been bragging about the Cleveland Indians to his buddies only "to be let down."

Sergt. Knight, whose home is at 3692 W. 140th Street, was the subject of much ribbing by his pals. That story touched the heart of Chester J. Koch, city coordinator of patriotic activities and faithful follower of Loveland's articles from abroad, so Koch went to the Cleveland Baseball Co. to see what he could do to bolster up the sergeant's flagging morale.

Koch decided the thing that would help the sergeant's morale most would be for the Indians to win, but until that D-Day of Cleveland baseball fans occurred a baseball autographed by the players was the best substitute for the good sergeant.

David E. Huntley

Images courtesy of Diane Plogger, the Knight family historian

Another interesting and poignant letter I have transcribed from Diane's archives was addressed to Mrs. Stocker, Albert's grandmother. Cpl Kenneth Birmbaum wrote it. I do not know how Mrs. Stocker knew the Corporal, nor how she had asked him to visit the grave of her grandson, Albert, and to describe aspects of the grave and cemetery where he was buried.

We should remember that in 1945, the war still has a couple of more months before peace was made. It was rare for anyone to have a camera and film during the war. The film would have to be developed and prints made. The future of the iPhone© would have been pure science fiction. Thus, the eloquent description that Birmbaum paints of the scene of Albert's burial is beautiful and touching. It gives anyone a sense of the peaceful tranquility of the location in the verdant cemetery and surrounding English countryside.

March 5, 1945
Dear Mrs. Stocker,

I have just returned from Cambridge and want to pass on the information you asked for as best as possible.

They buried Albert in the U. S. Army Cambridge Cemetery at 8:00 PM August 15, 1944, with a complete Military Funeral led by a chaplain of his faith. He is in Plot K-Row 10 -Grave 21.

*Where ever you acquired the information about his body not being identified, I don't know that, but I can tell you this, as I was told by an officer that pointed out his grave and the one of his crew, that Albert's was the only one that **was** identified per se. There are (sic) a crew of nine men flying forts and there were eight men's names on the grave next to his. Dated the same, the same organization and buried at the same time, as you can plainly see, he was one of the nine.*

Truly, he had a grave of his own with his name, rank and serial number and date killed enscribed (sic) on the grave. So, you may rest assured they identified him & the rest were not. I'm sure this will please you.

The casket is of English elm. Quite attractive. To tell you of the Cemetery's surroundings, I'm sure you'd be pleased to know it is in the country where it is quite (sic), grass planted on the grave and flowers are laid upon the grave periodically by the U.S. Army. The Cemetery itself is on a hill and is most beautiful. Looking at the grave at 8:00 PM the sun is at your back and his cross at the head of the grave faces the setting sun and a large American flag. It is so truly a gorgeous sight as the surrounding country is very hilly and beautiful. At the base of the flag are many flowers of all different species.

The graves are taken care of as well as if he were buried in a cemetery in Ohio. You can be sure for I saw it with my own eyes.

As for the information as to how the plane crash occurred, I can not say, for I do not know, nor can I personally find out. It happened you can be sure, and he has had a wonderful burial.

The cross is of wood and white. You would be most proud of it, I can assure you. I do hope I have helped you. I was most pleased to do it and if there are any further questions I can answer, I'd be pleased to hear from you.

With prayers for Albert, and I remain affectionately yours.

*Kenneth Birmbaum
710 Bomb Squadron,
447 Bomb Group
APO 559 % (illegible)*

Another letter in the Albert Knight archives was from Johanna Sienkiewicz, Farringdon, Oxfordshire England. Johanna was a historian and had set herself a task of documenting and cataloging missing or crashed American B-17 bombers in Europe.

Johanna, together with Peter Halliday and Allen Ostrom, were members of the Chiltern Historical Society in Buckinghamshire and helped to research the early days of the Tomahawk Warrior crash.

In this letter to Albert's parents dated October 2, 1997, Johanna mentioned the **'mystery'** of Frank Snyder and other areas of interest to Albert's parents. I have only included portions of the letter that apply to the current areas of interest to the 398th Bomb Group or the Tomahawk Warrior.

Dear Glenn,

Not a lot happens in this tiny village – we are so isolated and to lose our bus service on the 25 October. The 398th plan is to visit England again next June (1998). The parties get smaller each year – due to age and the expense. I hope to go, but unless Ron is going and can take me; I have no way of getting there. We don't see each other much now – it is a long way for Ron to visit. I occasionally visit but I have to stay with my aunt over night as it's not possible to do it in a day.

Allen Ostrom doesn't send much research my way now. I think I have found all the B-17's they lost over England. To do any research into lost aircraft over Europe is an almost impossible task – so many years have elapsed and the countries have changed. I am trying to find out what happened to the crew of a Liberator near Vienna for another Bomb Group in America. This aircraft flew from North Italy to bomb the oil fields near Vienna but was shot down. Six of the crew have never been found. Of course, records are again difficult to trace as German and then Russian occupation, and now Austria is a country in its own right.

Records – such as I have – are in German and Russian. Well, I am still trying. Research needs lots of patience. One can go up to two years or more and not find anything.

I have been trying to find one of Alberts' crew members – Frank A Snyder. He did not fly with them on August 12, 1944. There seems to be a conspiracy of silence about him. I must have written 100 or more letters in trying to locate his relatives. (Author's note; I have edited out this portion of Johanna's letter and introduced it in more detail in the Snyder section of this chapter.

Where do you have to apply for medals? – do you have a central place like we do? Please let me know the address as I want to find out if that office supplies books on medals.

I do hope you can visit England again in the next few years. It would be lovely if we could all go to Duxford, and you can present Albert's medals personally to the museum. I would like very much to see them safely there. At present, Ron and Peter have made a beautiful case to keep things of Albert on display when they give any talk about the research we do. Unfortunately, I can very seldom get to any of them.

I would love to visit America again – San Diego was wonderful. I would also like to go to Wisconsin and See Charlotte France – the pilot's *sister – the flag which was used on the commemoration day at the crash site in Penn is in the local Legion club in the town of Phillips where she lives. It is in a place of honor of all the crew.*

I would also like to see where Albert lived and people who knew him. He is the one so close and I always like to think his mother left him here for us to care for. I place flowers on his grave this year as always – enclosed is an up-to-date photo. I wonder what he would have done with his life? It is such a beautiful place and must be a comfort for many of the relatives, as not all of them would have been able to come and visit. I expect some buried there never have anyone. I know that the rest of Albert's crew are buried in Arlington (that I would like to visit in respect for them as they were already re-buried when I had completed my research). Albert is never lonely with us here to care, and lovely to think his medals eventually will be near him.

The Rev. Muspratt has moved to Brecon in Wales now, but he and I still keep in touch. He is a great man. I hope to visit him one of these days. I know Brecon well as I used to go there most weekends when I was doing some research for the regimental museum, which was the HQ for the 24th Foot Regiment, which fought at Rorkes Drift in the Zulu War 1879.

I cannot think of any other news of interest – do you know anyone near you who is coming over with the 398 next June? I have looked on my map of America but cannot find North Olmsted anywhere – I expect it is like this place – very small. Where is the nearest town and I see you are – to my way of thinking – near Wisconsin – so if I ever can get to USA can I visit you?

My best wishes to you and Jean – A good start for Jean having her hip done on New Year's Eve – but she missed the celebrations.

Love to you both,

Johanna

The B-17 Tomahawk Warrior: A WWII Final Honor

The 398th Bomb Group 600th Squadron Patch

Albert l. Knight, 1943.

(Note) Albert Knight's grave in the American Cemetery Madingly, Cambridge England is shown in Chapter Three.

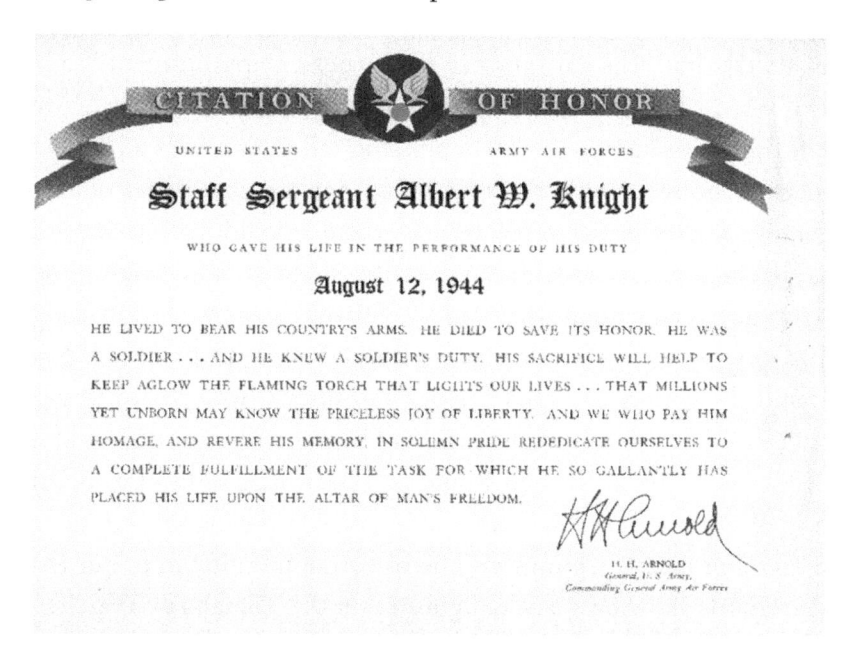

CITATION OF HONOR

UNITED STATES ARMY AIR FORCES

Staff Sergeant Albert W. Knight

WHO GAVE HIS LIFE IN THE PERFORMANCE OF HIS DUTY

August 12, 1944

HE LIVED TO BEAR HIS COUNTRY'S ARMS. HE DIED TO SAVE ITS HONOR. HE WAS A SOLDIER... AND HE KNEW A SOLDIER'S DUTY. HIS SACRIFICE WILL HELP TO KEEP AGLOW THE FLAMING TORCH THAT LIGHTS OUR LIVES... THAT MILLIONS YET UNBORN MAY KNOW THE PRICELESS JOY OF LIBERTY. AND WE WHO PAY HIM HOMAGE, AND REVERE HIS MEMORY, IN SOLEMN PRIDE REDEDICATE OURSELVES TO A COMPLETE FULFILLMENT OF THE TASK FOR WHICH HE SO GALLANTLY HAS PLACED HIS LIFE UPON THE ALTAR OF MAN'S FREEDOM.

H. H. ARNOLD
General, U. S. Army,
Commanding General Army Air Forces

All photos are courtesy of Diane Plogger, Knight family historian.

▲ ▲ ▲ ▲

THE FRANK SNYDER MYSTERY – PART ONE

THE MISTAKEN SNYDER

During my six plus years of research on the story of the Tomahawk Warrior, the reason Frank Snyder, the tail gunner, did not fly on its last mission has always been a nagging puzzle. Not just for me, but for numerous other people in years past.

Although, neither he, nor his descendant relatives are entitled to receive one of the British Honours that I describe in Chapter 12, I would still like to make it known for the record that Frank's name was on 29 of the 30 Loading Lists' Mission Reports of his crew. He did not miss a single mission except the last one.

One other factor concerning the Snyder mystery was that in a detailed newspaper report about the "Crash of the Tomahawk Warrior" by the Bucks Free Press in High Wycombe, England, on June 7, 1990, it was stated that "the tail gunner had a dental appointment." The reporter quoted Mr. Peter Halliday, the chairman of the Chiltern Historical Aircraft Association, who said, "the missing tail gunner was at the dentists in apparent agony." Neither Mr. Halliday, nor the newspaper offered any evidence how they got that information, and I could find nothing in the official declassified records to support the story. It is just one of several uncorroborated anecdotal stories of the Snyder mystery.

As I mentioned in my Preface, a local British historian told me he had found the widow of Frank Snyder and interviewed her on the phone around 2016. He also said that Frank had become a police officer after the war. Mrs. Anne Snyder denied Frank had been in a Bomb Group or had flown in B-17 bombers. She said, "he was just a mechanic and had never flown on a bomber as a gunner." The historian mentioned to her that the official records show he was a tail gunner on the Tomahawk Warrior.

I did not have any more information when I started to pay attention to this subject. I found an obituary of a Frank Snyder who had passed away at age 90. He had retired as a police officer in Fredericksburg, VA.

The obituary stated that Mr. Snyder was a World War II Army Air Corps veteran. He retired as a sergeant of Lakewood, NJ Police Dept in 1980 after 26 years. The obituary mentioned he was survived by his wife, Anne Snyder.

The photograph in the obituary had a certain resemblance to the missing Snyder and his history of being in the Army Air Corps and was sufficient information to investigate further. Because the historian had told me he had spoken to the widow Anne Snyder, it was obvious I had located the same person as the historian had.

Frank Snyder-policeman   Sgt. Frank A. Snyder

I contacted the police department in Lakewood, NJ, and was referred to Steven Wexlar, the retired C.I.D. officer and police historian. He told me that Anne Snyder had passed away in 2017, just two years after her husband. Her daughter, Marion Sandhoff, was still alive and living in Chesapeake, VA.

I telephoned her and her husband, John Sandhoff. After providing him with my credentials and details of the Tomahawk Warrior (TW) project, I had numerous telephone conversations with him regarding his father-in-law, Frank Snyder.

John said he had a very good personal relationship with Frank. After Frank retired from the Lakewood Police Department, he drove school buses as a part-time job. On weekends, the two of them attended many NASCAR Races. One day, they were in a pub and Frank, who rarely, if ever, mentioned WWII, disclosed he had lost friends in a plane crash. He then broke down in tears. John didn't ask any more about it as he felt it was a delicate and emotional subject. He said Frank mentioned nothing about the Tomahawk Warrior, or B-17 bombers, or being with a Bomb Group during his wartime service.

Was Frank's emotional incident at the pub a sign that he had been thinking of the Tomahawk Warrior accident, or was it something else? The answer to my question came when I received photographs and archival newspaper cuttings from Marion and John.

The photographs of Frank made me question if I had the right man. After examining the newspaper report, I noticed that Frank was a Private and not a Sergeant. The fact he was 19, at the time of the report as an armorer, for the 8th Fighter Command flying P51 Mustangs in England, did not add up for me. The photograph of Frank in the newspaper cutting of that period does not show a resemblance to Frank Snyder, the Tomahawk Warrior tail gunner.

The newspaper report also told of the squadron's actions in attacking the enemy before the invasion of France. The real Frank Snyder was already serving on the Tomahawk Warrior and could not have been in a fighter squadron. Furthermore, the real Snyder would have been of similar age to his fellow crew members, the very youngest of whom was 20 years old and the eldest 26. 30 missions were assigned to the Tomahawk Warrior and 28 completed by Frank which brought him up to the last mission he is officially recorded on, August 6, 1944. It would have been impossible to have transferred him from a tail gunner position to an armorer's position in a fighter group, as described in the newspaper report. Again, the tail gunner, Frank, had been on bombing missions before and during D-Day, which does not correlate with the newspaper report about the fighter group. Also, he would have to have been demoted from Sergeant to Private, an extremely unlikely event.

The B-17 Tomahawk Warrior: A WWII Final Honor

Finally, there was one last piece of information which confirmed everything I had postulated. I asked Marion Sandhoff if her father had a middle initial because he was simply referred to as Frank Snyder. Marion responded he had a middle initial of G, which stood for Grimm, a name he hated. It was the reason he never used a middle initial. The tail gunner on the Tomahawk Warrior was officially known as Frank A. Snyder. That information just by itself conclusively proves this Snyder was not the missing tail gunner from the Tomahawk Warrior!

Conclusion: I found that the historian had misidentified the widow and, thus, the airman, who just had had the same first and last name. Anne Snyder had been truthful with the historian when she told him her husband had never been part of a Bomb Group.

Even though this Frank Snyder was not part of the Tomahawk Warrior crew, I honor his service to his country and his contribution to helping to save the world from tyranny in WWII.

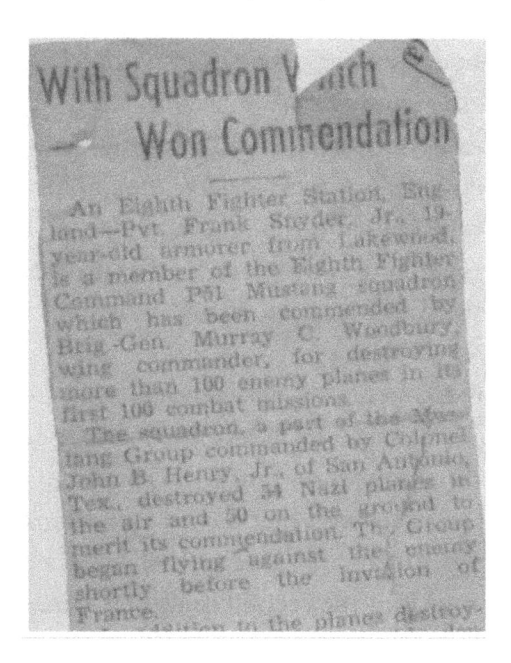

Pvt. Frank Snyder as an armorer in a fighter squadron

David E. Huntley

THE FRANK SNYDER MYSTERY – PART TWO

THE REAL FRANK SNYDER

ST. SGT. FRANK ALLEN SNYDER –TAIL GUNNER

Ms. Debbie Duay, my genealogist friend in Florida, sent me a link to the obituary of one of Frank Snyder's sisters. By exploring this link, it helped me to build a composite of the family tree.

I made extensive efforts to reach descendants and their grandchildren with very detailed, diplomatic, and courteous messages on the phone and through emails. Unfortunately, I was unable to elicit any response. The tone of my approach was always, my intention was to show that my search for Frank Snyder was to honor his WWII service in my book, and was related to a historical event.

It is possible, of course, that the contact information was too old or, perhaps, had changed, or the recipient had passed away. Interestingly, none of the emails bounced and none of my calls were returned.

There were other websites where 'relatives' had posted a photograph of Frank, or some artifacts, and two others a photograph of his grave. I messaged them. One did not respond, and the second said they were not related.

St. Sgt. Frank Allen Snyder's parents were Frank (Franklin) Stevenson

Snyder and Florence Ann Snyder (Sullivan). They had seven children, three boys and four girls. Of the four girls, one was the twin of Frank. Later, they had nine grandchildren.

I was not the first who looked for Frank's siblings and their descendants and failed to make contact. There were several anecdotal stories over the years of failed searches, as well as the misidentified Snyder that I described earlier in this chapter. Coincidentally, another letter in the Albert Knight's archives was from Johanna Sienkiewicz, the English historian mentioned previously.

In this letter to Albert's parents, dated October 2, 1997, she mentions the **'mystery'** of Frank Snyder and other areas of interest. I have only included portions of the letter, which apply to the 398th Bomb Group or the Tomahawk Warrior. This is an extract of her letter related only to the **'Snyder mystery.'**

Dear Glenn, October 2, 1997

"I have been trying to find one of Alberts' crew members – Frank A Snyder. He did not fly with them on August 12, 1944. There **seems to be a conspiracy of silence about him.** *I must have written 100 or more letters in trying to locate his relatives.*

I do know[128] *that the wife of Charles Searl – Albert's pilot – met Snyder in Chicago after the war but couldn't remember where he actually came from. Sadly, she died a few years ago.* (Author's Note: Cheryl Surfus, the pilot's daughter, has expressly denied to me that her mother ever met Snyder, either in Chicago, or as in another unsubstantiated rumor, in New York.)

"Allen Ostrom says he believes Snyder was killed in a road/rail accident in California some years after the war. Months after this, I found out that the town of Sacramento kept records of all unnatural deaths in

---

[128] Johanna offers no evidence as to how she 'knew'

California. I wrote there and paid for a search to be made of their records, but they had no record of a Frank A Snyder or of anyone with a similar name being involved in any such accident. I'm sure someone must know something of him. I have tried writing to other 398th aircrew who would have possibly known him – especially as it was rumored, he was returned to America soon after the B-17 crash, and that's the kind of thing people would remember."

As I thought about this so called, 'Snyder mystery,' was it Frank's intention not to be found? Did he leave instructions to his family to avoid discovery for some reason? Perhaps he did not want to be remembered as the guy who did not take his place in the tail gunner's position that fateful day? Did he, in fact, or, as it has been unofficially reported, have a dental appointment that day? I certainly could understand his feelings about this matter. Especially, the potential for misunderstandings that others might question him with, "so why were you not on the plane?"

If he were here today, I would want to put my arm around his shoulders and tell him, "Frank, I was there that dark morning when your crew mates died, and I just feel that none of them would begrudge you your freedom, or, because you were not with them that day.

"In fact, Frank, knowing them ethereally as I do, and having been so . . . close to their souls on that gloomy, blackened field that morning, I suppose, they would be pleased to learn that at least one of the men will go on to live a normal life in peacetime. Especially your buddy, Bert, the waist gunner, a good friend of yours and with whose father you communicated. I have the letter[129] you wrote that demonstrates your feelings about the crash. That handwritten letter will let the entire world understand that your dedication to your team mates was built on a foundation of life and

---

[129] See the Section of Chapter 10 St Sgt. Albert Knight. The full letter is published there.

death over the flak, and Luftwaffe ridden skies of Germany, and occupied France."

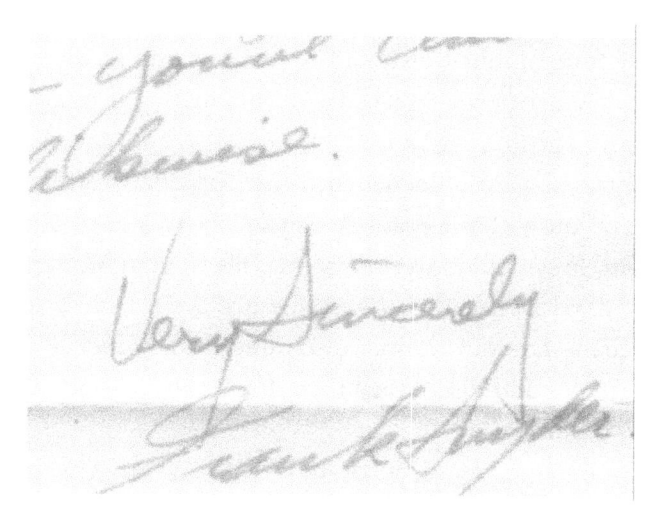

Frank's signature on the letter he wrote to Albert Knight's father in 1945. Courtesy of Diane Plogger – Albert Knight archives

Again, if Frank Snyder could be with me now, I would reassure him, "Frank, it's my duty and my honor, irrespective of whether your relatives remain unknown or untraceable, to document in my book your bravery and your personal story as a hero of WWII. You fought in those skies over Europe in sub-zero temperatures for sometimes as much as 11 hours at a time. You are listed on 29 of those missions and 28 were completed along with your fellow crew members, a great feat, considering that the chances of survival were so small.

"Your Distinguished Flying Cross and the Air Medal were well earned, and I shall make sure your legacy will live on in my book. You may be buried in The Holy Cross Cemetery, Fresno, California, but your soul is with your fellow crew in Arlington National Cemetery, as well as with your friend, Bert Knight, in the American Cemetery in Madingley, Cambridgeshire, England."

I am sure the Air Force veterans in the Fresno vicinity who will read my book, may, from now on, lay a wreath on Frank's grave on Memorial Day. He is not in Arlington National Cemetery. He may not have received a full military funeral, but we should remember him as the tail gunner of the Tomahawk Warrior who served with his deceased fellow crew on all but one of their wartime missions.

So, as I probed a little deeper into the **'Snyder mystery,'** let me tell you what I now know about Frank A. Snyder: he was born on June 9, 1920 in San Joaquin, Fresno County, California. He died in Madera, California, February 15, 1963 in a train/automobile accident. I have spoken to the Sheriff's office in Madera County. I also interviewed officials at the Madera Police Department and discovered they do not keep Accident Reports for more than four months.

It seems so tragic that a decorated WWII veteran who survived so many bombing missions over Germany and German occupied France would die so young in a civilian accident. The survival rate of American Bomber crews in combat over the skies in the European Theater was 31%[130] and that of British crews was 24%.[131]

Frank was a graduate of Fresno State College. I do not have a date for his graduation. His government Draft Card shows he was a student in 1941. I'm assuming, he resumed his studies after the war.

While in England on duty with the 600th Squadron, they gave the crew a couple of weeks off in June 1944 for rest and relaxation. While his fellow crew members went off to Southend on the South coast of England, Frank attended Oxford University[132]. I don't know what course he took, but evidently, he was a serious minded 24-year-old young man.

After the war, he worked for the Fresno County Welfare Department

---

[130] https://www.wearethemighty.com/mighty-history/bomber-crew-in-wwii-was-deadly/
[131] https://www.iwm.org.uk/history/life-and-death-in-bomber-command
[132] Reference the letter by Frank Snyder in this Chapter, under Albert Knight.

for several years. During this period, he served for a while with the State parole office. About three months before he died, Frank had quit the Fresno County Welfare Department and started a new job as a social worker for Madera County. Frank never married and was living with his brother, Robert, in Fresno.

On February 15, 1963, according to a report in the Madera Tribune newspaper, a Southern Pacific work train collided with the station wagon driven by Madera Welfare Department employee, Frank Allen Snyder, 42, of Madera. Snyder was killed when, the report indicated, he was thrown from the vehicle as it was pushed several hundred feet down the tracks.

'The body, badly mangled and torn, was found approximately 200 feet from the crossing.[133]'

---

[133] Madera Tribune, CA February 15, 1963

David E. Huntley

The B-17 Tomahawk Warrior: A WWII Final Honor

Welfare Employe Dies In Auto-Train Crash

A pocket watch, its hands stopped at 12:07, badly wrecked station wagon, and the body of a man.

This was all that remained after the station wagon was struck by a Southern Pacific work train this afternoon at the Rd. 24 crossing five miles north of Madera near U. S. 99.

Victim was Madera County Welfare Department employe Frank Allan Synder, 42, South J. st., Madera.

Snyder was killed when his Welfare Department station wagon was struck by a southbound Southern Pacific freight train at the Rd. 24 crossing, at 12:05 p.m.

Incomplete reports indicate that Snyder was thrown from the auto as it was pushed several hundred feet down the tracks. The vehicle and train engine remained intact as the train ground to a stop. The entire right side of the station wagon was ripped open by the impact, as the engine front speared through the vehicle.

Snyder, employed as a social worker, had been at the Madera Department since Dec. 3, 1962. He was single.

Ironically, seat belts which might have saved the victim's life were unfastened. The driver's side of the car was the least damaged.

Rd. 24 runs parallel to the tracks immediately before the crossing, but it is not definitely known in what direction the victim was traveling.

It is possible he was going south, the same direction of the Southern Pacific work train which claimed the life, pulling out in front of the trains.

The train carried the victim's station wagon one quarter mile up the tracks before coming to a stop.

The body, badly mangled and torn, was found approximately 200 feet south of the crossing.

Motorists, both south and northbound, who stopped to view the accident scene and take pictures, hampered efforts to clear the wreckage from the tracks.

The SP said that southbound passenger train 52 was about two hours late due to track blockage in Merced County caused by an earlier wreck.

Woody Tells Of New Bills On Firemen

Members of the newly formed Madera City Fire Fighters Association held

Courtesy of the California Digital Newspaper Collection, Center for Bibliographical Studies and Research University of California Riverside[134].

The report said the seat belts were unfastened, which, if had they been fastened, might have saved the victims' life. The driver's side of the car was hardly damaged, but the right side was ripped wide open.

A funeral mass was recited on February 18, 1963 at Our Lady of Victory Catholic Church. The burial took place at the Holy Cross Cemetery in Fresno. Frank was survived by his parents, two brothers, and four sisters, including his twin.

---

[134] Https://cdnc.ucr.edu

Courtesy of Karen Burns – Findagrave.com

In February 1964, Frank's parents filed a "wrongful death" lawsuit in the Superior Court. The named defendants were the Southern Pacific Co. and the engineer of the work train, which crashed into Frank's car on Ave. 24, in Madera one year previously on February 15, 1963. (Author: I did not pursue my investigation of which side prevailed).

The newspaper report of the Snyder accident is disturbing for me, because it tells how in this violent accident, his body was torn and mangled **like his fellow crew members 19 years earlier.** The image of 1944 that has remained with me all my life is reinforced now, with imagining Frank's broken and severed limbs being retrieved alongside those of his other friends. Was this the ultimate destiny of this man, but simply delayed in the matrix of the universe?

Is it possible that when the train ploughed into Frank's station wagon, he had an instantaneous vision of his predetermined fate before passing into God's realm? I hope my quest to solve the 'Snyder mystery' of the Tomahawk Warrior has been partially resolved. At least, he has been "found" so to speak, and I pray he will no longer lie there in Fresno a forgotten WWII hero. I hope a veterans' organization will take up my challenge to honor him each year, as we honor others who served their country. Rest in Peace, Frank.

(Author's Note: If any descendant relatives of the Frank A. Snyder, the tail gunner of the Tomahawk Warrior for 28 missions, read this story, please contact the publisher or the author directly. After verification of their qualification as a relative, I will gladly send them a copy of the British Scroll of Honour that was awarded to his fellow crew members.)

▲ ▲ ▲ ▲

SUB-CHAPTER:

THE CREW'S DESCENDANTS WHO HAVE NOT BEEN FOUND

Author Note: If any reader has information that would lead to the identification of any living descendant relatives of the following airmen of WWII, please contact the publisher. The verifiable closest living relative would be eligible to receive one of the five remaining Scrolls of Honour awarded by British Authorities, held by the author.

TECH SGT. JAMES A. BEATTY,   D.O.B. 10/3/1923

The Sgt. Beatty's last known address in 1943 was 210 Edison Avenue in Benton, AK.

I could not locate any surviving relatives or any war memorials in his name.

▲ ▲ ▲ ▲

S SGT. ALFRED BEUFFEL – BALL TURRET GUNNER, D.O.B. 9/9/1923

No relatives were traced for Alfred. He was single, and there were no descendant relatives at his previous address in Lynbrook, NY.

I was able to enlist the help of the Lynbrook American Legion Post 335 whose adjutant, Mr. Bill Marinaccio, kindly took photographs of the war memorials at Lynbrook Memorial Park, depicting Alfred Beuffel's name. Here is a copy of Mr. Marinaccio's email to me in May 2019.

Good morning, David,

Earlier this morning, I went down to our Lynbrook Memorial Park. I've attached six pictures regarding your request for info pertaining to Alfred Bueffel. Alfred's name appears on two monuments in the park. The first is on a wall of families who resided in Lynbrook at the time of WWII. You will find a picture of that monument as well as a closeup of Alfred Bueffel's

The B-17 Tomahawk Warrior: A WWII Final Honor

name. Note the star after his name, it denotes that he died in action. The other picture of our Doughboy Monument, which lists the names of those who died in WWI and WWII, again you will see Alfred's name. I also included a picture of our Memorial Park, which by the way was One of One Hundred Monuments selected by the United States Centennial Commission in Commemoration of the 100th Anniversary of the end of WWI. I spoke with our Post Historian to see if we can get any additional info. So far, it appears he lived on Abrams Place, nothing more to report at this time. If additional info should come forward, we will pass it along to you.

Bill Marinaccio
Adjutant
Lynbrook American Legion
Post 335

Photos courtesy of Bill Marinaccio, Adjutant of Lynbrook American Legion Post 335

▲ ▲ ▲ ▲

SGT. CECIL E. KENNEDY – RADIO OPERATOR, D.O.B. 5/27/1919

Cecil Kennedy was born May 27, 1919, and was unmarried. I have found no descendant relatives. His last known address in 1944 was simply KEOKEE VIRGINIA.

I could not locate any surviving relatives or any war memorials in his name.

▲ ▲ ▲ ▲

LT. LEO C. WALSH – BOMBARDIER, D.O.B. 10/3/1923

I approached the American Legion in Washington D.C. regarding 2nd Lt Leo Walsh but it yielded no results.

The American Legion is the nation's largest wartime veterans service organization aimed at advocating patriotism across the U.S. through diverse programs and member benefits. Their Headquarters are situated at the following address: 3408 Wisconsin Ave NW, Washington, DC 20016, United States

Leo Walsh was unmarried, and I have found no surviving descendant relatives. He was born in Washington D.C.

▲ ▲ ▲ ▲

SGT. ORVILLE M/ WILSON, WAIST GUNNER, D.O.B. 7/18/1924

Orville was from Mount Vernon, WA.

I was able to enlist the help of the Burlington American Legion Post 91, whose representative, Ms. April Patterson, kindly took photographs of the war memorials at the Burlington War memorial, depicting Orville Wilson's name. Here is a copy of Ms. Patterson's email to me on May 17, 2019.

"I found the gentleman you were looking for here at our own memorial. I found him in Arlington National Cemetery and then went and looked at our memorial out front and found his name!!! This is so exciting to know that he is being honored on the memorial. I am so happy and thankful that we have his name here. No man (or woman!) shall be forgotten! I will find out more information about relatives and get back to you. I can't wait to find out more!!" Talk to you soon." Respectfully, April Patterson"

Courtesy of April Patterson, representing the American Legion Burlington Post 91.

Orville was not married and I have found no surviving descendant relatives.

▲ ▲ ▲ ▲

PART 2

WWII AIR COMBAT HISTORY

This is for the readers who want to understand more about the machinery and operations of air combat during WWII. It is not a treatise but a basic summary of certain aspects of this period.

TRIBUTE TO THE TEXAS RAIDERS

▲▲▲▲

CHAPTER ELEVEN
THE B-17 FLYING FORTRESS AND WWII

▲ ▲ ▲ ▲

398th Bombardment Group History (Citation)

Brief history of the 398th Bombardment Group[135]. The Home of The Tomahawk Warrior Crew. I encourage readers to visit the 398th.org website, which is the home of the 398th Bomb Group Memorial Association, for an in-depth review of its history during WWII.

Overview

THE GROUP WAS CONSTITUTED AS 398th Bombardment Group [Heavy] on February 15, 1943 and was activated on March 1, 1943. It was prepared for combat with B-17s, but was interrupted during these activities from July to December 1943 to train replacement crews for other organizations.

The Group moved to England in April 1944 and was assigned to the Eighth Air Force. Entering combat in May 1944, and up until V-E Day it operated primarily against strategic objectives in Germany, attacking targets such as factories in Berlin, warehouses in Munich, marshalling yards in Saarbrucken, shipping facilities in Kiel, oil refineries in Merseburg, and aircraft plants in Munster.

The Group temporarily suspended strategic missions to attack coastal defenses and enemy troops on the Cherbourg Peninsula during the

---

[135] Courtesy of: https://398th.org/History/Group/History_398th.html

Normandy invasion in June 1944; to striking gun positions near Eindhoven, to support the air attack on Holland in September 1944, to raid power stations, railroads, and bridges during the Battle of the Bulge, December 1944-January 1945; and to attack airfields to aid the Allied assault across the Rhine in March 1945.

They flew their last combat mission by attacking an airfield in Pilsen, Czechoslovakia, on April 25, 1945. The Group transported liberated prisoners from Germany to France after V-E Day, and finally returned to the US, May-June 1945. Inactivated on September 1, 1945.

Stations

- Ephrata AAB, Wash, March 1, 1943
- Blythe, Calif, April 5, 1943
- Geiger Field, Wash, April 29. 1943
- Rapid City AAB, SD, June 10, 1943-April 4. 1944
- Nuthampstead, England, April 22,1944-May 26,1945
- Drew Field, Fla, July 3,-September 1, 1945

Campaigns

- American Theater
- Air Offensive, Europe
- Normandy; Northern France
- Rhineland; Ardennes-Alsace
- Central Europe

398th Bomb Group Combat Formations[136]

By Wally Blackwell, Pilot of the 601st Squadron (Citation)
December 2003

The use of the word "formation" by the 8th AF organizations of WWII referred to an orderly assembly of airplanes, lead(sic) by one of the airplanes, arranged together for their mutual protection, that could bomb a target in a coordinated and efficient manner. The group bombing formation used by the 398th Bomb Group when it arrived at Station 131 in April 1944 was called a Combat Box Formation. That particular formation was developed by General Curtis LeMay, learned from his experiences as an 8th AF strategic bomb group commander. The 8th AF Bomb Groups had used various formation schemes with some success beginning in 1942, but the Box Formation had eventually become a standard for all 8th AF group formations. The Box Formation was accepted at that time as the best arrangement of airplanes for maximum firepower, from all guns of all planes, while providing a bombing pattern with maximum effect.

The Combat Box Formation comprising a number of basic airplane relationships. From the smallest to the largest, these formations were:

> Element Formation: three planes
> Squadron Formation: four Elements – twelve planes
> Group Formation: three Squadrons – thirty-six planes
> Wing Formation: three Groups – one hundred and eight planes

Element Formation

An Element of three planes was the basic unit in all formations. The Element lead was responsible for maintaining his Element's position relative to the Squadron lead at all times. One plane flew off his left

---

[136] Courtesy of: https://398th.org/Research/8th_AF_Formations_Description.html

wing and one off his right wing. Those flying the left and right wing positions were responsible for staying in "tight formation" with the Element lead at all times, but on the bombing run to the target in particular. The Element wing positions tried to maintain their positions about the same altitude, one wing length horizontally from and one wing length behind the Element lead. See Diagram 1 for the Basic Element Formation.

(Author's Note: Major, Lucky Luckadoo, a WWII pilot who flew B-17s for the 'Bloody 100' Bomb Group out of Thorpe Abbotts offered me the following observation: "One of the basic features of the Box Formation, and that is that each of the wingmen in the element was slightly staggered at a higher or lower altitude than the element leader. This variation in altitude was necessary for the gunners in the wing positions to have the maximum range of fire without being impeded by the other ships in the formation."

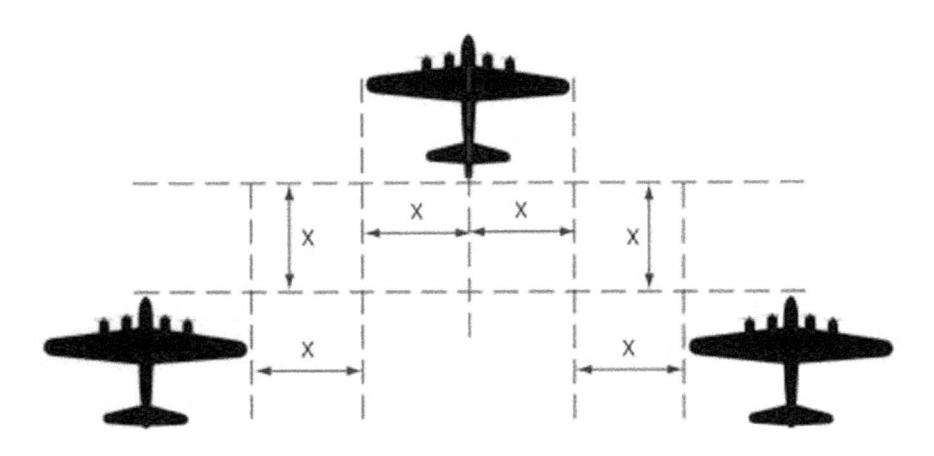

To learn more from the smallest to the largest of formations, see the footnote link.

A Unique Look at a Wartime B-17 Cockpit.

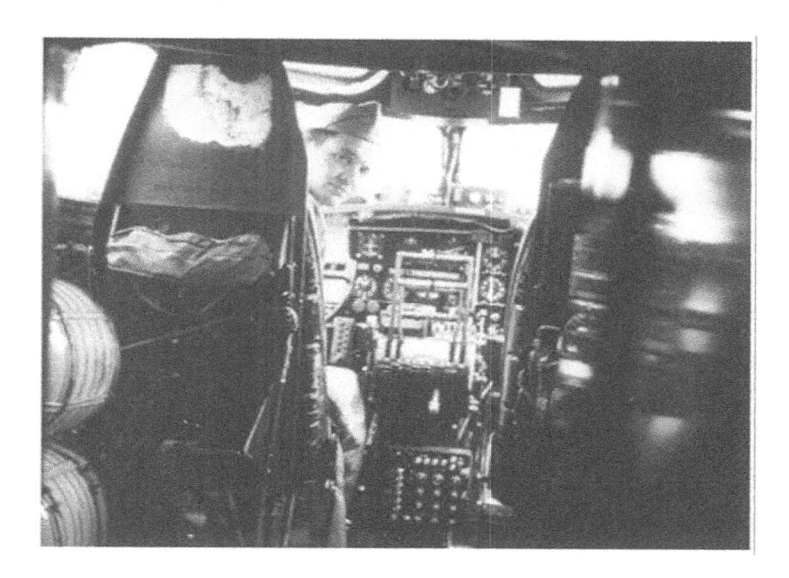

Courtesy of the 398th Bomb Group for image and ensuing comments below:

▲ ▲ ▲ ▲

(Citation) Pittsburgh Photo No. 1: This is a photo of Lt. Bob Welty[137] in a B-17 after the war in Pittsburgh. His father took the photo.

In May 2006, Wally Blackwell, former B-17 pilot, was asked to comment on what he saw in this very clear photo of the cockpit of a war time configured B-17. Here are his comments:

"Really special because it shows so much of the details you don't see in any restored B-17s."

"The yellow canisters are standard oxygen tanks. There were three on either side of the cockpit on the walls. The pilot's side for him and the

---

[137] https://www.398th.org/Images/Images_Welty/Text/Welty_AfterWar_Pittsburgh.html

navigator. The other side was for the co-pilot, engineer and bombardier. These systems were interconnected. There were another six or so under the cockpit floor for the back half of the plane. There was a tank or two in the radio room. A few smaller for a connecting walk around, one in the engineer turret and back in the radio room. One tank would last one individual for about 5 or 6 hours. It was the engineers responsibility to keep the oxygen balanced."

"The armor plate [on the back of the pilot's seats], really unique to see, was 1/2 inch thick or more. There were also some under the pilot's seats."

"The square box at the bottom is the autopilot and above that is the prop pitch controls. The white lever is to lock them into position when they are set. Above that, the throttle quadrant, configured to let each engine to be controlled individually, but also in unison. The bottom split bar for engines 2 and 3. The top for 1 and 4 (like for taxiing) and grasping the middle bar, moves them all in unison, like for take off. The red buttons are the 1 and 2 prop feathering, above that, altitude indicator, and above that, the old needle and ball. Below the red buttons, it looks like the right foot control for the rudder and right brake."

"The box on top of the dash was a distress call. If used like in a ditching, you picked up the cover over the switch on the left of the box. The cables up the middle of the windshield went up to radio equipment overhead on the bottom of the roof. A nice neat and tidy place to do business!"

Merwin Genung, former B-17 pilot, wrote that on the shelf on the back of the pilot's seat it looks like an Aviator's Kit Bag AN 6505-1 Property of the US government. We used it to carry our heavy jackets, etc. My wife has one in the garage.

Welty Photo No. 2007 (end Citation)

Here is another closeup of a B-17G cockpit showing detail of the controls and instrument cluster.

B-17G cockpit courtesy of Steve Hayes – AeonAviation Photography.com

Another wide-angle view.

Courtesy of Kamloops B.C. Canada

▲ ▲ ▲ ▲

The History of the Flying Fortress

My book is not any kind of treatise on the incredible B-17 bomber of WWII. There are many authors with highly acclaimed tomes and far more qualified than I to tell of the engineering masterpiece that was the B-17 of that era. Mine is more of a human story of the lives that were lost or of who came home safely after flying these machines in the severest of combat conditions. They could drop out of formation but only because of severe damage, making them an even easier target for the Luftwaffe to finish them off. Some enemy fighters were under orders to ram the rear of bombers after the fighter ran out of ammunition. They would attempt to slice into the tail of the B-17, even at the risk of being shot out of the air by the tail gunner.

Nevertheless, we must consider that some crews that came home after combat, even with an immense amount of damage to the B-17, with its frame, wings, and or controls literally torn to shreds.

One can imagine these young airmen staggering out of their last ship of hope, some with severe frostbite, because their electric heated suits had short-circuited due to flak damage to the aircraft systems in sub-zero temperatures, and kissing the ground they thought they would not see again. Those without injuries would be on their next flight in the following days, until they had completed the required number of missions.

"Not a small measure of this association with endurance were the occasions when Fortresses sustained extraordinary battle damage yet returned and landed safely at their bases when most contemporaries would have had to be abandoned in the air. Such incidents added to the legend, but the underlying factors were the sound construction and good flying characteristics of the aircraft." – Roger Freeman[138] 'The Flying Fortress Story.' Arms & Armour, a Cassell Imprint of Hatchette Publishing.

---

[138] The B-17 Flying Fortress Story: By Roger A. Freeman with David Osborne 1997 Hatchette

The B-17 Tomahawk Warrior: A WWII Final Honor

Over 50,000 Airmen[139] lost their lives in the four years of WWII and most of those losses were on bomber missions over Nazi Germany in B-17s and B-24s. The average age of the crew of a B-17 was less than 25, with four officers and six enlisted airmen manning the aircraft. Their chance of survival was less than 50 percent. (Author's note: Chapter 10, Snyder, I reference statistics of 31% survivability of American bomber crews and 24% among the British).

In the Fall of 1943, on one daylight mission known as "Black Thursday," during operations against industrial capability in Schweinfurt, Germany, more than 60 B-17's were lost to enemy fighter aircraft attacks.

Between 1935 and May 1945, 12,732 B-17's were produced. Of these aircraft, 4,735 were lost [140]during combat missions. Today, fewer than 100 B-17 airframes exist worldwide.

During the war, formations of over 1,000 B-17's assembled in the skies over England for bombing missions to enemy targets in Nazi occupied France, Belgium, and Germany.

As of December 2022, 18 B-17s are registered[141] with the Federal Aviation Administration (FAA). These include Nine-O-Nine (N93012, crashed in October 2019), Texas Raiders (N7227C, crashed in November[142] 2022, see my tribute in this chapter), and a B-17G registered in Granite Falls, Minnesota (N4960V) that was scrapped in 1962. Wikipedia lists the other 15.

Of the B-17s registered with a civil aviation authority, such as the FAA, less than 10 are being kept in airworthy condition, and some of those have not flown for over five years. Some other B-17s are being restored and may become airworthy in the future.

A fellow historian, Mr. Jing Zhou, whose website is often referenced by

---

[139] https://www.afa.org/publications-news/news/2019-10-03/afa-statement-on-loss-of-historic-b-17—painful-reminder-of-the-

[140] https://sage-answer.com/how-many-b-17s-were-lost-during-the-second-world-war/

[141] https://en.wikipedia.org/wiki/List_of_surviving_Boeing_B-17_Flying_Fortresses

[142] See Author's Tribute to "Texas Raiders" in this Chapter.

researchers and history enthusiasts, has developed an interactive world map depicting the locations of crashed B-17s in WWII. It looks better in color.

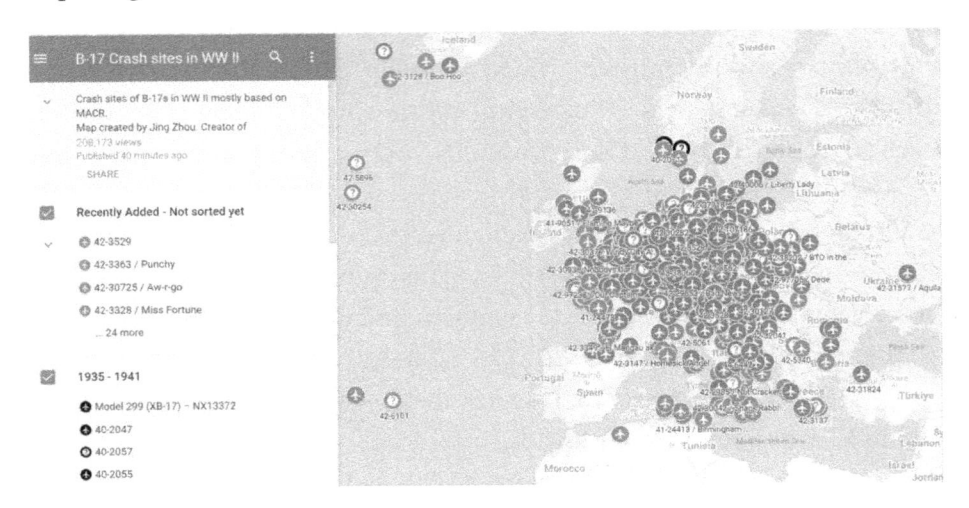

Courtesy of Jing Zhou map at https://tinyurl.com/4tzm6h95
Still a work-in-progress as of July 25,2023
You can also visit his web site for B-17 histories at Https://b17flyingfortress.de

An Example of The Tough Airworthiness of The B-17G and the Men Who Flew Them

Below is an extract from a remarkable story of the return from a bombing mission over Cologne, Germany, on October 15, 1944. With permission by the 398th BGMA. (Citation)

IT WAS A FORTRESS COMING HOME[143]
They Could Hear It Before They Could See it
By Allen Ostrom

They could hear it before they could see it!
Not all that unusual in those days as the personnel at Station 131

---

[143] https://398th.org/History/Articles/Remembrances/Ostrom_FortressHome.html

gathered around the tower and scattered hardstands to await the return of the B-17's sent out earlier that morning.

First comes the far off rumble and drone of the Cyclones. Then a speck on the East Anglia horizon. Soon a small cluster showing the lead squadron. Finally, the group.

Then the counting. 1-2-3-4-5.....

But that would have been normal. Today was different! It was too early for the group to return.

"They're 20 minutes early. Can't be the 398th."

They could hear it before they could see it! Something was coming home. But what?

All eyes turned toward the northeast, aligning with the main runway, each ground guy and stood down airman straining to make out this "wail of a Banshee," as one called it.

Not like a single B-17 with its characteristic deep roar of the engines blended with four thrashing propellers. This was a howl! Like a powerful wind blowing into a huge whistle.

Then it came into view. It WAS a B-17!

Low and pointing her nose at the 6,000 foot runway, it appeared for all the world to be crawling toward the earth, screaming in protest.

No need for the red flares. All who saw this Fort knew there was death aboard.

"Look at that nose!" they said as all eyes stared in amazement as this single, shattered remnant of a once beautiful airplane glided in for an unrealistic "hot" landing. She took all the runway as the "Banshee" noise finally abated, and came to an inglorious stop in the mud just beyond the concrete runway.

Men and machines raced to the now silent and lonely aircraft. The ambulance and medical staff were there first. The fire truck....ground and air personnel....jeeps, truck, bikes.....

Out came one of the crew members from the waist door, then another. Strangely quiet. The scene was almost weird. Men stood by as if in shock, not knowing whether to sing or cry.

Either would have been acceptable.

The medics quietly made their way to the nose by way of the waist door as the rest of the crew began exiting. And to answer the obvious question, "what happened?"

"What happened?" was easy to see. The nose was a scene of utter destruction. It was as though some giant aerial can opener had peeled the nose like an orange, relocating shreds of metal, plexiglass, wires, and tubes on the cockpit windshield and even up to the top turret. The left cheek gun hung limp, like a broken arm.

One man pointed to the crease in the chin turret. No mistaking that mark! A German 88 anti-aircraft shell had exploded in the lap of the togglier.

This would be George Abbott of Mt. Labanon, PA. He had been a waist gunner before training to take over the bombardier's role.

Still in the cockpit, physically and emotionally exhausted, were pilot Larry deLancey and co-pilot Phil Stahlman.

Navigator Ray LeDoux finally tapped deLancey on the shoulder and suggested they get out. Engineer turret gunner Ben Ruckel already had made his way to the waist was exiting along with radio operator Wendell Reed, ball turret gunner Al Albro, waist gunner Russell Lachman and tail gunner Herbert Guild.

Stahlman was flying his last scheduled mission as a replacement for regular co-pilot, Grady Cumbie. The latter had been hospitalized the day before with an ear problem. Lachman was also a "sub," filling in for Abbott in the waist.

DeLancey made it as far as the end of the runway, where he sat down with knees drawn up, arms crossed and head down. The ordeal was over, and now the drama was beginning a mental re-play.

Then a strange scene took place.

Group CO Col. Frank P. Hunter had arrived after viewing the landing from the tower and was about to approach deLancey. He was physically restrained by flight surgeon Dr. Robert Sweet.

"Colonel, that young man doesn't want to talk now. When he is ready, you can talk to him, but for now leave him alone."

Sweet handed pills out to each crew member and told them to go to their huts and sleep.

No dramatics, no cameras, no interviews. The crew would depart the next day for "flak leave" to shake off the stress. And then be expected back early in November. (Just in time to resume "normal" activities on a mission to Merseburg!)

Mission No. 98 from Nuthampstead had begun at 0400 that morning of October 15, 1944. It would be Cologne (again), led by CA pilots Robert Templeman of the 602nd, Frank Schofield of the 601st and Charles Khourie of the 603rd.

Tragedy and death appeared quickly and early that day. Templeman and pilot Bill Scott got the 602nd off at the scheduled 0630 hour, but at approximately 0645 Khouri and pilot Bill Meyran and their entire crew crashed on takeoff in the town of Anstey. All were killed. Schofield and Harold Stallcup followed successfully with the 601st, with deLancey flying on their left wing in the lead element.

The ride to the target was routine until the flak started becoming "unroutinely" accurate.

"We were going through heavy flak on the bomb run," remembered deLancey.

"I felt the plane lift as we dropped the bombs, then suddenly we were rocked by a violent explosion. My first thought – a bomb exploded in the bomb bay'–was immediately discarded as the top of the nose section peeled back over the cockpit blocking the forward view."

"It seemed like the entire world exploded in front of us," added Stahlman. "The instrument panel all but disintegrated and layers of quilted batting exploded in a million pieces. It was like a momentary snowstorm in the cockpit."

It had been a direct hit in the nose. Killed instantly was the togglier, Abbott. Navigator LeDoux, only three feet behind Abbott, was knocked unconscious for a moment, but miraculously was alive.

Although stunned and bleeding, LeDoux made his way to the cockpit to find the two pilots struggling to maintain control of an airplane that by all rights should have been in its death plunge. LeDoux said there was nothing anyone could do for Abbott, while Ruckel opened the door to the bomb bay and signaled to the four crewmen in the radio room that all was OK–for the time being.

The blast had torn away the top and much of the sides of the nose. Depositing enough of the metal on the windshield to make it difficult for either of the pilots to see.

"It tore the instrument panel loose and all the flight instruments were inoperative except for the magnetic compass mounted in the panel above the windshield. And its accuracy was questionable. The radio and intercom were gone, the oxygen lines broken, and there was a ruptured hydraulic line under my rudder pedals," said deLancey.

All this complicated by the sub-zero temperature at 27,000 feet blasting into the cockpit.

"It was apparent that the damage was severe enough that we could not continue to fly in formation or at high altitude. My first concern was to avoid the other aircraft in the formation, and to get clear of the other planes in case we had to bail out. We eased out of formation, and at the same time removed our oxygen masks as they were collapsing on our faces as the tanks were empty."

At this point the formation continued on its prescribed course for home–a long, slow turn southeast of Cologne and finally westward.

DeLancey and Stahlman turned left, descending rapidly and hoping, they were heading west. (And also, not into the gun sights of German fighters.) Without maps and navigation aids, they had difficulty getting a fix. By this time they were down to 2,000 feet.

"We finally agreed that we were over Belgium and were flying in a southwesterly direction," said the pilot.

"About this time a pair of P-51's showed up and flew a loose formation on us across Belgium. I often wondered what they thought as they looked at the mess up front."

"We hit the coast right along the Belgium-Holland border, farther north than we had estimated. Ray said we were just south of Walcheren Island."

Still in an area of ground fighting, the plane received some small arms fire. This gesture was returned in kind by Albro, shooting from one of the waist guns.

"We might have tried for one of the airfields in France, but having no maps this also was questionable. Besides, the controls and engines seemed to be OK, so I made the decision to try for home."

"Once over England, LeDoux soon picked up landmarks and gave me course corrections taking us directly to Nuthampstead. It was just a great bit of navigation. Ray just stood there on the flight deck and gave us the headings from memory."

Nearing the field, Stahlman let the landing gear down. That was an assurance. But a check of the hydraulic pump sent another spray of oil to the cockpit floor. Probably no brakes!

Nevertheless, a flare from Ruckel's pistol had to announce the "ready or not" landing. No "downwind leg" and "final approach" this time. Straight in!

"The landing was strictly by guess and feel," said DeLancey. "Without instruments, I suspect I came in a little hot. Also, I had to lean to the left to see straight ahead. The landing was satisfactory, and I had sufficient braking to slow the plane down some. However, as I neared the taxiway, I could feel the brakes getting 'soft'. I felt that losing control and blocking the taxiway would cause more problems than leaving the plane at the end of the runway."

That consideration was for the rest of the group. Soon three squadrons of B-17's would be returning, and they didn't need a derelict airplane blocking the way to their respective hardstands.

Stahlman, supremely thankful that his career with the 398th had come to an end, soon returned home and in due course became a captain with Eastern Airlines. Retired in 1984, Stahlman said his final Eastern flight "was a bit more routine" than the one 40 years before.

DeLancey and LeDoux received decorations on December 11, 1944 for their parts in the October 15 drama. DeLancey was awarded the Silver Star for his "miraculous feat of flying skill and ability" on behalf of General Doolittle, CO of the Eighth Air Force. LeDoux for his "extraordinary navigation skill", received the Distinguished Flying Cross.

The following deLancey 1944 article was transcribed from the 398th BG Historical Microfilm. Note: due to wartime security, Nuthampstead is not mentioned, and the route deLancey flew home is referred to in general terms.

TO: STARS AND STRIPES FOR GENERAL RELEASE

AN EIGHTH AIR FORCE BOMBER STATION, ENGLAND – After literally losing the nose of his B-17 Flying Fortress as the result of a direct hit by flak over Cologne, Germany on October 15, 1944, 1st Lt. Lawrence M. deLancey, 25, of Corvallis, Oregon returned to England and landed the crew safely at his home base. Each man walked away from the plane except the togglier, Staff Sergeant George E. Abbott, Mt. Lebanon, Pennsylvania, who was killed instantly when the flak struck.

It was only the combined skill and teamwork of Lt. deLancey and 2nd Lt. Raymond J. LeDoux, of Mt. Angel, Oregon, navigator, that enabled the plane and crew to return safely.

"Just after we dropped our bombs and started to turn away from the target", Lt. deLancey explained, "a flak burst hit directly in the nose and blew practically the entire nose section to threads.(sic) Part of the nose peeled back and obstructed my vision and that of my co-pilot, 1st Lt. Phillip H. Stahlman of Shippenville, Pennsylvania. What little there was left in front of me looked like a scrap heap. The wind was rushing through. It exposed our feet to the open air at nearly 30,000 feet above the ground and the temperature was unbearable."

"There we were, in a heavily defended flak area with no nose, and practically no instruments. The instrument panel was bent toward me as the result of the impact. My altimeter and magnetic compass were about the only instruments still operating and I couldn't depend on their accuracy too well. Naturally, I headed for home immediately. The hit which had killed S/Sgt. Abbott also knocked Lt. LeDoux back in the catwalk (just below where I was sitting). Our oxygen system also was out, so I descended to a safe altitude."

"Lt. LeDoux who had lost all his instruments and maps in the nose, did a superb piece of navigating to even find England."

During the route home, flak again was encountered, but because of evasive action Lt. deLancey was able to return to friendly territory. Lt. LeDoux navigated the ship directly to his home field.

Although the plane was off balance with no nose section, without any brakes (there was no hydraulic pressure left), and with obstructed vision, Lt. deLancey made a beautiful landing to the complete amazement of all personnel at this field who still are wondering how the feat was accomplished.

The other members of the crew include:

- Technical Sergeant Benjamin H. Ruckel, Roscoe, California, engineer top turret gunner;
- Technical Sergeant Wendell A. Reed, Shelby, Michigan, radio operator gunner;
- Technical Sergeant Russell A. Lachman, Rockport, Mass., waist gunner;
- Staff Sergeant Albert Albro, Antioch, California, ball turret gunner and
- Staff Sergeant Herbert D. Guild, Bronx, New York, tail gunner.

Originally printed in 398th Bomb Group Remembrances by Allen Ostrom, pages 45-46, published 1989.

Transcribed September 2003 by Lee Anne Bradley, 398th Bomb Group Historian.

The crippled B-17 Lt. DeLancey brought home courtesy of 398th.org

_____(End citation)

B-17G #42-38050 Thunderbird

Another example of the B-17's toughness and durability can be found on the 303rd Bomb Group website[144] where the story of the B-17G #42-38050 Thunderbird resides. It contains a wealth of information on that great B-17, including all 538 crewmen who flew on her 134 recorded flights.

COURTESY OF GARY MONCUR-HISTORIAN 303RDBG.COM

---

[144] Www.303rdBG.COM

This website is a memorial to B-17G #42-38050 (BN-U) Thunderbird and her original crew. Old reliable Thunderbird flew 112 bombing missions from Molesworth, England, for the 303rd Bomb Group. The original Thunderbird Crew, piloted by Lt. Vern L. Moncur, was the first crew in the 303rd Bomb Group to complete their combat missions with no one on board being injured. Lt Moncur's crew was the only crew ever assigned to Thunderbird as their primary aircraft. After Moncur's Crew finished their 28-mission combat tour, Thunderbird became a "first mission ship," given to new crews to get them off to a good start—and a good start it was, as no regular crew member was ever injured on a Thunderbird mission.

▲ ▲ ▲ ▲

CREW DUTIES

With the cooperation and permission of Mr. Gary L. Moncur, historian[145] for the 303rd Bombardment Group (Heavy), the "Hell's Angels" of the Mighty Eighth Air Force, I have reproduced some extracts of the crews' duties from the Training Manual of a B-17 – 1943. (**Citation**)

Duties and Responsibilities
THE AIRPLANE COMMANDER
From the B-17 Pilot Training Manual -1943

Your assignment to the B-17 airplane means you are no longer just a pilot. You are now an airplane commander, charged with all the duties and responsibilities of a command post.

You are now flying a 10-man weapon. It is your airplane and your crew. You always handle the safety and efficiency of the crew—not just when you

---

[145] Gary L. Moncur 303rd Bomb Group "Hell's Angels" Historianglm@303rdBG. comWebsite: https://www.303rdBG.com Facebook: www.facebook.com/groups/303rdBG/

are flying and fighting, but for the full 24 hours of every day while you are in command.

Your crew comprises specialists. Each man — whether he is the navigator, bombardier, engineer, radio operator, or one of the gunners — is an expert in his line. But how well he does his job, and how efficiently he plays his part as a member of your combat team, will depend to a great extent on how well you play your own part as the airplane commander.

Get to know each member of your crew as an individual. Know his personal idiosyncrasies, his capabilities, his shortcomings. Take a personal interest in his problems, his ambitions, his need for specific training.

See that your men are properly quartered, clothed, and fed. There will be many times when your airplane and crew are away from the home base, when you may even have to carry your interest to the extent of financing them yourself. Remember always that you are the commanding officer of a miniature army — a specialized army; and that morale is one of the biggest problems for the commander of any army, large or small.

Crew Discipline

Your success as the airplane commander will depend in a large measure on the respect, confidence, and trust which the crew feels for you. It will depend also on how well you maintain crew discipline.

Your position commands obedience and respect. This does not mean that you have to be stiff-necked, overbearing, or aloof. Such characteristics most certainly will defeat your purpose. Be friendly, understanding, but firm. Know your job; and, by the way you perform your duties daily, impress upon the crew that you do know your job. Keep close to your men and let them realize that their interests are uppermost in your mind. Make fair decisions, after due consideration of all the facts involved; but make them in such a way as to impress upon your crew that your decisions are to stick. Crew discipline is vitally important, but it need not be as difficult a problem as it sounds. Good discipline in an air crew breeds comradeship and high morale, and the combination is unbeatable.

You can be a good CO and still be a regular guy. You can command respect from your men and still be one of them.

"To associate discipline with informality, comradeship, a leveling of rank, and at times a shift in actual command away from the leader, may seem paradoxical," says a brigadier general, formerly a Group commander in the VIII Bomber Command. "Certainly, it isn't down the military groove. But it is discipline just the same — and the kind of discipline that brings success in the air."

Crew Training

Train your crew as a team. Keep abreast of their training. It won't be possible for you to follow each man's courses of instruction, but you can keep a close check on his record and progress.

Get to know each man's duties and problems. Know his job, and try to devise ways and means of helping him to perform it more efficiently.

Each crew member naturally feels great pride in the importance of his particular specialty. You can help him to develop his pride to include the manner in which he performs that duty. To do that, you must possess and maintain a thorough knowledge of each man's job and the problems he has to deal with in performing his duties.

Duties and Responsibilities of;
THE COPILOT

The copilot is the executive officer — your chief assistant, understudy, and strong right arm. He must be familiar enough with every one of your duties — both as pilot and as airplane commander — to take over and act in your place at any time.

He must be able to fly the airplane under all conditions as well as you would fly it yourself.

He must be extremely proficient in engine operation, and know instinctively what to do to keep the airplane flying smoothly even though he is not handling the controls.

He must have a thorough knowledge of cruising control data, and know how to apply it at the proper time.

He is also the engineering officer aboard the airplane and maintains a complete log of performance data.

He must be a qualified instrument pilot.

He must be able to fly good formation in any assigned position, day or night.

He must be qualified to navigate by day or at night by pilotage, dead reckoning, and by use of radio aids.

He must be proficient in the operation of all radio equipment in the pilot's compartment.

In formation flying, he must be able to make engine adjustments almost automatically.

He must be prepared to take over on instruments when the formation is climbing through an overcast, thus enabling you to watch the rest of the formation.

Always remember that the copilot is a fully trained, rated pilot, just like yourself. He is subordinate to you only by virtue of your position as the airplane commander. The B-17 is a lot of airplane; more airplane than any one pilot can handle alone over a long period of time. Therefore, you have been provided with a second pilot who will share the duties of a flight operation.

Treat your copilot as a brother pilot. Remember that the more proficient he is as a pilot, the more efficiently he will be able to perform the duties of the vital post he holds as your second in command.

Be sure that he is allowed to do his share of the flying, in the pilot's seat, on takeoffs, landings, and on instruments.

The importance of the copilot is eloquently testified to by airplane commanders overseas. There have been many cases in which the pilot has been disabled or killed in flight and the copilot has taken full command of both airplane and crew, completed the mission, and returned safely to the home base. Usually, the copilots who have distinguished themselves under such conditions have been copilots who have been respected and trained by the airplane commander as pilots.

Remember the pilot in the right-hand seat of your airplane is preparing himself for an airplane commander's post too. Allow him every chance to develop his ability and to profit from your experience.

Duties and Responsibilities of;
THE NAVIGATOR

The navigator's job is to direct your flight from departure to destination and return. He must always know the exact position of the airplane.

Navigation is the art of determining geographic positions by means of (a) pilotage, (b) dead reckoning, (c) radio, or (d) celestial navigation, or any combination of these 4 methods. By any one or combination of methods, the navigator determines the position of the airplane in relation to the earth.

(Author's Note: we covered these navigational methods in Chapter 8, but the pilot must ensure the navigator maintains his efficiency and ancillary duties. I have included here an abbreviated version of other duties).

Instrument Calibration

Instrument calibration is an important duty of the navigator. All navigation depends directly on the accuracy of his instruments. Correct calibration requires close cooperation and extremely careful flying by the pilot.

Pilot-Navigator Preflight Planning

Pilot and navigator must study flight plan of the route to be flown and select alternate air fields.

Study the weather with the navigator. Know what weather you are likely to encounter. Decide what action is to be taken. Know the weather conditions at the alternate airfields.

Inform your navigator at what airspeed and altitude you wish to fly so that he can prepare his flight plan.

Learn what type of navigation the navigator intends to use: pilotage, dead reckoning, radio, celestial, or a combination of all methods.

Determine check points; plan to make radio fixes.

Work out an effective communication method with your navigator to be used in flight.

Synchronize your watch with your navigator's.

Pilot-Navigator in Flight

Constant course – For accurate navigation, the pilot — you — must fly a constant course. The navigator has many computations and entries to make in his log. Constantly changing course makes his job more difficult.

Constant airspeed must be held as nearly as possible. This is as important to the navigator as is a constant course in determining position.

Precision flying by the pilot greatly affects the accuracy of the navigator's instrument readings, particularly celestial readings. A slight error in celestial reading can cause considerable error in determining positions. You can help the navigator by providing as steady a platform as possible from which he can take readings.

Notify the navigator of any change in flight, such as a change in altitude, course, or airspeed. If a change in flight plan is to be made, consult the navigator. Talk over the proposed change so that he can plan the flight and advise you about it.

If there is doubt about the position of the airplane, pilot and navigator should get together, refer to the navigator's flight log, talk the problem over and decide together the best course of action to take.

Check your compasses at intervals with those of the navigator, noting any deviation.

Require your navigator to give position reports at intervals.

You are ultimately responsible for getting the airplane to its destination. Therefore, it is your duty to know your position at all times.

Encourage your navigator to use as many navigation methods as possible to double-checking.

Post-flight Critique

After every flight, get together with the navigator and discuss the flight and compare notes. Go over the navigator's log. If there have been serious navigational errors, discuss them with the navigator and determine their cause. If the navigator has been at fault, caution him it is his job to see that the same mistake does not occur again. If the error has been caused by faulty instruments, see that they are corrected before another navigation mission is attempted. If your flying has contributed to inaccuracy in navigation, try to fly a better course next time.

Miscellaneous Duties

The navigator's primary duty is navigating your airplane with a high degree of accuracy. But as a member of the team, he must also have a general knowledge of the entire operation of the airplane.

He has a .50-cal. machine gun at his station, and he must be able to use it skillfully and to service it in emergencies.

He must be familiar with the oxygen system, know how to operate the turrets, radio equipment, and fuel transfer system.

He must know the location of all fuses and spare fuses, lights and spare lights, affecting navigation.

He must be familiar with emergency procedures, such as the manual operation of landing gear, bomb bay doors, and flaps, and the proper procedures for crash landings, ditching, bailout, etc.

Duties and Responsibilities of;
THE BOMBARDIER

Accurate and effective bombing is the ultimate purpose of your entire airplane and crew. Every other function is preparatory to hitting and destroying the target.

That's your bombardier's job. The success or failure of the mission depends upon what he accomplishes in that short interval of the bombing run.

When the bombardier takes over the airplane for the run on the target, he is in absolute command. He will tell you what he wants done, and until he tells you "Bombs away," his word is law.

A great deal, therefore, depends on the understanding between bombardier and pilot. You expect your bombardier to know his job when he takes over. He expects you to understand the problems involved in his job, and to give him full cooperation. Teamwork between pilot and bombardier is essential.

Under any given set of conditions — ground speed, altitude, direction, etc. — there is only one point in space where a bomb may be released from the airplane to hit a predetermined object on the ground.

There are many things with which a bombardier must be thoroughly familiar in order to release his bombs at the right point to hit this predetermined target.

He must know and understand his bombsight, what it does, and how it does it.

He must thoroughly understand the operation and upkeep of his bombing instruments and equipment.

He must know that his racks, switches, controls, releases, doors, linkage, etc., are in first class operating condition.

He must understand the automatic pilot as it pertains to bombing.

He must know how to set it up, make any adjustments and minor repairs while in flight.

He must know how to operate all the gun positions in the airplane.

He must know how to load and clear simple stoppages and jams of machine guns while in flight.

He must be able to load and fuse his own bombs.

He must understand the destructive power of bombs and must know the vulnerable spots on various types of targets.

He must understand the bombing problem, bombing probabilities, bombing errors, etc.

He must be thoroughly versed in target identification and in aircraft identification.

The bombardier should be familiar with the duties of all members of the crew and should be able to assist the navigator in case the navigator becomes incapacitated.

For the bombardier to be able to do his job, the pilot of the aircraft must place the aircraft in the proper position to arrive at a point on a circle about the target from which the bombs can be released to hit the target.

Consider the following conditions which affect the bomb dropped from an airplane:

ALTITUDE: Controlled by the pilot. Determines the length of time the bomb is sustained in flight and affected by atmospheric conditions, thus affecting the range (forward travel of the bomb) and deflection (distance the bomb drifts in a crosswind with respect to airplane's ground track).

TRUE AIRSPEED: Controlled by the pilot. The measure of the speed of the airplane through the air. It is this speed which is imparted to the bomb and which gives the bomb its initial forward velocity and, therefore, affects the trail of the bomb, or the distance the bomb lags behind the airplane at the instant of impact.

BOMB BALLISTICS: Size, shape, and density of the bomb, which determines its air resistance. Bombardier uses bomb ballistics tables to account for the type of bomb.

TRAIL: Horizontal distance, the bomb is behind the airplane at the instant of impact. This value, obtained from bombing tables, is set in the sight by the bombardier. Trail is affected by altitude, airspeed, bomb ballistics and air density, the first three factors being controlled by the pilot.

ACTUAL TIME OF FALL: Length of time, the bomb is sustained in air from instant of release to instant of impact. Affected by altitude, type of bomb and air density. Pilot controls altitude to get a definite actual time of fall.

GROUNDSPEED: The speed of the airplane in relation to the earth's surface. Groundspeed affects the range of the bomb and varies with the airspeed, controlled by the pilot. Bombardier enters groundspeed in the bombsight through synchronization on the target. During this process, the pilot must maintain the correct altitude and constant airspeed.

DRIFT: Determined by the direction and velocity of the wind, which determines the distance the bomb will travel downwind from the airplane from the instant the bomb is released to its instant of impact. Drift is set on the bombsight by the bombardier during the process of synchronization and setting up a course.

The above conditions indicate that the pilot plays an important part in determining the proper point of the release of the bomb. Throughout the course of the run, as explained below, there are certain preliminaries and techniques which the pilot must understand insuring accuracy and minimum loss of time.

Prior to takeoff, the pilot must ascertain that the airplane's flight instruments have been checked and found accurate. These are the altimeter, airspeed indicator, free air temperature gauge and all gyro instruments. These instruments must be used to determine accurately the airplane's attitude.

The Pilot's Preliminaries

The autopilot and PDI (Pilot Direction Indicator[146]) should be checked for proper operation. It is very important that PDI and autopilot function perfectly in the air; otherwise, it will be impossible for the bombardier to set up an accurate course on the bombing run. The pilot should

---

[146] https://en.wikipedia.org/wiki/Pilot_direction_indicator

thoroughly familiarize himself with the function of both the C-1 autopilot and the PDI.

If the run is to be made on the autopilot, the pilot must carefully adjust the autopilot before reaching the target area. The autopilot must be adjusted under the same conditions that will exist on the bombing run over the target. For this reason, the following factors should be taken into consideration and duplicated for initial adjustment.

(Author's Note; A full extract of the Bombardiers duties in Pilot's Manual are found at 303rdBG.com. I have only included the above basic duties to give the reader a glimpse of the role).

Duties and Responsibilities of;
THE ENGINEER

Size up the man who is to be your engineer. This man is supposed to know more about the airplane you are to fly than any other member of the crew.

He has been trained in the Air Force's highly specialized technical schools. Probably he has served some time as a crew chief. There may be some inevitable blank spots in his training which you, as a pilot and airplane commander, may be able to fill in.

Think back on your own training. In many courses of instruction, you had a lot of things thrown at you from right and left. You had to concentrate on how to fly; and where your equipment was concerned you learned to rely more and more on the enlisted personnel, particularly the crew chief and the engineer, to advise you about things that were not taught to you because of lack of time and the arrangement of the training program.

Both pilot and engineer have a responsibility to work closely together to supplement and fill in the blank spots in each other's education. To be a qualified combat engineer, a man must know his airplane, his engines, and his armament equipment thoroughly. This is an enormous responsibility:

the lives of the entire crew, the safety of the equipment, the success of the mission depend upon it squarely.

He must work closely with the copilot, checking engine operation, fuel consumption, and the operation of all equipment. He must be able to work with the bombardier, and know how to cock, lock, and load the bomb racks. It is up to you, the airplane commander, to see that he is familiar with these duties, and, if he is hazy concerning them, to have the bombardier give him special help and instruction.

He must be thoroughly familiar with the armament equipment, and know how to strip, clean, and re-assemble the guns.

He should have a general knowledge of radio equipment and be able to assist in tuning transmitters and receivers.

Your engineer should be your chief source of information concerning the airplane. He should know more about the equipment than any other crew member — yourself included.

You, in turn, are his source of information concerning flying. Bear this in mind in all your discussions with the engineer. The more complete you can make his knowledge of the reasons behind every function of the equipment, the more valuable he will be as a member of the crew. Who knows? Someday that little bit of extra knowledge in the engineer's mind may save the day in some emergency.

Generally, in emergencies, the engineer will be the man to whom you turn first. Build up his pride, his confidence, his knowledge. Know him personally; check on the extent of his knowledge. Make him a man upon whom you can rely.

Duties and Responsibilities of;
THE RADIO OPERATOR

There is a lot of radio equipment in today's B-17s. There is one man in particular who is supposed to know all there is to know about this equipment.

Sometimes he does, but often he doesn't. And when the radio operator's deficiencies do not become apparent until the crew is in the combat zone, it is then too late. Too often the lives of pilots and crew are lost because the radio operator has accepted his responsibility indifferently.

Radio is a subject that cannot be learned in a day. It cannot be mastered in 6 weeks, but sufficient knowledge can be imparted to the radio man during his period of training in the United States if he will study. It is imperative that you check your radio operator's ability to handle his job before taking him overseas as part of your crew. To do this, you may have to check the various departments to find any weakness in the radio operator's training and proficiency and to aid the instructors in overcoming such weaknesses.

Training in the various phases of the heavy bomber program is designed to fit each member of the crew for the handling of his jobs. The radio operator will be required to:

Render position reports every 30 minutes.
Assist the navigator in taking fixes.
Keep the liaison and command sets properly tuned and in good operating order.
Understand from an operational point of view:
Instrument landing
IFF
VHF
and other navigational aids equipment in the airplane.
Maintain a log.

Besides being a radio operator, the radio man is also a gunner. During periods of combat, he will be required to leave his watch at the radio and take up his guns. He is often required to learn photography. Radio operators took some of the best pictures taken in the Southwest Pacific. The radio operator who cannot perform his job properly may be the weakest member of your crew — and the crew is no stronger than its weakest member.

Duties and Responsibilities of;
THE GUNNERS

The B-17 is a most effective gun platform, but its effectiveness can be either applied or defeated by the way the gunners in your crew perform their duties in action.

Your gunners belong to one of two distinct categories: turret gunners and flexible gunners.

The power turret gunners require many mental and physical qualities similar to what we know as inherent flying ability, since the operation of the power turret and gunsight are much like that of airplane flight operation.

While the flexible gunners do not require the same delicate touch as the turret gunner, they must have a fine sense of timing and be familiar with the rudiments of exterior ballistics.

All gunners should be familiar with the coverage area of all gun positions, and be prepared to bring the proper gun to bear as the conditions may warrant.

They should be experts in aircraft identification. Where the Sperry turret is used, failure to set the target dimension dial properly on the K-type sight will cause miscalculation of range.

They must be thoroughly familiar with the Browning aircraft machine gun. They should know how to maintain the guns, how to clear jams and stoppages, and how to harmonize the sights with the guns. While participating in training flights, the gunners should be operating their turrets constantly, tracking with the flexible guns even when actual firing is not practical. Other airplanes flying in the vicinity offer excellent tracking targets, as do automobiles, houses, and other ground objects during low altitude flights.

We cannot overemphasize the importance of teamwork. One poorly trained gunner, or one man not on the alert, can be the weak link because of which the entire crew may be lost.

Keep the interest of your gunners alive at all times. Any form of competition among the gunners themselves should stimulate interest to a high degree.

Finally, each gunner should fire the guns at each station to familiarize himself with the other man's position and to insure knowledge of operation in the event of an emergency. **(End citation)**

▲ ▲ ▲ ▲

TRIBUTE TO THE TEXAS RAIDERS OF THE COMMEMORATIVE AIR FORCE (CAF)

Because of my work on the book about The Tomahawk Warrior, I had become associated with the people of the Commemorative Air Force, or CAF, where the restored WWII B-17G nicknamed the "Texas Raiders", was displayed.

Each time they exhibited or put on an air display in the Dallas/Fort Worth Metroplex area, they would invite me as a guest, and I got to enjoy the company of many members of their organization. On those occasions, it was Nancy Kwiecien, Executive Officer, Commemorative Air Force, Gulf Wing, and Maddi Crawford, Qualified B-17 Load Master.

So, it was with great sadness that on November 12, 2022, during a "Wings Over Dallas" show, I learned of a terrible accident when a P-63 KingCobra slammed into the B-17G, the crash, killing all 5 of the bomber crew and the pilot of the P-63. I could not attend the show on the day of the accident, but had planned on visiting it the following day. They instead canceled it.

I personally knew two of the B-17 crew, Terry Barker and Kevin "K5" Michels, and made an acquaintance of a third, Len Root. I only met Terry one time. I liked him straight away. I told him about my book "The B-17

Tomahawk Warrior: A WWII Final Honor," and he immediately expressed interest in it. He was keen to know when it would appear in bookstores.

I will be happy to present a signed copy of my book, when published, to Terry's wife and family.

Terry was a top-rated pilot for well over 40 years. He retired from a successful career with American Airlines, where he was a Check Airman on the Fokker 100, Airbus A300, and the Boeing 777. As a firearms enthusiast, he was especially proud to be a Federal Flight Deck Officer.

He also was the Maintenance Officer for the Gulf Coast Wing of the Commemorative Air Force and a member of the Greg Eagles. Terry loved to help and serve. He served the Keller community in Texas as a member of the Planning and Zoning Commission from 1995 to 1999 and was elected for two terms on the Keller City Council.

R.I.P. Terry, you are now soaring in heaven with your silver wings.

Kevin Dimitri Michels earned a BS in Electrical Engineering Technology (EET). He later received his MBA at St. Edward University in Austin, TX. Kevin started his career as a Field Engineer for GE Medical, maintaining MRI machines at three of the large hospitals in western Los Angeles. He moved on to Semiconductor Manufacturing. His career then took a turn to marketing and he founded a very successful company.

Kevin retired early and turned his passion toward the Commemorative Air Force, specifically the B-17 Flying Fortress "Texas Raiders." He volunteered his time, working as part of their crew, as a loadmaster, media representative, and Wing Historian. He traveled the country with the B-17, sharing his extensive knowledge of this magnificent war bird. Few things made him happier than educating the public, especially the children, on her history.

I had a great chat with him and Lt. Col Walt Thompson, another stalwart of the close-knit Commemorative Air Force family. The one thing I remember about Kevin was his infectious laugh. One couldn't help smiling when around him. You can see that in the photo that my daughter, Martine Huntley Wilson, took of the three of us that day.

It is indeed ironic that I am connected to the tragedy of two B-17 bombers in my 86-year-old lifetime.

The late Terry Barker. Courtesy of his widow, Karen Barker, with sincere thanks

L-R the late Kevin Michels, Lt. Col Walt Thompson, and author, 2021

L-R Lee Brown, the lead flight engineer, the late Len Root, Wing Leader and Command Pilot lost on November 12, 2022, Major Lucky Luckadoo a WWII B-17 pilot, the late Terry Barker, Co-pilot also lost November 12, 2022 Copyright Huntley Associates Dallas, Inc. Photo taken 2021.

▲ ▲ ▲ ▲

OTHER ASPECTS OF AIR COMBAT IN WWII

Physiological Problems of Bomber Crews in Eighth Air Force in WWII

(Citation) A research paper by James Carroll[147] for Air Command College, titled "Physiological Problems of Bomber Crews in Eighth Air Force in WWII," examines the physiological problems faced by bomber crews in

---

[147] https://www.airuniversity.af.edu/ACSC

the Eighth Air Force during World War II. The study primarily focuses on the effects of high altitude on the human body, including hypoxia, hypobaria, and cold exposure, as well as the psychological effects of combat stress and fatigue. This paper also discusses the measures that were taken to mitigate these problems, such as the use of oxygen masks, pressurized cabins, and flight clothing. The conclusion of the paper highlights the need for ongoing research in the areas of high-altitude physiology and psychology to improve the performance and survival of air crews.

The paper explains how the human body is affected by high altitude, starting with the physiological effects of hypoxia, which can cause headaches, fatigue, and confusion. The paper goes on to discuss the effects of hypobaria, which can cause barotrauma, a condition that can result in injury to the lungs and sinuses. Cold exposure is also discussed as a problem, which can cause frostbite and hypothermia.

The study then goes on to discuss the psychological effects of combat stress and fatigue on bomber crews. Combat stress can cause a wide range of mental health issues, such as anxiety, depression, and post-traumatic stress disorder. Fatigue is also discussed as a problem, which can cause cognitive impairment, decreased reaction time, and increased risk of accidents.

The paper then describes the various measures that were taken to mitigate these problems, such as the use of oxygen masks, pressurized cabins, and flight clothing. The paper also highlights the importance of training, which can help prepare air crews for the unique challenges of high altitude flying.

In conclusion, the paper highlights the need for ongoing research in the areas of high-altitude physiology and psychology to improve the performance and survival of air crews. The paper emphasizes that understanding the physiological and psychological problems faced by bomber crews during WWII will help researchers to develop better equipment, procedures and training that will help protect the health and safety of air crews in the future.

The research paper by James Carroll does not express any concern that the war planners did not take the physiological and psychological problems of bomber crews into account during WWII. However, it suggests that they did not fully understand the effects of high altitude on the human body at the time, and that more research was needed to improve the performance and survival of air crews. The author states that "the importance of understanding the unique problems of high-altitude flight cannot be overemphasized."

It also seems that some of the physiological and psychological problems faced by bomber crews were considered the "price of doing business," as they acknowledged that air crews were exposed to high levels of risk and danger. The author mentions that the "high altitude environment, with its low temperatures, low pressures, and lack of oxygen, presents a formidable challenge to the human body and mind." The author also notes that "the psychological stresses of combat and fatigue only add to the physiological stresses of high-altitude flight."

In summary, the author of the paper does not express concern that the war planners did not take these issues into account and it was considered the "price of doing business" but the author emphasizes the importance of understanding the unique problems of high-altitude flight and the ongoing research in the areas of high-altitude physiology and psychology to improve the performance and survival of air crews. (End Citation)

Path Finder Force Bombing Method (PFF)[148] (Citation)

PFF stands for "Pathfinder Force." PFF was a method of bombing developed by the Royal Air Force (RAF) during World War II to improve the accuracy of bombing at night and in poor visibility.

The PFF method involved using a small group of aircraft, known as "pathfinders," to fly ahead of the main bomber force and drop flares or

---

[148] Compiled from various sources including the 398th.org

markers to show the target area. These flares or markers would light up the target area, making it easier for the main bomber force to accurately drop their bombs.

The pathfinder aircraft were usually equipped with advanced navigation equipment, such as radar and H2S (a radar-like device), and were often manned by specially trained crews. They would mark the target using flares, special bombs, or other markers and then the main bomber force would follow to drop their bombs.

This method of bombing was widely used by the RAF Bomber Command during the war, and credited with significantly improving the accuracy of bombing in night and poor visibility conditions.

There were problems with accuracy when using the PFF (Pathfinder Force) bombing method in WWII. The marker flares used to mark the target could drift in the wind, causing the bombs dropped by the primary force of bombers to fall off target. Additionally, the flares were often visible to the enemy, allowing them to take evasive action. To address these issues, the PFF developed techniques such as using radar to guide the bombers to the target, and dropping the flares at a higher altitude to reduce the impact of wind drift.

By dropping the flares at a higher altitude, the impact of wind drift on their descent would be reduced, making them more accurate markers for the main force of bombers to follow. This was one of the techniques used by the PFF to improve the accuracy of the bombing runs. Additionally, the PFF also used radar to guide the bombers to the target, which could overcome some of the challenges posed by wind drift and visibility.

In WWII, radar technology was still relatively new and not as advanced as it is today. While radar could guide bombers to a general area, it was not always accurate enough to identify small targets, such as rail stations. Hazy conditions could also make it difficult for radar to detect targets.

To overcome these limitations, the PFF used a combination of techniques, including radar, marker flares, and visual cues from the lead navigator to locate and mark targets. The lead navigator would often fly ahead of the primary force of bombers and drop flares to mark the target, while the radar operator would use radar to guide the bombers to the general area. The combination of these techniques allowed the PFF to locate and bomb small and well-defended targets, such as rail stations, but it was still a difficult and challenging task. (End citation)

Types Of Explosives Used In WWII (Citation)

Torpex is a high explosive mixture that was used extensively in World War II. It is a blend of TNT, RDX (cyclonite), and aluminum powder, and was developed to provide a more powerful and reliable explosive for use in depth charges and torpedoes. They also used Torpex in a variety of other weapons, including naval mines and bombs.

RDX (Research Department Explosive) is a powerful, stable, and relatively insensitive explosive that was widely used at that time. It was developed in the late 19th century and was initially used as a military explosive during World War I. RDX was used in a variety of applications, including as the primary explosive in bombs, shells, and land mines. It was also used as a booster explosive to initiate the detonation of other, less sensitive, explosives, such as TNT.

In anti-submarine warfare during WWII, it used Torpex as the explosive charge in depth charges, which were dropped by ships and aircraft to attack submarines. The powerful explosion created by the Torpex charge would damage or sink the submarine. They also used Torpex in the British "hedgehog" anti-submarine weapon, which fired a pattern of small projectiles ahead of a ship, each carrying a Torpex charge. When a submarine was detected in the area, the hedgehog would be fired and the Torpex charges would explode against the submarine's hull, causing significant damage.

In air force bombing missions, it used Torpex in the British Tallboy and Grand Slam bombs, which were developed specifically to attack hardened targets such as underground bunkers, bridges, and dams. The bombs were dropped from high altitude and used a combination of their colossal size, weight and the explosive power of Torpex to create a deep, penetrating and devastating effect.

RDX was primarily used in the United States as the main explosive ingredient in block-buster bombs, general-purpose bombs, incendiary bombs, and in some torpedoes, as well as by the USAAF as the main explosive in the M-47 bomb, which was employed to attack submarine pens, naval bases, and other heavily reinforced targets.

In British bombing missions, RDX was also a primary explosive in the "Cookie" bomb, in attacks at heavily fortified targets, such as submarine pens and industrial complexes. The "Cookie" bomb could cause significant damage because of the combined effect of its enormous size, weight, and the explosive power of RDX. (End Citation)

The RDX explosive was a sensitive product to deal with, as described in the excerpt by Paul Brown, a Radio Operator with the 601st squadron, 398th Bomb Group. (Reproduced with permission from the 398th Bomb Group Memorial Association, and website www.398th.org. Printed in *Flak News* Volume 3, Number 1, Page(s) 4, January 1988.) **(Citation)**

It Should Have Been A Milk Run: BOMBS KISSED IN MID-AIR By Paul Brown 601 Radio Operator

For many of us on the Palant crew, it was supposed to be our 35th and final mission. And it was supposed to be the easiest of them all. A real milk run.

But it didn't work out as planned. It quickly became a nightmare which has taken a long time to fade into comfortable memory.

Our pilot, Sam Palant, was assigned to fly deputy lead on CA Tom Marchbanks and pilot Art Taylor. Our target, while in flight, was changed from Bad Kleinen to Neumunster, some 40 miles due north of Hamburg.

We would attack the city's marshalling yards with 10 "RDX" bombs in each of the group's B-17s.

These very special bombs yielded a very high explosive force, but were also very touchy. We were all cautioned that they had to be handled with care.

Everything was as briefed to the target. No flak and no enemy fighters. And it was a beautiful day, both in England and on the continent.

At the words, "bombs away!" I poked my head into the bomb bay to confirm that the load had been dumped. As deputy, we were to drop on the lead ship, and I could see the smoke marker from Taylor's aircraft.

I immediately hollered into the intercom that our bombs were still in there. Nothing happened! There was a flurry of conversation on the intercom, and I continued looking into the bomb bay, waiting for the bombs to go. After what seemed like several minutes, they all let go. All at once!

Then, in just a few seconds, I saw a tremendous orange flash through the open bomb bay. At first I thought our plane had exploded, then I realized that what I had seen was the reflection of an explosion beneath our plane.

Our tail-gunner on this trip was the squadron armament officer named Lt. Orie Hedges. He had been hit. Byron Cunningham, in the waist, crawled to the tail and dragged Hedges back to the waist door. Hedges' own chute was still back in the tail, so Cunningham placed his own chute on the injured lieutenant and readied him for position to bail out.

We had suffered heavy damage from the explosion, were losing altitude and there was a fire in the right wing! It was all bad. By the time we had dropped to 12,000 feet, Palant ordered us to bail out. By the time I got to the waist door, the others had gone: Hedges, Cunningham, waist gunner Robert Sanford and ball turret gunner Tom Coleman.

I could see the others plummeting to earth, and I quickly joined them. I tugged on what I thought was the handle, but with no success. Finally, I realized I had been pulling on the carry handle, not the metal red handle that popped the chute. Being left-handed almost cost me my life.

Cunningham, who made a delayed jump, evaded capture for 24 hours. The rest of us were caught quickly and taken to an interrogation center at Pinneberg, near Hamburg.

During our passage through Hamburg, the 8th Air Force came over the city on their way to some other target. They herded us into a railroad tunnel which served as a shelter. The townspeople, having experienced some of the heaviest bombing by the Allies, turned on us with shouts and curses. I felt lucky that Hamburg wasn't the target because if one bomb had fallen that day, I'm sure the natives would have set on us and we would not have survived. The British liberated us on May 2, 1945. **(End Citation)**

603rd Squadron in action – 1944 or early 1945.
Photo courtesy of the 398th.org.
Planes 1,2, and 3 have just released their bomb loads.

▲ ▲ ▲ ▲

PART 3

HONOR-A HISTORICAL MOMENT-& A LINK TO AMERICA'S INDEPENDENCE

▲▲▲▲

CHAPTER TWELVE

REQUEST FOR POSTHUMOUS HONORS

▲ ▲ ▲ ▲

An Application To Request A US Honor for 1st Lt. Charles Searl

You may remember that in Chapter 3, I had mentioned that I saw a significant number of concrete pillars positioned in the meadows near our cottage in Loudwater village. The purpose of these obstacles was to prevent German troop gliders from landing during any attempted invasion[149].

Quoting from British wartime regulations:

> "Open areas were considered vulnerable to invasion from the air, a landing by paratroops, glider-borne troops or powered aircraft which could land and take off again. Open areas with a straight length of 500 yards (460 m) or more within five miles (8 km) of the coast or an airfield were considered vulnerable. Trenches, wooden or concrete obstacles, and old cars blocked them."

Lt. Searl and his crew could probably see in the murky darkness of breaking dawn that the fields below were strewn with obstacles preventing a forced landing. He was already at a very low altitude because of circumstances that I described in Chapter 7. So low, in fact, I thought it was

---

[149] https://en.wikipedia.org/wiki/British_anti-invasion_preparations_of_the_Second_World_War#Airfields_and_open_areas

coming down on our cottage until it passed right overhead, only to crash around 30 to 40 seconds later.

I presented this evidence to the United States Army and to the United States Senator Ron Johnson of Wisconsin to have Lt. Searl and his crew awarded a posthumous medal for valor in saving many lives that day at the cost of his own, and that of his crew. Sadly, the Army regulations that govern the award process, requires support and sanction by the lieutenant's commanding officers and because they were no longer alive, the process was automatically closed.

I will not burden the reader with the lengthy and detailed declarations required to initiate and sustain this application, as well as the necessary signatures, not just of myself, but of Mrs. Cheryl Surfus, Lt. Searl's daughter. There were many email interactions with Senator Ron Johnson's office through his Veterans and Military Affairs Constituent Services Representative.

I did receive a confirming letter from Lieutenant Colonel Christopher L. Moore, U.S. Army Chief, Awards and Decorations Branch, which gave a very comprehensive explanation why the Army could not make an award. It was in detail, but not in rationale, in my humble opinion. In essence, the decision to decline was that Lt. Searl's Commanding Officers would be required to sanction or approve such an award. This was, of course, impossible. They were all dead!

I thought I would try a different approach as the effort would not show a result in the USA.

▲ ▲ ▲ ▲

Request for a British Posthumous Honor

I had exhausted my efforts to get recognition for Searl's crew in the United States for saving lives in the villages of Loudwater and Penn in England, so I turned my direction toward England.

Through my prior business connections at the highest levels, I made important contacts in the political and business spheres of the United Kingdom.

Knowing the importance of networking and without providing unnecessary details of the chain of events, I contacted the Hon. Steve Baker, the Member of Parliament for the area in Buckinghamshire County where the plane crash had occurred. After some discussions with Mr. Baker and further interaction with his parliamentary secretary, Sue Hynard, I informed them of my intention to attend the Remembrance Day service at the Holy Trinity church in Penn, when the community honors both their own World War fallen, and the American airmen from the Tomahawk Warrior.

I added that certain descendants of the airmen I had traced would accompany me. I was exploring the possibilities of whether the authorities would consider offering a posthumous honor for the sacrifice the American Airmen made in 1944.

After my discussions with Mr. Baker, on August 15, 2019. I received the following email from a Mr. Joe Bradshaw, with the Civic and Lieutenancy Office, of her Majesty's Lord Lieutenants Office

Dear David (if I may),
I would like to introduce myself to you in the hope that we can put something together for you should you decide to visit the United Kingdom. In my role here at County Hall I support Her Majesty's Lord-Lieutenant of Buckinghamshire and also the Chairman of Buckinghamshire County Council and it would be a great honour if we can arrange something that will offer belated thanks to the crew on behalf of the people of High Wycombe and the surrounding area for the bravery of the crew who diverted the aircraft away from the populated area on 12th August 1944.

For my part, I live in High Wycombe and served with the Royal Air Force for 28 years and had the good fortune of serving alongside members of the United States Air Force in several postings across the world. For the past 18 years, I have supported the Buckinghamshire Lieutenancy and Buckinghamshire County Council by providing Civic and Ceremonial guidance and support.

It would be good to have an understanding about your travel dates

so that we can put some sort of programme together for you and your party. It would also be worth hearing your views on whether we should also provide scrolls for other crew members and perhaps any other expectations that you might have. Councillor Brian Roberts, who is the current Chairman of Buckinghamshire County Council, would like to present the scroll if the visit goes ahead.

If I can make the arrangements, would any of the following appeal to you?:

1. *A Service of Thanksgiving for the Crew at Penn Church.*
2. *Afternoon Tea at Penn House–the official residence of The Earl and Countess Howe*
3. *A visit to RAF High Wycombe–it is now the home of Headquarters Air Command, but as you know, in WW2 it was the home of Headquarters Bomber Command.*

We would, of course, invite the US Ambassador (or a member of his staff) to the event too.

I am probably running before I have learned to walk, but please let me know what your outline plans are and we will do our best to assist you. I have a 15-seater minibus at my disposal, so transportation to collect you from London Heathrow Airport would be very easy as it is only 25 minutes away by motorway.

Sincerely
Joe Bradshaw

Dear Joe, (likewise, if I may)

First, thanks to Sue Hynard for connecting me to your office.

I am, of course, extremely grateful to you for your very kind proposal to provide the late 1st Lt. Charles Searl and his crew with a posthumous award of thanks for diverting his aircraft and saving many lives on August 12th 1944.

You have probably seen the material I sent to Mrs. Hynard and are familiar with the details of how I came to be involved. I listed a summary of who might attend the proposed ceremony in November in this synopsis.

Upon discovering the facts of the TW in 2016 and how it confirmed what I had witnessed in 1944, it led to further discovery. After researching in more depth, I tracked down Lt. Searl's only surviving daughter, Mrs. Cheryl Surfus. Later, I discovered a diary that the Navigator of the plane had written, 2nd Lt. Saul Kempner. Using various methods at my disposal, I located Saul's surviving nieces (the daughters of his twin brother, Irving Kempner). Their names are Andrea Blake (Kempner) and Janice Morgan.

I have found no any other relatives yet, but this could change.

Kind Regards
David Huntley

These initial contacts became the basis for continuing communications over several months and establishing the dates when an official presentation would take place.

▲ ▲ ▲ ▲

Presentation Of The Scrolls Of Honour

I will not tax the reader's patience by giving a tedious and very detailed account of the extensive number of emails and phone calls it took to bring all the parties involved, together, in England and in the USA, to agree on the schedule and format. I will instead provide a more visual account and a brief description.

The Lord-Lieutenant's Office sent the following invitations out to the parties involved.

Here is the itinerary for the Tomahawk Warrior award ceremony in the U.K. on Remembrance Day, November 10th 2019.

10:00 am The Rev. Mike Bissett, Vicar of the Holy Trinity Church in Penn, will hold a service, followed by a reading of war dead names, and laying of wreaths at the War Memorial.

Penn House 2:00 pm Guests arrive 2.30 pm Welcome by The Countess Howe

2.35 pm Short speech by Mr. Brian Roberts, Chairman of Buckinghamshire County Council, who will then present the scroll to the families

2.40 pm Response by Mr. David Huntley, who will recount that day in 1944.

Afternoon Tea Served

4:00 pm Carriages

Dignitaries attending with the Countess of Howe and Mr. Roberts, members from RAF High Wycombe, the local Royal British Legion, local RAFA members, local Parish Council and several local dignitaries including, The Hon. Steve Baker, Member of Parliament. The US Embassy has been invited to send a representative to today's function. We will also have a number of our Deputy Lieutenants in attendance.

Here is the link to Penn House http://www.pennhouse.org.uk/

Monday November 11th 2019

The Group will tour RAF High Wycombe and visit the historical office of "Bomber Harris."

The group from the USA, comprising Mrs. Janice Kempner Morgan, Dr. Alex Morgan, Andrea Kempner Blake, her partner, Dr Ian Zitron, and David E. Huntley who will also represent Mrs. Cheryl Surfus, the daughter of the pilot 1st Lt. Charles Searl. Mrs. Surfus could not travel from the USA.

We assembled at the Holy Trinity Church as the bells were ringing for the morning service. Remembrance Sunday 10th November and the start of the morning service was at 10:00 am so that the congregation could observe, with millions around the country, the traditional United Kingdom two-minute silence at 11:00 am. The morning was a little overcast, with a mild temperature and a fresh breeze. The pathway leading to the church entrance had British Flags on each side representing the fallen soldiers from the local Parish in both world wars. There were American flags representing the nine airmen of the Tomahawk Warrior neatly displayed with the other flags. There were also placed small wooden crosses next to each flag.

To get an idea of the historical holiness of this little church in the English bucolic countryside below, I include the extract of the description of the magnificent piece of architectural history written by a local historian, Miles Green, with whom I have had many communications over the years. (Citation)

"Christians have prayed and worshiped in Holy Trinity since its foundation just over 800 years ago. The nave is late 12th-century (also the font, consecration crosses and stone tomb), the south aisle and low tower are early 14th-century with the chancel and Lady Chapel largely rebuilt in brick in the 1730s. A clerestory and the fine queen-post roof with arcading were added in c.1400. They built the nave of flint, with clunch and tiles incorporated into parts of the quoins, buttresses and porch. They removed all the exterior roughcast in 1952 to reveal the flint-work and stone."

"The 'Penn Doom', one of only five surviving wooden tympanums in the country, is a 12-foot wide painting of the 'Last Judgement' on oak panels and hangs above the chancel arch. It has twice been on display in the Victoria & Albert Museum in London."

"There is also an attractive arrangement of 14th-century Penn floor tiles set into the floor of the Lady Chapel, and a fine collection of Tudor and Stuart brasses of the Penn family. There is a well-preserved example of Queen Anne's arms on the nave wall. Six grandchildren of William Penn, the Quaker, founder of Pennsylvania, are buried in a large family vault under the centre of the nave. Heraldic shields on the roof corbels portray eight centuries of English history. There is a particularly fine collection of 18th and early 19th-century wall monuments mainly to the Curzons and Howes."

"In the churchyard there are many well-known names, two of which are notorious: **Donald Maclean, who defected to Russia in 1951,** and **David Blakeley,** who was shot in 1955 by **Ruth Ellis,** the last woman to be hanged in England."

"In the Second World War, the church tower was an observation post of the Home Guard's nightly watch from a wooden sentry box erected on the roof. They could see Windsor Castle, Ascot racecourse, Northolt airport and the outskirts of London, as well as American planes landing at Brackley in Northampton some 40 miles away." *(Miles Green) (End Citation)*

The service began inside the church and the Vicar, Rev. Mike Bissett, arranged for the two nieces of Lt. Saul Kempner, Andrea Blake and Janice Morgan, to come forward with a wreath for a blessing. After a wonderful sermon and hymns sung, the congregation and the U.S. visitors walked to the War Memorial across the street. The Vicar had Andrea and Janice read the names of the nine American airmen out loud and place the wreath on the Memorial. A member of the congregation did the same for the fallen military of the local Parish community.

The pathway to Holy Trinity church lined with British flags for local parishioners fallen in two world wars and American flags for nine airmen who died in Penn in 1944

The B-17 Tomahawk Warrior: A WWII Final Honor

Copyright, Huntley Associates Dallas, Inc.

*Andrea and Janice at the War Memorial after
reading out the names who perished*
Copyright, Huntley Associates Dallas, Inc.

One interesting point to note is that after the service, while I was speaking with a Deacon of the church, I enumerated some of the amazing and bizarre coincidences I had experienced while working on my book. The Deacon, after listening attentively, turned to me and said, "David, these are not coincidences. This is God telling you, you must write this story."

Many more aspects of the story have come to light since then, and touched me deeply. It seems as if an unseen hand has guided me forward and given me an ever deeper connection to the souls of these airmen.

After leaving the church and the War Memorial, we drove to a delightful pub nearby, The Crown, dating back to the 17th century. Happily, the food was of the 21st century and quite delicious. With some great conversation about today's event so far and feeling content after such a good meal, we set off for the Penn House Estate to meet Lord and Countess Howe.

We drove into the grounds of a lovely English country estate and parked close to the house. The Penn House Estate, Penn Street, near Amersham, Buckinghamshire, situated in one of the prettiest parts of the Chilterns Hills, has been passed down in a direct family line since the Middle Ages. Earl Howe, the present custodian, is the successor of at least fifteen previous generations of the Penn, Curzon, and Howe families who have made Penn their home. As it stands today, the estate owes much to grants of land made by Henry VIII and his son, Edward VI, to David and Sybil Penn in recognition of the latter's role as nursemaid to the royal children during the 1530s and 40s.

We were met in the foyer by the gracious Countess Howe and introduced to other members of the gathering, including my primary contact in the U.K. who had made all the preceding arrangements, Joe Bradshaw, of the Lord Lieutenant's office in the Buckinghamshire County Council.

Lord Howe joined us and gave a brief speech welcoming everyone to his residence. (The Earl, at the time of the ceremony, was the Deputy Leader of the House of Lords, and was a previous Minister of Defense in the British Cabinet)

The Hon. Brian Roberts, Chairman of the Bucks County Council, made a brief speech of how the Council was pleased to honor posthumously, the Tomahawk Warrior crew for their sacrifice in WWII and to present Scrolls of Honour.

I stepped forward to receive the Scroll in Honour of 1st Lt. Charles Searl on behalf of his daughter Cheryl Surfus, who was unable to attend. The nieces of 2nd Lt. Saul Kempner, Andrea Blake and Janice Morgan received another framed Scroll.

I was asked to make my address describing the reason this Award was given and my thanks for the presentation.

The B-17 Tomahawk Warrior: A WWII Final Honor

Address by David E. Huntley to the Scroll Ceremony for the Tomahawk Warrior Crew- Remembrance Day, November 10th 2019, United Kingdom

"My Lord, Mr. Chairman, Distinguished Guests, Ladies and Gentlemen, this has been a long journey. As a WWII survivor of the London Blitz and my late wife Sophie having lived under Nazi occupation of France, her own brother sent to work under forced labor in German factories, together, we always had our admiration for the sacrifice of the Americans and Allies who saved us all from tyranny.

"My family had come through four years of the bombing of London, when seeing the effects of the V1 rockets, my father decided in June or July 1944 to move some of us to Loudwater to live temporarily with an aunt at her cottage on Station Road. He left our two sisters in London as they had good-paying jobs, but later, when the V2s began raining down around September of that year, they became terrified.

"One morning at approximately 6:30 just as it was getting light, a frightening noise and vibration came toward us and shook our cottage to its foundations, waking up my brothers and me from our sleep, as a plane with stuttering engines flew directly over us. Around 30 to 40 seconds later there was a massive explosion.

"My brother Bob said, "That thing is down. Come on, let's see it."

"My thought at the time was, *I should be able to add to my shrapnel collection*. It would enhance my standing at the local school, whose students were not too fond of this foreigner – me from London.

"We ran headlong up Derehams Lane and across various fields and stiles, following the smoke we could see in the distance and coming out at Whitehorse Lane and onto Outgate Lane. We eventually reached a metal fence or a gate, which gave us a clear view of a devastating image. It stayed with me thereafter all my life.

"I had seen people pulled from rubble in London, but they were still whole human beings. This was much different, as there were auxiliary crew picking up body parts and placing them in these galvanized bins or tubs. There were parachutes lying in places, and one was in a hedge nearby. I asked my brother, 'Surely they couldn't have tried to bale out, could they?' Of course, it was later when I realized these were being used as shrouds.

"One man called over to another man who then approached us and told us firmly to 'Shove off, you are not allowed to be here.' He used different words to 'Shove off.'

"I did not take any debris. I suppose I was afraid of what I may pick up! It was 72 years later when I saw the official story of this crash and posted it on my website describing how I had witnessed it. It must have been a terrifying moment for the pilot, 1st Lt. Charles Searl, knowing he had safely brought his crew through so many successful bombing missions, only to now bravely navigate his crippled aircraft away from populated areas and tragically crashing in open farmland. I then took on representing the souls of these brave men, tracing the surviving families, and bringing them together for the first time in 75 years later.

"Therefore, we are here now, and I wish to offer my sincere thanks to Lord Howe and Countess Howe for hosting us today, to Mr. Brian Roberts, Chairman of the Buckinghamshire County Council for authorizing and presenting the Scrolls, and finally to Mr. Joe Bradshaw of Her Majesty's Lord Lieutenant's Office who I personally cannot thank enough for the way he received my initial inquiry and request. He has been simply amazing and frankly, your efforts, Joe, have brought me a sense of immense achievement. Apart from my 62 years marriage to Sophie, this has been the pinnacle of my life's successes, more than my business developments over two continents, or the Founding of a British/American business organization in the USA, or even as my appointment as a Director of Historic Royal Palaces, this, today, crowns it all!

Thank you."

The gathering mingled and held pockets of conversation while partaking of tea and sandwiches. It was a most elegant occasion held in a historic house, with walls hung with portraits and scenes of British history. Some aspects of the family history go back to Henry VIII.

Both Lord Howe and Lady Howe were gracious hosts and very engaging.

Mr. Roberts and the author
Courtesy of Angela Howard

David E. Huntley

Mr. Roberts, myself, Janice, and Andrea
Courtesy of Angela Howard

L-R Lord Howe, Janice Morgan, Andrea Morgan, the author, Countess Howe
Photo courtesy of Angela Howard

The B-17 Tomahawk Warrior: A WWII Final Honor

To these gallant American airmen, collectively known as the "Tomahawk Warrior Crew" who on August 12, 1944, sacrificed their lives to prevent their aircraft from crashing on the homes of the residents of Loudwater & Penn in the County of Buckinghamshire & who dedicate this memorial in grateful memory.

1st Lt. Charles J. Searl
2nd Lt. Albert L. Dion
2nd Lt. Saul J. Kempner
2nd Lt. Leo C. Welsh
S/Sgt. James A. Beaty
Sgt. Orville M. Wilson
Sgt. Alfred Bueffel
Sgt. Albert W. Knight
Sgt. Cecil E. Kennedy

Commemorated in perpetuity
by the residents of Buckinghamshire

Mr Brian Roberts
Chairman, Buckinghamshire County Council

A copy of the Scroll of Honour from the people of Buckinghamshire, England, Issued on Remembrance Sunday, November 10, 2019, in Penn, Bucks, England
Image copyright Huntley Associates Dallas, Inc.

I would like to make it clear, as I have done throughout this book, that I wanted to ensure the wording of this award reflected the accuracy of its statement and the proper sense of its intention. This book is not about a plane nicknamed, 'The Tomahawk Warrior,' but about the crew who were known as the 'Tomahawk Warriors.' In any event, the plane they flew the day of the crash was not their usual plane, and it was one they had never flown before.

No, this is not a post-mortem of aircraft machinery, it's the story of nine human beings, young men in their prime, who had risked their lives successfully flying twenty-eight missions at 28,000 ft in sub-zero temperatures, for as long as 11 hours, usually, while being shot at by flak from the ground and Luftwaffe fighters in the air. Then, on one fatal day, they became torn and mangled pieces of flesh and blood, being retrieved by auxiliary personnel from among the debris of aircraft strewn over a wide area.

It would be for a time in the future, when I would be old enough to recognize these souls needed to be brought home to their loved ones and their actions to save my life and of my future family, to be officially recognized. They can rest in peace knowing that their sacrifice had not been in vain.

▲ ▲ ▲ ▲

A Tribute to the Rev. Oscar Muspratt, Vicar of Pen 1944

The following article reproduced by courtesy of Flak News, the official news publication of the 398th Bomb Group Association, is a tribute to the Rev. Oscar Muspratt who played such an important role of identifying the names of the crew who died on August 12, 1944. He developed important contacts with the parents and loved ones of the deceased crew.

Muspratt, Penn Vicar, Dead at 93 By Allen Ostrom

Rev. Oscar Muspratt, former vicar of Penn Church, Buckinghamshire, England, died March 8, 2000, at 93. While only one of many, many vicars to serve the Penn Church during its 900-year history, Rev. Muspratt will is remembered as the one who went directly to Gen. Jimmy Doolittle at 8th Air Force Headquarters to seek names. These would be the names of the nine members of a 398th crew that perished near his church in 1944. He wanted to honor the men and to write to their relatives in the United States. Gen. Doolittle obliged and Rev. Muspratt followed through not only with the letters but also had their names inscribed on the church's 'Book of Honour'. In 1990, the 398th Tour to England and Scotland visited Penn, and Rev. Muspratt, and saw not only the venerable book but also a row of American flags representing each of the deceased crew members. The tour also took in the very location where Charles Searl's B-17 and crew crashed at a place known as Lude Farm. Ron Setter was a boy of 12 living on the farm at the time and he vividly recalled being thrown from his bed when the plane and all its bombs exploded some two hundred yards from his home. Ron, Peter Halliday and Johanna Sienkiewicz combined to arrange for the 398th travel party to visit Penn. They were part of the Chiltern Historical Aircraft Preservation Group, and combined to do the research on the Searl crash. Rev. Muspratt, the 55th in an ecclesiastical lineage dating back to 1349, connected the little town of Penn with William Penn, founder of the state of Pennsylvania. He wrote, 'If the Tomahawk Warriors (name of the Searl B-17) perished defending a church and a parish descended from a founder of the great democracy which, at the time America was itself defending in war, then, don't you see, the Tomahawk Warriors sacrificed their lives defending an American shrine.' "My church was the shrine, right here, in the hinterland of England."

Printed in Flak News Volume 15, Number 3, Page(s) 9, July 2000

There were many letters between the Rev. Muspratt, the Army and the families. His actions ensured that the American crew would never be forgotten.

▲ ▲ ▲ ▲

The incumbent vicar, the Rev. Mike Bissett, of both the Holy Trinity Church of Penn and St. Margaret's Church of Tylers Green, continues the tradition of his predecessors by holding an annual Memorial Service on Remembrance Sunday. While they read out the names of the local parishioners who gave their lives in wars, they also remember the nine Americans who made the ultimate sacrifice in 1944.

In 2019, the service included our delegation from America. We attended the church prior to the Award Ceremony at Lord Howe's residence hosted by Countess Howe.

Rev. Bissett, Ms. Morgan and Ms. Blake.
Photo copyright Huntley Associates, Inc.

Rev. Bissett, who retired in 2022, was the 63rd Vicar in the history of the Holy Trinity Church in the village of Penn, Buckinghamshire, U.K.

The following is an extract of a tribute from the Penn and Tylers Green Blog,[150] by Peter Brown.

Mike, 66, took on the role of vicar of both Holy Trinity, Penn and St Margaret's, Tylers Green in 2004. Previously the churches had separate incumbents.

A friend in stressful times... MIKE WILL be greatly missed in Penn and Tylers Green.

He has great warmth and understanding, meeting challenging times in the community and stressful times within local families with calmness and positivity. A spiritual leader and a reliable friend to many, with or without faith.

It didn't take long for Mike and Ali, his wife of nearly 40 years, and their children Chris, James and Suzy to become an integral and important part of the Penn and Tylers Green community. They will leave with the love and best wishes of so many people.

▲ ▲ ▲ ▲

---

[150] https://pennandtylersgreen.com/2021/11/15/mike-bisset-penn-and-tylers-greens-first-combined-vicar-calls-it-a-day/

CHAPTER THIRTEEN

THE COMMEMORATIVE MARKER

▲ ▲ ▲ ▲

Designing, Making, and Placing of the Commemorative Marker

WHILE MY SUGGESTION IN 2019 to have a commemorative marker established to honor the nine American airmen who died in Penn in 1944 met with general enthusiasm, the location of where to place it became fraught with many logistical and bureaucratic difficulties.

Originally, the discussion with Joe Bradshaw of the Lord Lieutenants Office, who was my principal liaison with the Bucks County, in England, concerned the position of a marker on the roadside nearest the farm field where the crash had occurred. After several communications between Joe Bradshaw and the County Council, Joe said it appears to be difficult based on the letter he received.

I will not tax the reader's patience with a long explanation, but I will let you know that the response came from the Senior Road Safety Engineer, Transport For Buckinghamshire, Network Safety Team. It comprised 19 paragraphs of 538 words saying in effect, that no permanent roadside memorials are allowed for road safety reasons by the distraction to motorists.

This policy relates primarily to many memorials that are placed at the roadside following a fatal road traffic collision. I could understand how this could lead to many unregulated memorials, but I felt that an important historical marker should receive a more flexible examination of its merits.

Nevertheless, I had no choice but to accept the status quo and seek other ways of establishing a permanent marker.

It was the Earl, Lord Frederick Howe, and his wife Countess Elizabeth Howe, who became the catalyst in moving my efforts in the right direction. In a conversation with Lord Howe, I expressed my concern about my lack of progress. We were at an impasse with getting the Marker established, and he said the quest for a historical marker was "a worthy cause." I felt that the only way we could establish this marker would be on a private property nearby to the crash site. He said he would think about it and give me his thoughts.

In the meantime, I had already found that the current owner of Lude Farm, which had been the scene of the crash, had suggested to the Penn Parish Council, the local authority, that a marker should be set up at the War Memorial near the Holy Trinity church. He felt this would be more suitable and will prevent motorists and visitors from clogging already very narrow access roads near his farm.

My opinion on this subject differed because there would never be hordes of visitors. Only a few descendant relatives and, perhaps, a few avid readers of my book who wished to pay their respects.

I wrote to the farm owner with a personal appeal to have the marker established on a public footpath on his property next to the crash site. It was some weeks later when I received a reply from his secretary advising that because of the bad weather in recent months; the farmer was much too busy to deal with this issue, but would give it his consideration later that year. I did not receive any further communication.

It was soon after this, when Lord Howe introduced me to a local landowner named Mr. Paddy Hopkirk, MBE and his wife Mrs. Jenny Hopkirk, DL. Paddy had expressed a keen interest in perhaps having the Marker on his property, at Parsonage Farm. He suggested we could place it on his property boundary line with a public footpath facing SSE in a direct line of sight to the crash site on the neighboring Lude Farm.

The dialog between Paddy and me began in early 2020. His Irish humor, together with my banter, gave the two of us old codgers a "raison d'être." He had the same desire as I did to honor the contribution made by America toward the British Isles in the Second World War. Sadly, and much to my dismay, as I was writing these last few chapters of this tome in 2022, Paddy Hopkirk, MBE, passed away at age 89. As I had been in touch with him just a couple of weeks prior to him leaving us, it was quite a shock to realize I would never hear his Irish brogue again. I shall never forget the conversations we have had on our WhatsApp communications and the Irish humor that kept us both smiling. I feel so bad for his wife Jenny for her very sad loss. Jenny too, had also been a keen 'behind the scenes' supporter of our project.

The tradition of Public Footpaths[151] in England was one of the first issues we faced. One of the unique aspects of footpaths in England, Scotland, and Wales is that one can virtually traverse the length and breadth of the country almost using footpaths alone. Now that we no longer had to be concerned about county road safety issues, it was necessary to ensure we did not contravene any footpath rules of access. I made the acquaintance of Kate Ashbrook, General Secretary of The Open Spaces Society[152] (OSS), the society, with its country-wide membership, which maintains and monitors the free access to public and sometimes private lands. "It funds legal action by the society and its members in defence (sic) of commons, paths and open spaces." The OSS has successfully taken farmers to court for blocking public footpaths and preventing access.

These cases include ploughing up footpaths on farm fields, planting crops on footpaths, and preventing access to the public. Guilty parties have had to pay hefty fines and finish up with criminal records. Yes, public access to lands on designated footpaths, or in certain cases bridle-paths, has been the law for many centuries in England.

Most of the work of determining the location for the sign, its design

---

[151] https://www.gov.uk > right-of-way-open-access-land > use-public-rights-of-way
[152] *Https://www.oss.org.uk*

The B-17 Tomahawk Warrior: A WWII Final Honor

and size, its manufacture and final installation was conducted during the period of Covid in 2020. There were many months of communication between me in the USA and a team Paddy and I had 'assembled' in the U.K.

Let me introduce you to the team that helped make this project happen. Mr. Paddy Hopkirk would address me to the group in various capacities such as David Huntley, Project Leader USA (Witness to the immediate aftermath of the crash), or sometimes as The Boss, or Godfather. Oh, how I miss his Irish humor!

Paddy always insisted that he wanted to remain anonymous. He wanted no accolades from helping in this project. While he was generously willing to allow the Commemorative Marker to be placed on his property, he was very apprehensive about visitors straying from the footpath and stumbling into his property and invading his personal privacy, which was Parsonage Farm. This was very understandable when you consider he was one of England's most famous personalities. After all, it was he who put the Cooper Mini on the world map when he won the Monte Carlo Rally in 1964. I'm sure there are, and will be, many more biographies written about Paddy and his achievements both in and out of motor sports.

Thinking about him now, and wishing he were still here, I believe I would tell him, "So, Paddy, you cannot set Bertie, your dog, on me now, just because I spilled the beans on your fame. After all, your humble approach to my quest and the diligent manner you set about helping me speaks volumes about why you should be recognized. I simply could never have completed the task without your input.

As you often said, like me, you did it because without the sacrifice of America back then, we might all be speaking German today. It isn't a bad thing, but in 1944 it would have been terrible."

Paddy Hopkirk MBE has been the full driving force of my team in England, and this could never have reached completion without him. The relatives of the Tomahawk Warrior crew and I will be forever grateful to him for his contribution and advice.

Let me introduce to you the other members of the team:

- Joe Bradshaw, Town Clerk of High Wycombe, was previously with the office of The Lord Lieutenant of Buckinghamshire and was my first primary contact with the British Authorities. Joe really went above and beyond to help attain recognition for the Tomahawk Warrior crew.
- Craig Smith, the Director of Aces-High Art Gallery[153], had his in-house artist to design the Marker, **free of charge,** for which we are extremely grateful.
- Richard Taylor, the artist with Aces-High, produced the artistic work of the design of the Marker.
- Colin Hudson, also of Aces-High, was the one who introduced me to Craig.
- Mike Hayes, of Signal Display Brokers,[154] manufactured the actual Marker Sign from the design by Aces-High. His company also produced this **free of charge,** as their contribution to this effort. Again, with sincere thanks from me on behalf of all the relatives.
- Matthew O'Keeffe, the owner of the oldest pub in England, The Royal England Standard,[155] which is situated close by to our site. Matthew has offered to provide directions to visitors at his establishment to the Commemorative Marker. Since the Marker is in an obscure location, having a place in the vicinity where accurate directions can be obtained is a valuable asset. The food and hospitality are another good reason to visit his establishment.

---

[153] https://www.aces-high.com/
[154] https://signanddisplaybrokers.com
[155] https://theoldestpub.com/gallery

- Sean Smith, kindly provided some overhead drone footage of the Marker.
- Kate Ashbrooke, the Head of the Open Spaces Organization in England, gave me valuable advice on the Public Footpath and Bridle Path laws and protocols.
- Ian McEnnis of the Buckinghamshire County Council cleared the permission process.

Other people who have provided input to me or Paddy during the period of the development of the Marker, or have an interest in the history of this region:

- Geoff Rice -Trustee of the Nuthampstead Airfield Museum, which was the home of the USAAF 398th Bomb Group in WWII (Author's note; Sadly, as I was writing this chapter, I received a note from his wife, Marilyn, that Geoff had passed away on Christmas Eve 2022. Many will miss him for his tireless work supporting the legacy of the 398th Bomb Group of the United States 8th Air Force. (R.I.P.)
- Marilyn-Rice Gibbs – President of the 398th Bomb Group Memorial Association.
- Ian James, a local resident, and historian with extensive knowledge of the 1944 event and was helpful to me and especially to Paddy Hopkirk.
- David Hardie, a relative to a local resident and a commercial national airline pilot with extensive knowledge of aviation, and this tragedy in particular,[156] has been very supportive of me, and with whom I have exchanged many important emails.
- Brian Roberts, previous Chairman of Buckinghamshire County Council and who had presented the Scrolls of Honor in 2019.

---

[156] Chapter 7, Likely Cause of the Crash.

- Miles Green, the Penn Village official Historian.
- Mike Bissett, the Vicar of Penn Holy Trinity Church, where an annual tribute is conducted for the deceased crew of the Tomahawk Warrior.
- Jeff Lipman, a local resident.
- Dan Dorehill, a local resident.
- Peggy and John Walker, whose windows got blown out, and a wall cracked in their house when the plane crashed and exploded. (According to Ian James, a local historian).

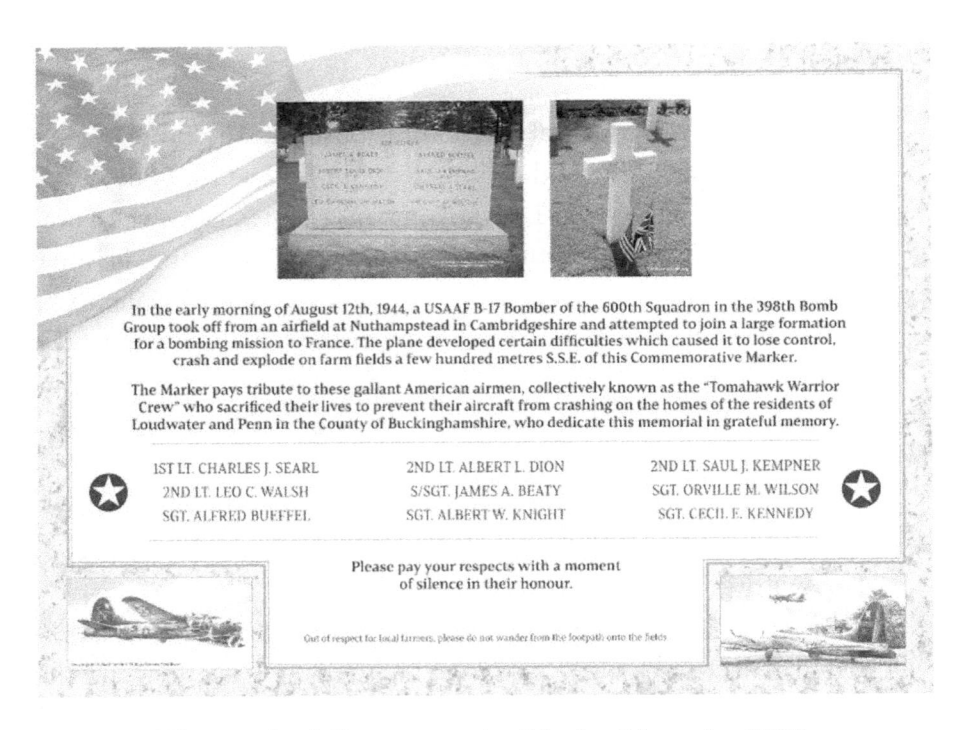

The completed Commemorative Marker, November 2020.
The exact location of the crash site is **51° 36' 57" N and 0° 40' 51" W**

The B-17 Tomahawk Warrior: A WWII Final Honor

Office of the Mayor

August 22, 2021

To: The Earl, Lord Frederick Howe, and Countess Howe, Her Majesty's Lord-Lieutenant of Buckinghamshire.

On behalf of the City of McKinney, Texas, and its citizens, I wish to offer our special greetings, and our deep gratitude for the kind support you have shown toward David E. Huntley. Mr. Huntley is an engaged McKinney resident that has been instrumental in posthumously honoring the American crew of the B-17 bomber which crashed in Penn, Buckinghamshire, on the 12th of August 1944. This endeavor has revived the human element to a tragic event that took place many years ago.

We are particularly grateful for your personal introduction to Mr. Paddy Hopkirk, MBE, and Mrs. Jenny Hopkirk, DL, who proved to be invaluable in helping Mr. Huntley in getting the Commemorative Marker designed, produced, and installed on their property. With this accomplishment, the grateful men and women can pay their respects for the sacrifice this brave American crew made during WWII.

Sincerely,

Mayor George Fuller

222 N. Tennessee • P.O. Box 517 • McKinney, Texas • 75070
972.547.7507 • Fax 972.547.2607

The Letter of Thanks from the Mayor of the City of McKinney, Texas, to Lord Howe.

*Paddy and Jenny with the new sign.
Courtesy of the late Paddy Hopkirk*

*David presenting Lord and Lady Howe a letter from
Mayor George Fuller, of McKinney, Texas.*

The B-17 Tomahawk Warrior: A WWII Final Honor

*Mission accomplished – Paddy, the author, & Bertie.
Copyright Huntley Associates Dallas, Inc.*

▲ ▲ ▲ ▲

Why Is This Story Important to So Many People?

Nowadays, we hear many stories about finding lost WWII ships under the ocean, war planes discovered in jungles or buried in sand dunes. Invariably, the narrative of those discoveries revolves around the machines. What caused them to crash, sink, or disappear is investigated, often in depth. Perhaps the names of who died in the wrecks are discovered. It is rare, however, to explore deeply enough the lives of the heroes and to bring their own unique stories to life for the benefit of their descendants and their future generations.

I don't ask you to take note of any accolade directed at me personally but, more importantly, of the joy, relief, and comfort these descendants have experienced because of my efforts. I take my motto from Victor Hugo, **"Our minds are enriched by what we receive, our hearts by what we give."**

The following is a message from Mrs. Shelly Surfus Loe, the granddaughter of the pilot of the Tomahawk Warrior, 1st Lt. Charles Searl. She talks about her mother, Mrs. Cheryl Surfus, with whom I have since interviewed extensively.

I cannot even express to you what finding you have done for my mom. She literally thanks me every day. We have always heard the stories and talked about my grandpa and what he did. My mom is just... filled with emotions ever since you two have talked. I am truly grateful that she could connect with you! It's hard to put into words how truly amazing all of this is. My mom told me about you and your Sophie. True love is really remarkable, and I will think of you often during the next couple of weeks. Merry Christmas to you and all of your family.

Here are some comments from other family members I had brought together because of my research. If I do nothing else in life, I feel I have accomplished something worthwhile in bringing these families together after almost 79 years, since their loved ones sacrificed their lives for all of us.

The following quotes are from Andrea Kempner Blake, the niece of the Navigator, 2nd Lt. Saul Kempner and her sister Janice Morgan.

Andrea Kempner Blake: You are a fine man, David Huntley. I don't quite understand it, but then again, maybe I don't have to. I do, however, believe that God sent you as a messenger to my family and to the families of the other crew members to help in honoring their memory and telling the story of their sacrifice.

Cheryl Searl Surfus called, and we had a lovely conversation. She had the same response to your initial call as I had, shock, disbelief, and gratitude. But now my connection with my Uncle Saul is that much stronger. I have read all that you forwarded to me. What a compilation, what work!

April 25, 2019
Andrea Kempner Blake again:
Thank you so much for your visit, David.

They are rare moments indeed when you have the chance to cross paths with someone who impacts your life on a deeply personal, emotional, spiritual level.

You are, for me, one of those rare individuals. You are a truly extraordinary, special man. Your Tomahawk Warrior Project brought us together. You helped us feel more connected to our deceased Uncle Saul than we ever had before. You are a link in our family, bridging the gap between his life and ours. And now <u>you</u> are like family. You witnessed the story and now we know it, and so do our children and our children's children. What you did for our family is impossible to repay. We are now more committed than ever to keeping his memory alive. We know that on the anniversary of his death, August 12, 1944, which corresponds to 23rd of Av, 5704, on the Jewish calendar, we will honor his life by lighting a memorial candle, and with a tribute and special prayers at our Synagogue. We will continue to remember him telling the story of his sacrifice that day. You helped bring this all into focus for us. I am grateful that God brought you into our lives. It is like a beautiful and poignant dream.

"I hope we meet again.
Please stay well, and remember, you have family in Detroit.
Much love and appreciation,
Andrea.

Andrea's sister, Janice Kempner Morgan, wrote this poignant note in *2019*:

Dear David,
I wanted to take a moment during the season of miracles to say thank you for all you've done for me and my family this year. You have taken me on an adventure I never could have expected. You have introduced me to an uncle I never knew and allowed me to see a side of my father I had never considered.

You facilitated the return of Uncle Saul's diary, which my father and grandparents thought lost forever. We now have an heirloom to enrich our family history. You enlightened us to his and the crew of the Tomahawk Warrior's heroism, giving us a proud story to pass on to our children and grandchildren.

But you didn't stop there. You continued to seek recognition and honors for the crew of that fateful flight. You lead on us on a pilgrimage to England to touch the soil where my uncle gave his life and to meet strangers who 75 years later continue to honor him and his crew. We received and will treasure the certificate recognizing Saul J. Kempner's sacrifice.

Best of all, you've become a dear friend, and one can never have too many of those. Please enjoy the enclosed memories.

Wishing you the warmest holiday season.
Janice Morgan

(Author's note; Janice had presented me with a book of photographs memorializing the time when Saul Kempner's diary finally returned to the safekeeping of the family.)

▲ ▲ ▲ ▲

CHAPTER FOURTEEN

A MOMENT IN AMERICAN HISTORY

▲ ▲ ▲ ▲

Joseph Kennedy Jr. And The Tomahawk Warrior Connection

Public domain US Navy file photo of Joseph P. Kennedy, Jr.

IN SEARL'S EARLY LIFE, CHAPTER 7, I described the 'Five Musketeers' as Searl and his four boyhood friends were known. One of the boys, Joe Chvala, (pronounced Kwa-la) became a navy pilot. Another *irony* in the story of the Tomahawk Warrior is that this particular 'Musketeer', was asked by Joseph Kennedy, the older brother of John F. Kennedy, to join him on a special secret mission, which Chvala ultimately declined. Joe Kennedy died on that mission together with Lt. Wilfred Willy, his engineer technician and co-pilot, when his plane exploded over the English Channel on **12ᵗʰ August 1944!** The very **same date** of the Tomahawk Warrior tragedy.

During his campaign trip to Dallas/Fort Worth in 1960, John F. Kennedy made a stop to honor Edna Willy, the widow of Lt. Wilfred Willy. You can see historic photos of that day in the Dallas Morning News Archives.

Joe Chvala passed away in 2000 at seventy-nine. Later, his younger brother, Jack, who also served in the Navy at the end of the war, gave an interview to Jed Buelow, a reporter from the Tomahawk Leader newspaper.

In his interview, he described how the 'Five Musketeers' each became a war hero. Regarding his own brother, he described how Joe left the University of Wisconsin-Oshkosh to volunteer in the Navy. He co-piloted a PBY-1 (B-24 equivalent) bomber for 33 missions in Erope. He took part in sinking U-boats in the Bay of Biscay and the English Channel.

Jack described how on one mission Joe, as co-pilot, had to force-land the PBY-1 single-handedly after the pilot next to him got shot and killed. For this action and his other wartime service, they awarded him with the Navy's Air Medal, among other recognitions.

Jack continued to say that Joseph Kennedy Jr. asked his brother Joe, to co-pilot a mission called Operation Aphrodite after Joe completed his last mission. Joe declined because he had already completed three extra missions and was ready to return to the United States. Kennedy died on his mission when his plane exploded over Southern England on August 12, 1944.

Jack told the reporter that when Joe returned after the war, he didn't have the same enthusiasm about flying. "From that moment on, the glamor of flying left me."

After tracing a nephew of Joe Chvala, a Mr. Chuck Chvala, in Madison, Wisconsin, the story of his uncle Joe became even more interesting. Later, I learned how close a friend he may have become to Joseph Kennedy. Chuck introduced me to his cousin, Robert (Bob) Chvala, who was Joe Chvala's son.

Bob spent many hours with Joe, his father; although they did a lot of hunting and fishing together, he rarely talked about the war.

Still, Bob remembers he had heard from his dad about the forced landing, that there were other injured crew on the plane besides the dead pilot. It's one reason they did not bail out. Instead, they voted on trying to bring it in with the landing gear not locked in position, which turned out to be reasonably successful.

Joe told Bob that he took the plane out and around to dump the fuel. He prayed they had enough to bring her in!

Joeseph Chvala and the Navy BBY-1 B-24 he crashed-landed, -courtesy of Chavala family archives

There were several little snippets of stories Joe revealed to either Bob or his other siblings. By combining these anecdotes from different family members, it appears that Joe had a close relationship with Joe Kennedy.

There are no records or photos of the two men together. Both Joe Chvala and Joe Kennedy were Catholics and Chvala's family understood the two would attend Mass together.

According to Bob Chvala, his father Joe had been invited by Joe Kennedy to attend his sister's wedding in London. Kathleen 'Kick'

Kennedy married William Cavendish, Lord Hartington on May 6, 1944. Lord Hartington was heir to the Duke of Devonshire.

Joe Kennedy was the only Kennedy who attended his sister's wedding because the parents were furious that 'Kick' a Catholic, was marrying a Protestant against their express wishes. Joe appears in the wedding photo below.

The wedding at the Chelsea Register Office in Caxton, London on May 6, 1944-Getty Images

Lt. Joseph Kennedy in his US Navy uniform is seen smiling in the background.

Kathleen Kennedy was the youngest daughter of Joseph P. Kennedy, the past US Ambassador to England who had returned to the USA. Kathleen had returned with her father but went back to England as a volunteer for the Red Cross. It was then she had met Lord Hartington.

News reports said: the bride in her pink frock, a turban of blue and pink feathers, and a pink nose veil, looked very well against her groom's Captain's Coldstream Guards's uniform.

Best man was the captain's fellow officer, the Duke of Rutland. Lord

Hartington placed an old family ring on the bride's finger. The Register was signed by the Duke of Devonshire, Lord Hartington's father, and Lt. Joseph Kennedy as a witness.

Many of the bride's fellow Red Cross workers also attended the wedding. Because of those invitations, it was more than likely that Kathleen had told Joe he could bring his Navy friends to the wedding. We do not know how many other pilots in his squadron were invited, but Joe Chvala had told his son Bob Chvala, on one of their fishing trips, that Kennedy had invited him to the wedding. In fact, Bob said that the reception was a posh affair and his father told him he had embarrassed himself when some peas on the plate he was holding began rolling off on to the floor.

They held the reception for 200 at 94 Eaton Square, Belgravia, London. The couple took off for their honeymoon by train to Eastbourne. They would stay at Compton Place, one of the residences of the Duke of Devonshire. Sadly, Kathleen became widowed four months later when Captain Hartington died on 9 September 1944, at the age of 26. A sniper killed him whilst leading a company trying to capture the town of Heppen in Belgium from troops of the German Waffen-SS.

While the preceding anecdote that Joe Chvala told his son about attending the Kennedy wedding provides an interesting but unconfirmed story, the following report is well documented. The official record suggests that Chvala and Kennedy were close, which adds credibility to Chvala's family stories.

Joe Chvala defended Joe Kennedy from a false report in a newspaper years after the war, since Kennedy had passed away and couldn't defend himself.

An article in the Chicago Tribune of 1986 reproduced a story from a German newspaper, which claimed that Joe Kennedy got shot down over France. He allegedly was captured, tried to escape, and was shot and killed. The Germans buried him in an unknown grave.

Joe Chvala, who served alongside Kennedy in the squadron, promptly rejected the baseless German assertion. This very act of his speaks volumes

David E. Huntley

about Joe's respect not just for his fellow Navy aviator, but to his friend and comrade-in-arms even though it was over 40 years earlier. The article is reproduced here:

Section 1 Chicago Tribune, Monday, November 10, 1986

Nation/world

Ex-German officer gives new version of a Kennedy death

BONN [UPI]—Joseph P. Kennedy Jr., the older brother of President John F. Kennedy and Sen. Edward Kennedy, was shot to death by Nazi SS soldiers in July, 1944, as he tried to escape, a West German newspaper reported Sunday.

Standard history texts say Kennedy, 29, was lost in action when explosives packed into the B-17 bomber he was piloting detonated on a flight over Europe.

The copyrighted story, published in the nationwide Bild am Sonntag newspaper, was based on an interview with a former German antiaircraft officer who said he interrogated Kennedy after his plane was shot down and he was captured.

Karl Heinz Wehn, 65, told Bild am Sonntag that he was a lieutenant in an antiaircraft unit fighting 11 miles southwest of the French city of Caen when he shot down a plane from which Kennedy parachuted to safety.

Wehn reported that the American, during interrogation, said he was Joe Kennedy of Hyannisport. Kennedy and another downed American airman were shot later that day as they tried to escape across a river, Wehn said.

Wehn told the newspaper he saw 12 American B-17s flying back to England after a bombing raid July 14, 1944. Wehn said he fired at one B-17 Flying Fortress, which caught fire and went into a spin.

He said two men parachuted from the plane and landed in woods 1,000 yards from him. Ten minutes later, two Americans came out with raised hands, captives of infantrymen from the 12th German Panzer Division.

Wehn, a member of the 1st Regiment of the Third Flak Corps, said both captives were brought to his bunker where he questioned one in English. He said the man wore olive-green aviator's coveralls, chewed gum and looked very pale under dark blond hair.

"What's your name?" Wehn said he asked.

"Joe Kennedy," the man replied, adding in a somewhat softer voice, "First lieutenant, U.S. Air Force."

Wehn said the interrogation lasted 40 minutes and then the two SS soldiers took both prisoners to an assembly point.

Lt. Joseph P. Kennedy Jr. in July, 1941, a year before his B-17 bomber disappeared.

Wehn said that at 9:45 p.m. on the same day, he heard several loud shouts from the direction of the Orne River, then five shots from light machine guns, followed by silence.

He said he later learned that the two prisoners had run away from their captors when one was using a field telephone and the other had gone without permission to get some French apple wine.

Wehn said a general alarm was sounded along the river and SS soldiers there said they saw two men wearing aviator uniforms running toward the water only a few yards away. He said the men jumped into the river as the soldiers fired. Five minutes later German medical orderlies found Kennedy and the other captive dead, Wehn said.

The two men, Wehn said, probably had learned from maps left in the woods that English troops were on the other side of the Orne River. He said the men were buried by German infantrymen in two simple graves.

The above document is by the courtesy of the Department of Veteran's Affairs Museum in Madison, Wisconsin

358

The B-17 Tomahawk Warrior: A WWII Final Honor

Below is the letter by Joe Chvala to the Chief Editor of the Chicago Tribune.

Boushea, Chvala & Johnson Law Offices

Leighton W. Boushea
Charles J. Chvala
Stan C. Johnson
Sharon A. Segall

5708 MONONA DRIVE
MONONA, WISCONSIN 53716
(608) 221-0079

COMMUNITY NATIONAL BANK
733 NORTH MAIN STREET
OREGON, WISCONSIN 53575
(608) 835-7646

November 26, 1986

The Editor of the Chicago Tribune
Chicago, Illinois

RE: Your article on Joe Kennedy, November 10, 1986

Dear Sir:

Attached is a cut out of an article in your paper. I would like to set the record straight about the death of Joe Kennedy vs. the attached article.

I was a Navy pilot in the same squardron with Joe Kennedy and was with the squardron at the time of Joe's demise.

I have underlined four points in the article.

    1. Joe Kennedy was flying a B-24 better known in the Navy jargon as a PB4Y1 and not a B-17 bomber.

    2, His ill-fated aircraft, which was loaded full of explosives, exploded over the coast of England. Joe had volunteered to take this plane, get it up in the air and turn it over to an escorting British aircraft for the mission they were on. Their mission was to fly this plane load of explosives down into target on the coast of France. Joe was killed when trying to transfer the command to the escort plane. This plane blew up killing Joe instantly.

    3. Joe was a Navy pilot and our squardron mission was to fly anti-sub and anti-shipping in the waters around Europe. He did not fly any B-17s and he did not participate in any bombing raids.

    4. Joe was a full lieutenant in the Navy air corp and not a first lieutenant in the U. S. Air Force.

All of the squardron members were very sorry to lose Joe as well as the great loss of all our fallen members. Other members of the squardron went on to carry out the hazardous volunteer mission. Joe did not die in vain, in that the work accomplished during his mission was improved for future missions.

David E. Huntley

```
The Editor of the Chicago Tribune
Page Two
November 26, 1986
```

By now you may have received other letters trying to set the record straight on Joe. If not, there are other pilots and squadron members that would be interested in giving testimony if anybody thought it worthwhile.

                         Sincerely,

                         Joseph Chvala

```
JC:cb
Enclosure
cc   Mr. Lloyd Koth
```

Courtesy of Chvala family archives.

In conclusion of the Chvala story, it is fitting to say that even the smallest link to the Tomahawk Warrior seems to fulfill a larger role in American history. This is reinforced again in the closing chapter. In the meantime, I once again thank the Tomahawk Warrior crew, Joe Chvala, Joe Kennedy, and every WWII veteran for their bravery and sacrifice.

Although the secret mission of Joe Kennedy is well documented in various historical reports, in the interests of continuity of my story about its link to the Tomahawk Warrior, here is a description of the project, which was code named 'Aphrodite.'

The idea following the success of the German V1s and V2s inspired the Americans to develop an unmanned guided bomb. This involved taking a war-weary but still flyable B-17 bomber and stripping it of everything unnecessary to fly it. This meant all gun mountings, interior equipment like radios, except the radio used by the pilot, bomb racks, etc. The aim was to save around 12,000 to 13,000 lbs in valuable weight.

They would completely cut off the canopy of the cockpit surrounding the pilot and his engineer. The two would bale out of the craft once it was airborne.

Next, they would load the ship with between 21,000 to 30,000 lbs of Torpex that had 50 percent more power than ordinary dynamite. An Azon radio remote-control system was then installed. The Azon system was developed to create the first smart bomb and was successfully used in Burma, as well as some targets in Europe. The B-17 in the Aphrodite missions had early TV cameras that sent images to a following mother craft for remote piloting.

Once airborne and stabilized, the plane achieved flight at around 2000 or 3000 ft. The pilot would flip a switch to arm the Torpex explosive. Both men would then bale out of the open cockpit or the nose wheel bay, where there was a hatch escape. This was very dangerous and men died having their parachutes catch on the plane, or in the slipstream and be dashed against the fuselage.

The mother ship pilot, using the streaming TV image, guided the remotely controlled plane to the target. There were some successes, but there were many failures, and Aphrodite was eventually abandoned. It was, however, the basis for the development of a drone aircraft of the future.

There has been no clear evidence why Joe Kennedy's plane, known as BQ-8, blew up in mid-air. According to one report, he last radioed he was flipping the switch to arm the Torpex before baling out but, then the plane blew to pieces. The switch may have had a short circuit when thrown.

In another report, "A young officer called Earl Olsen had spotted a potentially(sic) defect in the control panel of the BQ-8 and reported it to his superiors. But since he wasn't a high-ranking officer and had no official qualifications in electronics, his concerns were dismissed, even by Joe Kennedy himself. What if they just would have listened to Earl Olsen?"

This photograph was taken by Earl Olsen just before Kennedy boarded his fatal flight. My thanks to Earl Olsen's son and Wikipedia Commons for the photo.

An analysis and report specifically of the Kennedy mission can be found on the website of the Norfolk and Suffolk Aviation Museum in England.

▲ ▲ ▲ ▲

A Broader and More Detailed Description of the Aphrodite Project

My research colleague of mine in Germany, Jing Zhou, has an extensive website[157] dedicated to the story of the "Flying Fortress." It provides some unique stories about the B-17 and gives a much broader description and details about the planes used in the "Aphrodite" missions.

The quality of the translation, however, was poorly done by an auto-translate technology in 2005. The owner gave me permission to provide a more up-to-date translation. It is translated below verbatim.

---

[157] A very informative site for the history of the B-17 Flying Fortress as well as a detailed analysis of the secret Aphrodite Project. https://B-17flyingfortress.de/en

(Citation) Project Aphrodite

By June, the English had become used to being roused from their morning slumber by the roar of airplane engines. The spectacle of a plane crashing or bursting into flames or exploding was not uncommon in East Anglia in 1944. However, when a Boeing B-17 crashed into a wood on the sunny afternoon of 4th August the explosion was far more than usual. Although the detonation was somewhat softened by numerous oak trees, three road workers still lost their hearing at a considerable distance.

Those arriving at the crash site were faced with a crater about 30 meters in diameter and trunks of mature oak trees were scattered within a radius of 60 meters. All that remained of the B-17 were metal fragments, the largest being the engine cylinders.

The heat from the explosion had melted much of the metal. Not surprising, since this machine was not a normal B-17 with a bomb load of 4,000 lbs (1,814 kg), but probably the deadliest missile to have ever come down over Britain. This and three other similarly equipped bombers formed the opening salvo in an experiment with guided weapons – named after the Greek goddess of love: "Project Aphrodite."

On June 13, the Germans began their offensive against London from launch pads in Pas de Calais with the "flying bomb" Fieseler Fi 103 (V1). The V1 was actually a pulsejet, non-reusable unmanned aircraft specially designed to carry a warhead. This forerunner of today's cruise missiles was a result of the research work on pulse jet engines begun in 1928 by the aerodynamicist Paul Schmidt.

The project ran under the alias FZG 76; the missile was given the designation Fi 103 and the weapon itself was christened V1 (i.e. Retribution Weapon 1) by Göbbels' propaganda machinery. The Londoners named it "Doodlebug" after its first hit on June 13, 1944 because of its unmistakable sound. (Author's Note: For those of us who lived through the blitz, we also called it a "buzzbomb").

While the V1 was not the first "guided missile," its mass deployment sparked increased interest in the Allied camp of single-use weapon carriers.

Various staffs had already considered the use of unmanned, radio-controlled, conventional military aircraft loaded with explosives. In view of the threat of V-weapons, this possibility was now taken up by Major General Carl A. Spaatz at the suggestion of the USSTAF (US Strategic Air Forces in Europe).

Major General Spaatz, veteran WW1 fighter pilot, returned to England in January 1944 and assumed command of the USSTAF, which had become the 8th Air Force at Bushy Park, Middlesex, and was now the 8th and 15th Subordinate to the US Air Force.

Operational equipment that was no longer required should be removed from obsolete or flown heavy bombers and radio receivers should be installed in their place and connected to the autopilot. Finally, the machines should be loaded with about ten tons of explosives. The aircraft, manned by a pilot and a radio operator, was to be started and leveled normally by the crew. As soon as the radio remote control was taken over from a "mother aircraft" (command aircraft), the crew should leave with the parachute, which would then be steered to the intended target by radio.

However, the rapid disembarkation of the crew of two proved to be problematic, on the one hand because of the very small hatch located directly in front of the engines on the left side of the fuselage and on the other hand because of the extremely strong current. Therefore, at least on some machines, the hatch was enlarged and a wind deflector was attached in front of the hatch.

AZON – At first only a makeshift

On June 20, 1944, General Spaatz informed General Henry H. "Hap" Arnold about the start of the project and demanded that corresponding tests be carried out in the USA as well. As a result, a program called "Weary Willie" was launched at the US Air Force testing facility in Florida. However, it appears to have been pursued only half-heartedly, having little impact on the works in England.

Project Aphrodite was ordered by the USSTAF on June 23, 1944 with the provision that the US 8th Air Force conduct development and testing.

The Operational Engineering Section, which was directly involved, described the radio control used at the time for testing the steerable AZON bomb (AZON = azimuth only; i.e. only steerable in azimuth) as the most suitable. In practice, however, it was only a makeshift until special equipment arrived from the USA.

Major Henry Rand, the technical expert on the AZON system, was instructed to leave the AZON device at Horsham St Faith and proceed to Burton Wood, while three crews trained on the AZON system went to Bovingdon, where the first remote controlled bombers should be tested.

Old aircraft with new descent behavior

Meanwhile, the US 8th Air Fleet had tasked the 3rd Bomb Division with splitting up the Aphrodite unit. Volunteer pilots and radio operators, recruited from the division's bomber squads for a "secret and dangerous" mission, were dispatched to Honington Air Depot, where the 1st Strategic Air Depot was busy plowing out 10 war-weary B-17F/G bombers – with a total of 65 planned – to remove the equipment that is not required.

All armor, machine gun emplacements, bomb and oxygen equipment, the co-pilot's seat and everything not required for the one-off flight were removed. This allowed the weight of the Flying Fortresses to be reduced to around 32,000 lbs (14,500 kg).

However, this weight reduction of 5,000 lbs (2,268 kg) had an impact on the flight behavior, so that data on the changed descent behavior of the B-17 had to be collected. This was largely done with the help of the roughly equally heavy transport version of Major General Earle E. Partridge's B-17F.

On one machine, the B-17F, 42-30595, the entire cabin structure was detached to facilitate loading with torpedoes. According to the latest findings, the German battleship "Tirpitz" was to be attacked with it. However, after the daring undertaking was dropped, the machine with its open cockpit was only used for training purposes, but no longer as a "baby."

After removing unnecessary equipment at Honington, the B-17s were flown to Burton Wood, where they found two AZON receivers (one for rudder and one for elevator) coupled to the autopilot, an antenna, the necessary wiring and a radio altimeter received for automatic height maintenance. In addition, the bomb bay was sealed and reinforced with crossbeams to accommodate seven tons of the planned ten-ton load of explosives; the remaining three tons went into the front fuselage area. Initially, three AZON-B-24 of the 458th Bomb Group were used as command aircraft. But a B-17G was also fitted with AZON transmitters in Burton Wood.

A suicide mission in the cockpit during test flights

After their conversion, the machines were transferred to Bovington, where the conversion training began on July 1, 1944 in the strictest secrecy. The crews received 25 flight hours of training and intensive training in destination and route navigation. The AZON guidance appeared to work satisfactorily, with the RC bomber's flight stability appearing to be the only major problem. For safety reasons, there was always a pilot in the cockpit of the remote-controlled bomber known as "Baby" on all test flights, including those with radio remote control.

The construction of the large V1-positions at Pas de Calais gave rise to growing concern and calls for the operations to begin as soon as possible grew louder. The RAF agreed to use the extra long runway at Woodbridge as a launch pad. As a result, the commander of the Aphrodite unit, Lt.Col. James Turner, with 10 B-17 "Babies", one B-17 and three Consolidated B-24 Liberator command aircraft for guidance and observation, and eight P-47 Thunderbolts assigned by a fighter group for escort protection on July 7 to Woodbridge.

Nine of the guided bombers received a payload of 20,000 lbs (9,072 kg) of TNT, the tenth an equal amount of petroleum gel (napalm). The loaded machines were parked scattered among the pines, causing uneasiness among the field's personnel, who continued to use it as an emergency landing pad for damaged machines returning from missions. Many of these "invalids" spun out of control on landing and the thought of one ramming into one of the loaded Aphrodite planes was frightening.

Because of the limited radio frequencies, only two "babies" could be launched at a time. Two task forces were planned, each consisting of two command aircraft and one remote-controlled bomber. The "Babies" were to take off conventionally and fly a planned route during which the remote control could be checked and the crew had the opportunity to parachute.

After the lead aircraft had steered their two "babies" to the destination, they were to fly back to their starting point, take over two other "babies" that had meanwhile taken off and steer them to the specified destination in the same way. The bomber loaded with the gasoline gel should be kept in readiness to be able to completely eliminate a hit target.

Airport change for confidentiality reasons

However, the basic prerequisite for every Aphrodite mission was clear weather. However, in the days following the arrival of the Aphrodite unit, the weather was never favorable in the intended target areas.

In the meantime, it had been decided to move the Aphrodite unit to a more remote location, Fersfield, for reasons of secrecy. Fersfield was an airfield built for US 8th Air Force bombers, but had not previously been used by any operational unit. The decision itself was made on July 12 and just three days later the relocation of the Aphrodite unit from Woodbridge to Fersfield began.

Fersfield was run as a branch of the nearby 388th Bomb Group. The ground personnel of the 560th Bomb Squadron, 388th Bomb Group, moved from Knettishall to Fersfield as a maintenance unit in August and their squadron commander, Lt.Col. Roy Forrest, became commander of the squadron. However, the B-17s of the 560th BS at Knettishall continued to participate in regular operations with the support of ground crews from the three other squadrons of the 388th BG.

Among the units transferred to Fersfield was the Special Air Unit No. 1 (SAU-1) of the US Navy with volunteers from the Anti-submarine

Squadron based in Dunkeswell, South West England. The US Navy had already considered a similar project for the Pacific region, using radio-controlled drones from carriers for single-use operations, and wanted to be involved in this first US robotic warfare venture. Their work in Fersfield went under the alias "Anvil" (kick-off).

To further complicate matters, a special unit, codenamed "Batty", who had just arrived in Britain from Wright Field, USA, intended to carry out test missions with TV-guided bombs, was also transferred to Fersfield.

Main target: The V1 launch pads

Equipped with remote control and a TV guidance system and loaded with 25,000 lbs (11,340 kg) of torpex explosives, the SAU-1's PB4Y-1 Liberator was piloted by a PV1 Ventura motherplane. The PB4Y-1 took off with a crew of two, taking the machine to 2,000 feet (600 m) and heading for V1 positions in France before parachuting.

Despite several alerts over the previous weeks, the first Aphrodite mission took place in the early afternoon of August 4th when two "babies" weighing 64,000 lbs (29,000 kg) each took off from Fersfield 5 minutes apart and large concrete V1s aimed at launch pads near the French Channel coast.

The two AZON command aircraft had already climbed 45 minutes earlier in order to be able to reach a fixed checkpoint at an altitude of 20,000 feet (6,000 m). The two "babies" were guided to the checkpoints with the help of a B-17 guide plane, where the guide planes took over radio control. Then the "babies" flew a 50-mile square course at 2,000 feet, during which the remote control could be checked.

A B-24 command aircraft was provided for each "baby" as well as a B-17 as a reserve command aircraft in case the radio link should fail en route. The "Babies" had the top of the wings and the fin painted white for better recognition. A Mosquito weather observation plane flew ahead and another B-17 served as a relay station for weather information.

Tumbled to death

The crew of the first "Babies" disembarked between Woodbridge and the coastal overflight point at Orfordness. The flight of the second "baby" ended in disaster:

When switching to radio remote control, the machine went into a slight climb. The pilot brought them back to level flight, but the error reappeared when they switched again. On the third attempt, the climb resulted in a stall and the Fortress went into a spin. The radio operator was able to save himself with the parachute, the pilot 1st Lt. John Fischer, however, was killed when he only got out of the plane immediately before the impact and explosion. The water-filled crater is still there today.

The first "Baby" (B-17F 42-30342) was successfully steered across the English Channel, but then a malfunction in the altitude control occurred and during further control maneuvers the machine crashed northwest of Gravelines some distance from its target, the V-1 position in Watten. The reason was probably an anti-aircraft hit. The explosion shattered the B-17 into tiny fragments, which were scattered over an area of about 5 km.

As the lead aircraft returned to its home base, two more "babies" took off, this time against V1 positions at Wizernes and Mimoyecques. The course over the county of Suffolk and the coastal crossing point were the same as before. Both crews were able to parachute; however, two of the men were slightly injured. The "baby" destined for Wizernes went out of sight in the low clouds on approach to the target and only hit the target behind – the radio operator on the mother plane had miscalculated the effect of the elevator.

After anti-aircraft crews reported the downing of B-17s intended for the attack on Watten and their unusual behavior, the crash site was investigated. But despite the lack of bodies and machine guns, and the enormous size of the crater, the incident was not recognized (by the Germans) (sic) as a use of a special weapon.

Again and again problems with the radio control

The next Aphrodite mission took place on the morning of August 6th with the launch of two more "babies." Procedures were the same as the first two missions, with a main and reserve command aircraft at 15,000 feet (4,572 m) for each "baby" and a test course over Suffolk before leaving the coast at Orfordness.

The crew of the first "Babies" had parachuted out of their plane. However, when approaching the enemy coast, the lead aircraft lost radio contact and the Fortress, loaded with explosives, fell into the sea. Problems with the radio control also occurred with the "Baby" which followed at an interval of 10 minutes. After the crew jumped off and flew over the Channel coast, the machine went into uncontrollable left turns and also fell into the sea.

Dissatisfaction with the limited capabilities of the double AZON receivers, which were only intended for temporary trials, led to them being replaced by much more sophisticated devices that had meanwhile arrived from the USA, and more precise control with greater sensitivity promised. During the installation work and tests, no further Aphrodite assignments took place for a month. Although the Aphrodite aircraft equipped with the new devices were given the new code name "Castor", the designation "Aphrodite" was retained as a generic term for the guided missile program of the USSTAF in Fersfield.

Lt. Joseph Kennedy in action with his Liberator PBY-1

The crew of the first "Babies" disembarked between Woodbridge and the coastal overflight point at Orfordness. The flight of the second "baby" ended in disaster:

The US Navy launched its first guided aircraft under the Anvil program on the afternoon of **August 12** with the goal of destroying the V-weapon site at Mimoyecques. The US Navy, always concerned about its independence, had brought two of its own PV1 Ventura command aircraft with it and also equipped them itself. The "baby" was that of Lt. Joe P. Kennedy (pictured above), son of the US Ambassador to Great Britain and brother of the future President, John F. Kennedy, flown a PB4Y-1 Liberator (Bu. No. 32271). The place of the radio operator was taken by Lt. W. J. "Bud" Willy.

The start took place at 5:52 p.m. The 150-mile (240-km) route headed southeast across the English Channel. The PB4Y-1 was able to reach a good 150 knots fully loaded, making the 7:00 p.m. estimated arrival time over the target easy to meet. Eighteen minutes after takeoff, flying at 2,000 feet (600 m), Lt. Kennedy trimmed the machine, warmed up and engaged the autopilot. "Spade Flush" he reported the readiness to hand over to Lt. Anderson, the pilot of the lead aircraft flying behind him. From this point on, Anderson carefully steered Kennedy's machine with the so-called "Peter Pilot" (small joystick) on the console in front of him. He relied on radar echoes and visual observations by the co-pilot of the reserve command aircraft, since his TV screen only showed snow flurries. Together with Kennedy, he began to check the individual controls: elevator, aileron and rudder, just as he had done half an hour earlier with the "baby" still on the ground.

Five minutes later, the aircraft, call sign T-11, was supposed to be on the inland leg of the route, but was 12 miles (20 km) off course towards the sea during controls checks. It was a mile south of the River Blythe near the town of Beccle. Col. Elliot Roosevelt, son of the US President in his Mosquito photo-reconnaissance aircraft, had gotten within a few hundred feet of the machine to take a few pictures. Vapor trails from the accompanying Mustangs dotted the slightly overcast sky overhead.

Commander Smith in the bow of the B-17 piloted by Lt.Col. Forrest, which should have landed far to the south near Dover in half an hour and was to pick up the two parachuted crew members, had Kennedy's plane been in front and well below. Forrest, began a slight descent and tried to catch up. Both Kennedy and Willy were recognizable in their "baby": Kennedy in the cockpit and Willy behind his Plexiglas dome in the bow. The TV picture in Anderson's lead plane from the area below Kennedy's machine was still poor, but the "baby" provided a good picture to LT. Demlein in the reserve command aircraft. Since it was Demlein who would pilot the "baby" on its final approach for 40 minutes, everything seemed fine.

Explodes in the air

Escorted by P-51 "Mustang" fighters, plus navigation and other support aircraft from Fersfield, the US Navy Assault Unit was on its way to the coastal flyover point at Southwold.

Anderson steered Kennedy's machine into a slight left turn. At that moment, at exactly 18:20 GMT, the "Baby" suddenly exploded with two massive detonations a second apart at 2,000 feet (600 m) above Newdelight Wood. There was no indication of a possible cause of the explosion in the debris of the machine scattered around near the village of Blythburgh. The detonation of 24,000 lbs (11,000 kg) of explosives had shattered the entire aircraft into tiny fragments, with the exception of the engine blocks. Subsequent investigations came to the conclusion that the most likely cause was a fault in the electrical system, which had been switched on before the crew jumped out.

In August 1944, three baby missions were carried out with radio-controlled GB-4 bombs equipped with a TV camera. These attempts were not exactly a resounding success, mainly due to interference from radio equipment and reflections on the water surface.

Based on a 2,000 lb (900 kg) bomb, the GB-4 featured small wings, articulated tail fins, radio control equipment and a head-mounted TV camera. Two of the bombs were attached to external bomb carriers of a B-17 command aircraft. All operations were carried out with the B-17G, 42-40043 and a crew from the 388th BG.

After three attempts with the GB-4 on English training areas, the first real operation took place on August 13th, the destination was the port of Le Havre. A B-17 observation aircraft accompanied the Batty machine. Each crew included two or five experts from Wright Field who had been involved in the development of the GB-4. Colonel Forrest watched the action from his "Droop Snoot" P-38. A Mosquito photo reconnaissance aircraft got too close to one of the concrete bombs and crashed, hit by shrapnel. The TV receiver built into the lead aircraft, which unfortunately did not work properly, delivered too weak images to be able to precisely control the bombs. So one suggested about a mile, the other a mile to the right of the port of Le Havre.

Camera shutter just didn't do it

The second Batty operation, conducted a week later against the submarine bunker at La Pallice, was even less successful. When the first bomb was released, the camera shutter closed and prevented further image transmission. The second GB-4 went into an uncontrollable spin. The third and final attempt by the GB-4 took place on August 26 and was aimed at facilities in Ijmuiden. With a cloud cover of 8/10, however, the target area could no longer be recognized and the mission had to be aborted. After this third unsuccessful use, the command decided to postpone the project for further development.

In retrospect, one has to say that the technology at that time was not yet mature enough to ensure the necessary precise control and reliability.

On the other side of the world, Japan deployed its version of the V1 against US Navy task forces operating in the Pacific. The Yokosuka MXY-8 Ohka (sakura; Allied code name was Baka, Japanese for fool) was carried under the wing of the 721st Kokutai's Mitsubishi G4M-2 Betty. The first use on March 21, 1945 was directed against US Task Force FV58.

Target Helgoland

The US Navy's second and last Anvil mission took place on September 3, 1944. After the Allies had already captured the large V-weapons positions, the submarine base on Helgoland was chosen as the target. This time the mission was successful, but the man at the radio remote control had confused the island with the neighboring island dune and had the "Liberator" open there. The force of the explosion destroyed houses almost a kilometer from the point of impact. The FM system used by the US Navy used a TV camera in the bomb's head, which provided images to the lead aircraft.

Castor operations began in September using a remote control system similar to the US Navy's FM system with a TV camera in the nose of the aircraft. Helgoland and Heide/Hemmingstedt were chosen as targets, as these only required a short penetration into enemy territory and the danger of being shot down by flak was therefore lower.

Instead of a double AZON device, a standard AN/ARW-1 radio control receiver was installed on the Castor aircraft and the associated AN/ARW-18 transmitter on the lead aircraft. Although the machines still started with a crew of two, a co-pilot now replaced the radio operator. Eureka/Rebecca navigation systems were used to locate the aircraft should it disappear from the observer's field of view in poor visibility.

Additional aids to maintaining visual contact were a smoke generator in the Castor aircraft that could be switched on and off by radio from the mother aircraft and the eye-catching yellow paint job on the upper side of the aircraft.

The first Castor launch was on September 11, when a machine loaded with 21,855 lbs (9,913 kg) of Torpex was deployed against Heligoland. The procedure was the same as for the Aphrodite missions using the Doppe-AZON devices, except that the lead aircraft was level with the "Baby" at 2,000 to 2,500 feet (600 to 760 m) but separated by two to three kilometers behind and increased this distance to ten to twelve kilometers as it approached the target.

The remote control during the flight over 400 kilometers was called perfect, until the "baby" received an anti-aircraft hit just 10 seconds before the target, crashed into the sea and exploded about 200 meters from the beach.

Even though the Castor system showed significant improvements over the earlier systems used, its use was tragically tragic. When the pilot, 1Lt. Richard Lindahl, left his machine with the parachute, the bridle of his parachute was obviously not properly attached and he suffered a broken neck. Three days later, two Castor machines were used against an oil refinery in Hemmingstedt, but missed their target due to bad weather.

Hit a farm in Sweden instead of Heligoland!

On October 15th and 30th, Heligoland was again the target of two double attacks, but this time the "Babies" missed their target. A machine hit outside of the village of Helgoland, two others fell into the sea. The fourth lost radio contact, flew north-east and exploded on a farm near Trollhättan in Sweden. Apparently, the patient Swedes viewed this incident as another attempt by a damaged bomber to find salvation in their country. This can be concluded from the fact that they reported that the crew had jumped over Denmark.

On October 27, the USSTAF issued instructions to use the remaining Castor aircraft for attacks on industrial complexes in major German cities as far inland as possible. To do this, it was necessary to install an additional engine power control in order to be able to penetrate enemy territory at an altitude of 10,000 feet (3,000 m) and to reduce the flight altitude to 250 feet (75 m) near the target. Although an even higher entry altitude would have been desirable, it was not possible because of the oil pressure-controlled supercharger control, which had a tendency to ice up and thus to fail.

In November, after carving out Projects Batty and Anvil, the 3rd Division decided to move the Aphrodite unit back to the OU's home base of Knettishall. This was completed by the end of the month and already on December 5th the first two machines started from Knettishall with the destination Herford marshalling yard.

During the flight, however, the weather deteriorated and dense clouds prevented the station from being identified. Gaps in the clouds near the Dummersee enabled a descent in order to be able to identify suitable targets of opportunity. The first "baby" was aimed at Haldorf and exploded south of town. In the second, the engine performance dropped, probably due to carburetor icing and it fell into a square without exploding.

The crew of the accompanying Mosquito scout aircraft appeared to have escaped the machine unharmed. As a result, the escort flying hunters were instructed to destroy the "baby" with on-board weapons, but this was unsuccessful.

While the command assumed the enemy had managed to get their hands on an intact "baby", this does not appear to have been the case. A report suggests that the Castor bomber exploded shortly after the crash landing, killing some German soldiers who had begun examining the bomber.

Unnoticed by the Germans

German records of the Aphrodite missions show that none of these attacks had been identified as such at the time and gave reason to believe that if the bomber had exploded after landing, it was assumed to be a normal B-17 with a bomb load.

As fate would have it, the USSTAF was not aware that another Aphrodite bomber, albeit damaged, had fallen into German hands. On New Year's Day, the last two Castor B-17s still available were used against a power plant in Oldenburg. the first of the approaching "babies" received an anti-aircraft hit and crashed into a field on the outskirts of town without exploding, which the escort planes failed to notice.

This enabled Luftwaffe experts to examine the Castor bomber fairly closely and recover much of the radio and guidance equipment. The second "baby", presumably also hit by flak, crashed a few miles south-west of Oldenburg and exploded. These should have been the last sorties of the Castor planes, largely because they had suddenly become a political issue.

The last missions

In November, the USSTAF had proposed moving the launch site for Aphrodite operations to mainland Europe, from where the B-17s could have been used against industrial targets. When this proposal was put to the British High Command, they expressed concern that using this weapon against densely populated areas could provoke retaliatory strikes against

London, which was suffering from V2 attacks at the time. The British reluctantly agreed to the plan on January 15, despite serious concerns in some quarters.

This concern continued, eventually leading to the withdrawal of consent eleven days later. British fears also stemmed in part from a rethinking of the value of bombing densely populated areas to break popular morale.

The USSTAF, still anxious to proceed with its experiments, made representations to Washington and got **President Franklin D. Roosevelt** to telex March 29, 1945, demanding British approval of the plan to use Castor aircraft against the Ruhr. to repeat. **Churchill's** reply telex, although full approval, was written in Churchill's own style. that the concerns expressed therein would deter Roosevelt.

However, the death of the President and the collapse of Germany put an end to the plan. No more Castor aircraft were being prepared for take-off at Knettishall and those involved awaited the project being shelved. The Aphrodite command planes and crews were forgotten for several weeks. It was not until April 27th that the project, which used the largest single amount of conventional explosives against enemy targets in World War II, was finally shelved.

Aphrodite-Missions, Aircraft and Crews

Date	Target	Baby	Crew
04. Aug. 44	Watten	B-17F 42-30342 (ex- 95th BG "Taint A Bird")	1Lt F. H. Pool, S/Sgt P. Enterline
04. Aug. 44	Siracourt	B-17G 42-39835 (ex-351st BG "Wantta Spa")	1Lt W. Fisher (KAS), T/SGT E. Most
04. Aug. 44	Wizernes	B-17F 42-3461 (ex-92nd BG)	1Lt F. L. Houston, T/Sgt W. D. Smith
04. Aug. 44	Mimoyecques	B-17F 41-24639 (ex-91st BG "The Careful Virgin")	1Lt C. A. Angel, T/Sgt C. A. Parsons
06. Aug. 44	Watten	B-17F 42-30212 (ex-388th BG "Quarterback")	1Lt J. P. Andrecheck, T/Sgt R. Healy

06. Aug. 44	Watten	B-17G 42-31394 (ex-379th BG)	1Lt. J. Sollars, T/Sgt H. Graves
12. Aug. 44	Mimoyecques	PB4Y-1 32271 (Rufzeichen T-11)	Lt. J. Kennedy (USN) (KAS), Lt. W. J. Willy (USN) (KAS)
03. Sep. 44	Helgoland	B-24D 42-63954	Lt R. Spalding (USN)
11. Sep. 44	Helgoland	B-17F 42-30180 (ex-96th BG "Guzzlers")	1Lt R. W. Lindahl (KAS), 1Lt D. E. Salles
14. Sep. 44	Hemmingstedt	B-17F 42-30363 (ex-96th BG "Ruth L III")	1Lt M. P. Hardy, 1Lt E Hadley
14. Sep. 44	Hemmingstedt	B-17G 42-39827 (ex-306th BG)	1Lt W. G. Haller, /2Lt. C. L. Shinault
15. Oct. 44	Helgoland	B-17F 42-30039 (ex-384th BG "Liberty Belle")	1Lt R. Betts, 2Lt M. Garvin
15. Oct. 44	Helgoland	B-17G 42-37743 (ex-94th BG)	1Lt W. Patton, 1Lt J. W. Hinner
30. Oct. 44	Helgoland	B-17F 42-30066 (ex-100th BG "Mugwump")	1Lt G. A. Barnes, 1Lt R. McCauley
30. Oct. 44	Helgoland	B-17F 42-3438 (ex-96th BG)	1Lt W. C. Gaither, 1Lt W. M. Dunnuck
05. Dec. 44	Herford	B-17G 42-39824	1Lt T. H. Barton, 1Lt F. E. Bruno
05. Dec. 44	Herford	B-17F 42-30353 (ex-95th BG "Ten Knights In The Bar Room")	1Lt R. F. Butler, 1Lt K. T. Waters
01. Jan. 45	Oldenburg	B-17F 42-30178 (ex-95th BG "Darlin' Dolly")	2Lt J. Stein, 1Lt E. Morris
01. Jan. 45	Oldenburg	B-17F 42-30237 (ex-397th BG "Stump Jumper")	Capt J. Hodson, 1Lt L. Lawing. **(End of Citation)**

▲ ▲ ▲ ▲

CHAPTER FIFTEEN
TRIBUTE TO LORD HOWE

▲ ▲ ▲ ▲

The Remarkable Connection Between William Penn, Lord Howe, and his Ancestors and their Role in the American Revolution

IN MY PREVIOUS NEWSLETTERS AND within the narrative of this book, I have mentioned the names of Lord Howe and Countess Howe. They were a vital link in my quest to honor the crew of the American 8th Air Force B-17 bomber that crashed in England in 1944, and to which immediate aftermath I was a witness.

Frederick the 7th Earl Howe and his most gracious wife, Countess Elizabeth Howe, have been the strongest of supporters of my quest to establish a Commemorative Marker and the Scrolls of Honour for the nine American airmen known as the Tomahawk Warrior crew. They died on August 12, 1944, when their bomber crashed and exploded on Lude Farm.

Ironically, the plane crashed in the village of Penn, in Buckinghamshire, U.K. the original home of William Penn, one of the America's Founding Fathers. Further connections to American history became apparent as I began the investigation into the sacrifice the crew made on that fateful day, in which many lives were saved because of the pilot's actions. And it was in 2019, when Lord and Countess Howe offered their beautiful residence, the Penn House Estate, for the presentation of the Buckinghamshire County Council Official Scrolls of Honour to the members of the crew's descendants whom I had traced and brought to England for that purpose.

My Article Dedicated to Lord Howe.

During the period of requesting the British authorities for obtaining recognition to the Tomahawk Warrior crew, I had already set in motion the process of getting a Permanent Commemorative Marker near to the crash site. This attempt became beset with many difficulties, which are unnecessary to be itemized here. Suffice to say, once again, Lord Howe, who felt, "this was a worthy cause", stepped in to offer his help. He introduced me to a local landowner, Paddy Hopkirk, who agreed to allow a marker to be established on his property adjacent to the crash site. Paddy and his lovely wife Jenny, together with other volunteers, had the sign installed in November 2020.

None of this would have happened were it not for the kind help of Lord and Countess Howe, with whom I am now on first-name terms. I would like my readers to know a little more of the Earl's ancestry relating to the American history, before and after the American Revolution.

It is indeed ironic that the Howe dynasty should have such extensive significance to the American story. The family can trace its ancestry many centuries back, but for this article, I will begin with the 3rd Viscount Howe, George Augustus (1725-1758), who was the only British nobleman buried in the U.S. His story is the following: about 17 years before the American Revolution Viscount Howe was placed in charge as Deputy Commander of British Forces under Lord Abercrombie's Army at the time of what has been called The Seven Years War with the French. About 150 miles North of New York City, on the Hudson River sits the town of Albany. Although the area had first been reached in the 1600s by the English explorer Henry Hudson, for whom the river was named, it had become a Dutch settlement at that time. In 1755, George took command of the Royal American Regiment.

George became good friends with many of the local American colonial leaders and he admired their general pioneering efforts, and their ability to adapt to local conditions no matter what they may be. The area was heavily forested, to which the usual tactics of European armies were unsuited. He developed several innovations for those under his orders. He made a point of respecting American soldiers under his command, which was not common among many British officers at the time. An article in the Pennant quoted him as saying:

> "*Knowledge and respect for the varied manners and opinions of others will harmonise (sic) our great army and make it invincible. Any gentleman officer will find his equal in every regiment of the Americans. I know them well. Beware how you underestimate their abilities and feelings.*"

He also reformed the tactics and the dress for his men. He discarded scarlet and brass buttons in favor of more muted colors and woolen leggings, these being more practical. George shared the same rations as his men and instead of heavy furniture of the day for officers, he also slept in a tent but with a blanket and bear skin. He encouraged his officers to do the same.

He modified the muskets to make them easier to use in the forest terrain. Lord Abercrombie said of Viscount Howe, "*Howe was universally loved and respected throughout the Army and a favourite (sic) of the local Americans.*"

On July 6, 1758, Howe led one of four columns of the British troops, along with the Connecticut militia, from the shores of Lake George through the wooded terrain. They moved towards the French army at Fort Carillon, commanded by General Marquis de Montcalm, when they encountered a unit of French soldiers. In the ensuing skirmish, the British captured 148 French soldiers, causing twice that in casualties. Unfortunately, in their attack, a French soldier shot a musket ball into General Howe's chest. Reportedly, Howe died in the arms of Major Israel Putnam of the Connecticut militia (who in the future will become a general in the Continental Army during the American Revolution).

They buried General Howe in St. Peter's Church in Albany and there is also a historical marker at Trout Brook, the place of the skirmish with the French. The Massachusetts Assembly later voted £250 to place a monument in Howe's memory in Westminster Abbey[158] in London.

---

[158] https://www.westminster-abbey.org/abbey-commemorations/commemorations/george-howe

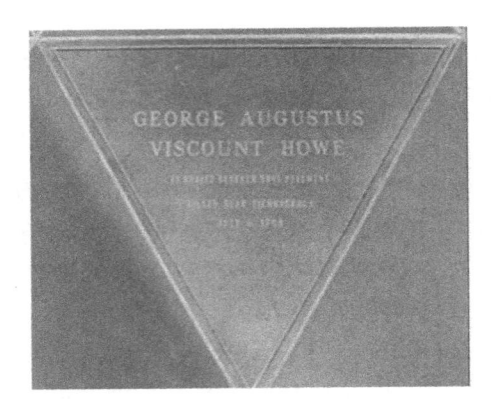

Tombstone in St Peter's Church, Albany, NY.

Historical Marker, Trout Brook.

John Stark, an American colonial officer and a great admirer of Howe, later commented that he became reconciled to Howe's death. "Had his great abilities been used against the American colonists during that War of Independence, its outcome might have been different."

It was Howe's younger brothers, Admiral Richard Howe and General William Howe, who eventually commanded the British Navy and the other the Army in the early years of the Revolutionary War. Both men were sympathetic to the colonists and, in fact, Admiral Howe had met with Benjamin Franklin. Although the two brothers had achieved some early success, they were replaced at their own request in 1778. They remained critical of the government policy and the resourcing of the war.

During my trip to England in September 2021, I was fortunate to be hosted by Mrs. Francine Vella-Roccia,[159] who also drove me to Penn, Buckinghamshire, to facilitate the inauguration of the Commemorative Marker for the Tomahawk Warrior crew. After the function for the Commemorative Marker, Francine and I accompanied Lord Howe to a private meeting at his residence at Penn House[160] on the beautiful grounds of the estate.

Penn House, courtesy of Lord Howe

Lord Howe kindly gave me a personal summary of his family history, a part of which I have outlined above.

His position in the British Government at the time of writing this book was that of the Deputy Leader of the House of Lords, and he previously held the position of Minister of Defence (sic). I am very privileged to call this kind and modest man a friend. His personal help to me in

---
[159] Mrs. Roccia's family had bought the house I lived in during the blitz, after we left in 1945. Francine had given me a nostalgic tour of the house in Clapham, London in 2021.

[160] https://pennhouse.org.uk/default.html

getting recognition for the crew of the Tomahawk Warrior is a testament to his friendship and acknowledgment of the support that America gave to Britain in World War Two.

The 7th Earl Frederick Howe

David E. Huntley–Author
January 2022

The Earl and his wife have three daughters, Anna, Flora, and Lucy and a son, Tom. Earl Howe has been an active parliamentarian in the House of Lords since he inherited the title. He is a Conservative hereditary peer and, after spells in Agriculture and Health Ministries, was their spokesperson for Defence (sic) and also Deputy Leader of the House of Lords.

Countess Howe was the High Sheriff of Buckinghamshire from 2010 to 2012. In June 2020 Her Majesty the Queen appointed Lady Howe to the post of Lord Lieutenant of Buckinghamshire[161]. She succeeded Sir Henry Aubrey-Fletcher Bt KCVO, the then current Lord Lieutenant in November 2020.

▲ ▲ ▲ ▲

---

[161] https://wendovernews.co.uk›news›countess-elizabeth-howe-is-the-new-lord-lieutenant

ACKNOWLEDGMENTS

▲ ▲ ▲ ▲

I may have been the lead actor in this saga of bringing posthumous honors to the Tomahawk Warrior crew for their heroic sacrifice in 1944. It would not have been possible without a magnificent supporting cast.

I am immensely grateful to the Hon. Steve Baker, who, at the time I was initiating contacts in the UK, was a Conservative Member of Parliament. He introduced me to Joe Bradshaw, of the Lord Lieutenant's Office in Buckinghamshire.

Much is owed to Joe Bradshaw for his detailed efforts and diligence in making my quest to honor the sacrifice of the Tomahawk Warrior crew known to the highest levels of local government, and in particular to Mr. Brian Roberts, Chairman of the Buckinghamshire County Council.

I have paid tribute to Lord Howe and his wife Countess Howe in a chapter in this book. However, it would be remiss if I did not state that without their help and cooperation, neither the presentation of the Scroll of Honor or the installation of the Commemorative Marker would have been realized. Thank you, Frederick, and Elizabeth.

My sincere thanks seem inadequate for the generosity offered by the late Paddy Hopkirk and his wife, Jenny. With Paddy's help, we gathered a team of volunteers and over one year; We established the Marker on Paddy's property next to the crash site. In Chapter 13, I mention several individuals for their contribution in getting the Commemorative Marker installed. I express my sincere thanks to them all.

A big thank you to Kate Ashbrook, the General Secretary of the Open Spaces Society. They monitor the centuries old laws of public and bridal footpaths in England. Her advice and guidance were invaluable when placing the location of the Commemorative Marker.

Many kudos to David Hardie, a British commercial airline pilot and local resident of Penn, Buckinghamshire. David had taken a keen interest in what had happened to the Tomahawk Warrior. His keen insight into some aspects of this event proved invaluable to me. Thank you, David, for your encouragement and support. I hope you like the conclusion. I'm sure you will be happy that the Historian for 398th Bomb Group Memorial Association, Lee Anne Bradley, was ecstatic about my book.

It is important for me to acknowledge the contribution made by several family members of the Tomahawk Warrior crew's descendants, without which this book would never have been possible. Namely, Mrs. Cheryl Surfus, the pilot's daughter who graciously hosted me as if I were family in Wisconsin. She granted me extensive interviews and access to her archives.

Martin and Angie Ginther, who tried to ensure that I came into possession of the navigator's diary that Martin's father Mr. Ed Ginther had found in 1944. Besides the diary and by drawing on the extensive wartime correspondence of Mr. Ginther Sr., I provided an interesting window into the period of his service in England.

The two nieces of the plane's navigator, Andrea Kempner Blake and Janice Kempner Morgan, could not have been more welcoming to me in my quest to learn more about their uncle Saul. I was fortunate to have been the link that brought the long-lost diary back to the family archives after its absence of 75 years. The additional documents I obtained for the Kempner family through my research gave them much comfort and new knowledge of their family history. Their comments of gratitude, which you have read in the preceding chapters, were enough to show me the importance of my work was to all these families.

I am also very grateful for another side of the Searl family, a Ms. Kathy Searl, a 2nd cousin of Lt. Charles Searl. She gave me additional photographs and important certifications of Searls' training. Kathy and her brother Charles initiated the installation of a paver stone in memory of Lt.

Searl at the City of Tomahawk war memorial. I also owe a debt of gratitude to Kathy for providing a valuable proofreading service.

Sue Wales, who was my primary contact with the Ducharme family, as well as Robyn Ducharme, helped me to construct a small profile of the co-pilot Lt. Albert Dion. Although it was 2 years after the presentation of the Scrolls of Honour in England, it pleased me I could send Ms. Wales one of the Scrolls I had brought back with me.

Similarly, it was late last year when I was able to contact Mrs. Diane Plogger, the family historian of the Knight family. It resulted in receiving a plethora, or I should say, an abundance of archival material. One can never have too much material in these circumstances, but what Diane provided was very impressive. Her material, besides some historical baseball memorabilia, and the life of Albert Knight, there was a letter in the personal handwriting of Frank A. Snyder, the mystery airman. My in-depth investigation of Snyder and his subsequent premature violent death was very emotional for me. I felt his pain as he lived out those final years thinking about his comrades who died, and not him. Thank you, Diane. Without you, this chapter would never have been written. I was pleased to send Diane one of the Scrolls of Honour for her uncle's archives.

It is thanks to Ms. Bradley who, by reading my draft, offered corrections of places and names from other documents not in my possession. She clarified aspects of certain missions from alternative material in the Association's archives.

Thanks also to 102-year-old Major Lucky Luckadoo, US Air Force (Ret) and wartime B-17 pilot in the 100th Bomb Group. He not only graciously endorsed my book but pointed out several issues which needed correcting when reading the draft. A big thank you for helping me with this book and for my first book, *Deathwatch Beetle: A Post WWII Historical Spy Thriller*, when you allowed me to address your group, 'Happy Warriors' in 2012/13.

I wish to thank the late Geoff Rice and his widow Marilyn Gibb-Rice. Geoff was the Trustee of the Nuthampstead Airfield Museum and Marilyn is the President of the 398th Bomb Group Memorial Association. Both Geoff and Marilyn had given me permission to use images and material from the Group's website with proper credits. In 2019, while visiting Geoff at the Airfield Museum, in England, I pledged to donate certain proceeds from the sale of this publication at my personal retail book signing events. I trust my readers will visit the 398th.org website and read much more about this Bomb Group's air combat accomplishments in WWII.

Thanks to John Saunders and his brother Neil, of Flackwell Heath, UK, who both vouched for my memory of concrete barriers in the meadows at Loudwater village. These were installed in wartime to prevent German gliders from landing. My evidence of this was a key point in substantiating my claim that the TW crew tried to avoid crashing on the village.

Upon my return to England for the second time in two years to inaugurate the Commemorative Marker, I was kindly hosted by my friend and fellow author, Ivy Ngeow, and her family. Ivy is a popular writer for Penguin Books.

Thanks too, to Francine Roccia for also hosting me during this visit to England. Francine's family had purchased the house I and my family lived in during the blitz. She now owns the house and gave me a nostalgic tour of the property. She also drove me to the ceremony for the Commemorative Marker and took the photographs. Much appreciated, Francine.

I am most grateful to Mary Stafford, President of Roll-Call.org the veterans' charity that I support, for her assistance with introductions to numerous WWII veterans, as well as Brigadier General Mitchell Hanson US Air Force, who kindly wrote the amazing Foreword to this book.

Some very helpful research assistance was given to me by Ms. Debbie Duay, the National Genealogist for the Daughters of the American Revolution.

I am most grateful to Mr. Chuck Chvala for helping to acquire the Getty image on Chapter Fourteen which highlighted the amazing link between the Tomahawk Warrior, his uncle, and Joseph P. Kennedy Jr.

Finally, I would like to thank my good friend, the award-winning author of WWII historical fiction books, Marina Osipova, for her help and advice during this period.

▲ ▲ ▲ ▲

ABOUT THE AUTHOR

▲ ▲ ▲ ▲

David E. Huntley, is a retired international business executive who has lived on three continents, Europe, Africa, and America.

Surviving the London Blitz of WWII, he became an engineer and company owner with extensive international experience.

He lives near Dallas, Texas. His late wife Sophie was also a survivor of WWII, having lived under the Nazi occupation of France.

David was the Founder and a past President of the British-American Commerce Association and a director of Historic Royal Palaces, a U.K. charity in the USA. He has been a guest speaker at many Forums and a frequent panelist on national public television.

In 2022, Huntley was awarded the National Americanism Medal by the Daughters of the American Revolution for his humanitarian work with WWII veterans. He is a popular public speaker on WWII from personal experience. His full biography can be seen here: https://tinyurl.com/2p9pkbf

His previous book, *Deathwatch Beetle: A Post WWII Historical Spy Thriller*, was a 2015 Chaucer Finalist in the Chanticleer International Book Awards for Historical Wartime Fiction. David was also awarded a Certificate of Appreciation by the Dallas Jewish War Veterans Group. To buy a signed copy with free delivery go here:

https://deathwatchbeetle.net/buy_book.html

His current book, *The B-17 Tomahawk Warrior: A WWII Final Honor*, resulted from almost seven years of extensive research, travel across two continents, and hundreds of interviews.

▲ ▲ ▲ ▲

INDEX

▲ ▲ ▲ ▲

381'st Bomb Group, 189
398th Bomb Group, 9
600th, 98–99, 120, 152–54, 157, 159, 205–6

A
Accounts of Downing of Rohrer Crew, 206
Advanced Navigation School, 129–30
   Mather Field, 132
Africa, 24, 389
Aircraft, 4–5, 95–97, 190–92, 194–95, 282–83, 369–74
Aircraft 42-107080, 99, 101–2
Aircrew, 260
Air Force, 29, 31, 130, 133, 219, 222–23
   398th Bomb Group of the United States Army Air Corps, 8th Air Force, 3
   1945, after the war when the WWII Bomber Command was closed, 22
   airfield in Picauville carved out of an apple orchard, 201
   crew of the Tomahawk Warrior were part of the 600th Squadron, 3
   General Jimmy Doolittle was the Commander, 22
   generous visitors with a stick of Wrigley's chewing gum, 22
   High Wycombe, but buried deep in underground bunkers, 22
   HQ of the U.S. Army Air Force Bomber Command, 22
   A NOTE TO MY CHILDREN AND GRANDCHILDREN, 25
   there were many 'Yanks, 22
Airplane commander, 293–97, 303–4
Albert, 237, 240, 244, 247–53
Albert Dion, xvii, 121, 236–39, 387

Allied Expeditionary Air Force, 171, 185
Allied ground forces, 191, 226
Allied Planes Hammer Nazi Targets, 188
Allied warplanes, 177
  1000 Bomber RAF Raids, 173
  Heavies, Fighters Sweep Europe Looking for a Scrap, but Nazis Refuse, 173
  stretched an aerial dragnet across the skies of western Europe, 173
American aircraft, 193
American bombers, 221, 262
  bombers were hammering Hitler's railway network, 175
  Crews reported intense flak over some targets, 175
  head of our camp was a German captain, 168
  Over 1,500 American bombers yesterday struck from two sides of Europe, 175
  roared out on their greatest mission of the war, 193
American History, 5, 353, 360
  the 3rd Viscount Howe, George Augustus (1725-1758, 380
  Countess Howe appointed by Queen Elizabeth to Lord Lieutenant of Buckinghamshire, 379
  historic incident in American history, 113
  In 1755, George took command of the Royal American Regiment, 380
  Joe Chvala, 113
  Lt. Joe Kennedy, (expected to be groomed for the American Presidency, 5
  the only British nobleman buried in the U.S, 380
  original home of William Penn, 379
  the plane crashed in the village of Penn, 379
  The Remarkable Connection Between, 379
  William Penn, Lord Howe, and his Ancestors and their Role in the American Revolution, 379
American Revolution, 240, 379–81, 388–89
American warplanes, 211, 220–21
And, 28
Andrea Kempner Blake, 326, 350, 386
Aphrodite, 361

Aphrodite
  21,000 tp 30,000 lbs of Torpex, 361
  the Americans to develop an unmanned guided bomb, 360
  guided missile program of the USSTAF, 370
  Joe Kennedy, 360
  taking a war-weary but still flyable B-17 bomber and stripping it, 360
Aphrodite missions, 361–62, 367, 374, 376
Arlington National Cemetery, 83, 147, 261–62, 272
Army Air Corps, 64, 83
  Albert Dion co-pilot, 237
  Albert Knight, waist gunner, 237
  American Legion in Tomahawk, 63
  Charles Joesph Searl, 63
  Ed Ginther, Sr, 46
  Irving Kempner, Flying Tigers in China, 83
  Saul Kempner, 46
AT-17, 119
  Charles's declassified pilot flight logs, 119
  twin-engined advanced trainer, 119
Azon system, 361, 365

B
B-17 bomber crew, 53
B-17 FlyingFortress.de.en, 105, 124
B-17 Flying Fortress Story, 97, 282
B-17G, 97, 154, 283–84, 292–93, 366, 372
B-17s, 183–87, 196–200, 202–7, 218–20, 282–83, 365–69
  12,732 were produced, xvi
  398th Bombardment Group, Tomahawk Warrior, 98
  fallen out of his chute, 161
  Ginther to Europe, check flights, 51
  Nuthamstead, 29
  Penultimate Mission, 226
  Plane Identification, 98
  received a direct hit, exploded, 164
  training in a Link Simulator, 120
  vulnerable to icing, 98
B-17 Tomahawk Warrior, xvi–xvii, 13–377, 381, 383, 387, 390
Beatty, 267
Belgium, 153, 172, 175–76, 194–95, 283, 288
Berlin, 152, 154–62, 168, 170, 204–5, 207–11
  19th of May, 29

German civilians who had witnessed my descent, were firing at me, 166
Me-110 had taken a shot at a parachute, DIRTY POOL! 205
Operations Officer assigned them 42-107191, 106
plane was spiraling down now, I was catapulted out into space, 166
received heavy flak damage that day, 52
target today was the Wilhelm-Strasse Railroad Station in the center of Berlin, 162
BGMA, 26, 28, 30, 157, 159, 230
Biber, Pearl, 140, 147–48
Bombardment Group, 37, 98, 275, 293
Bomb Group, 104–5, 123, 152–53, 277–78, 292–93, 366–67
Bomb Group Memorial Association, 28, 94, 96, 106–7, 160, 386–87
Geoff Rice, 95
website, 398th Bomb Group, 9
Bordeaux, 196–97, 199, 202
Boulogne, 183–85, 187
Our target was some gun emplacements, 180
target was just a little north of Pas de Calais, 180
We had to bomb PFF, 180
Britain, 172, 177, 184, 221–23, 363, 368
British bombings of Dresden, 21
directed at strategic targets, 181
One thousand Flying Fortresses and Liberators flew out, 175
was alone for the early part of the war, 21
British Double Summer Time, 4
British wartime regulations, Open areas were considered vulnerable to invasion, 321
Brunswick, 155, 157, 170
Buckinghamshire, 18, 20, 22, 335–36, 338, 383–86
Buckinghamshire County Council, Her Majesty's Lord-Lieutenant of Buckinghamshire, 323
Buckinghamshire County Council, Joe Bradshaw, 323
Bueffel, Alfred, xviii, 30, 32, 268

C

CAF. *See* COMMEMORATIVE AIR FORCE
Castor aircraft, 374, 377

Cessna AT-17 BobCat, 119–20
Chairman of Buckinghamshire County Council, 323, 326, 345
Councillor Brian Roberts, 324
Charles, 60–61, 70–73, 86–88, 111–15, 118–22, 124–25
I gure I should write you one last letter Page 27, 125
It seemed as if he had a sort of premonition Page 99, 124
Charles Searl, 29, 40–41, 69–70, 74–75, 88, 98–99
Cheryl Surfus, 59, 77, 79, 113–15, 322, 325–26
Cheryl is the second daughter of Lt. Charles Searl, 40
his first daughter, Charlene, 40
Mrs. Cheryl Surfus of Weston, Wisconsin, 40
Shelly Surfus Loe, Searl's Granddaughter, 40
Chicago Tribune, 357, 359
Churchill, 377
Combat Box Formation, 277
Commemorative Air Force, 307–8
COMMEMORATIVE AIR FORCE (CAF), 307–8
Commemorative Air Force, Kevin "K5" Michels, 307
Commemorative Air Force
Len Root, 307
Lt. Col Walt Thompson, 308
Terry Barker, 307
Texas Raiders, 307
Commemorative Marker, 340, 343–44, 379, 383, 385–86, 388
Joe Bradshaw, 340
Lord Frederick Howe & Countess Elizabeth Howe, 340
Paddy Hopkirk, MBE & Jenny Hopkirk, DL, 340
Parsonage Farm, 340
Penn, 340
Countess Howe, 324, 326, 330, 338, 379–80, 384
Crash site, 6, 9, 96, 230, 341, 380
Crew, 9-man, 120
CREW DUTIES, 293
Crew Training, 295

D

Dallas, 24, 51, 59, 66, 389
David Hardie, 92–94, 96–98, 106, 231, 240, 345
Davis, 68–69, 112
DESCENDANTS, 267
Diary, 37–39, 43–45, 77, 144–55, 157–59, 386–87

discovery of the diary had changed my attitude to this 1944 incident, 47

how the navigator's diary came into my possession, 5

Mrs. Janice Morgan Saul Kempner's niece Page 79, 80

navigator, 2nd Lt. Saul Kempner,^31 the author of the diary, 47

navigator of a plane nicknamed "Tomahawk Warrior" had written it, 37

Double Summer Time (DST), 92, 94

Duay, Debbie, 240, 258, 388

E

Eighth Air Force, 191, 193, 195, 198, 200, 224–25

250 to 500 Britain-based Fortresses and Liberators, 179

398th Bombardment Group [Heavy] on February 15, 1943, 275

600th Bombardment Squadron of the 398th Heavy Bombardment Group, 154

heavies flew two missions against the winged-bomb emplacements, V1s & V2s, 212

severely battered ten, targets in Germany, 228

study primarily focuses on the effects of high altitude, 311

The "Tomahawk Warrior" and its crew, 154, 308

Element Formation, 277

three planes, 277

Elwood crew, 34, 107

England, xvi–xviii, 50–51, 289–91, 335–37, 342–45, 386–88

English Channel, 354, 369, 371

Europe, 27–28, 186–87, 190, 250–51, 361, 364

Explosives, blend of TNT, RDX (cyclonite, Torpex), 314

F

FAA (Federal Aviation Administration), 283

Final Mission, 7, 229, 315

Five Musketeers, 112, 114, 353–54

Flak News, 31, 160–61, 165, 169, 315, 336

Flying Tigers, 83–84

Flying Tigers were an 'American Volunteer Group' (AVG), 83

nickname for the P-40's used

by the Flying Tigers was the:'Tomahawks, 84
poignant letter he wrote to his wife, Mary, 84
FOIA (Freedom of Information Act), 38, 106, 142, 145, 152
Fortresses and Liberators, 184–85, 189, 193, 200, 211, 220
France, 256
   raid on a German target near Versailles, 4
   Tomahawk Warrior crew took off from Nuthampstead at 6:18 a.m, 4
Frank Snyder, 255–59, 261–62
   He wrote this letter to Albert Knight, Bert's father, 242
   Johanna mentioned the '<:mystery:>' of Frank Snyder, 250
   simply another one of those strange coincidences, 241
   THE FRANK SNYDER MYSTERY – PART ONE THE MISTAKEN SNYDER, 254
   THE REAL FRANK SNYDER Page 258, 254
   this Snyder was not the missing tail gunner, 254
   was it Frank's intention not to be found? Page 260, 254
   written by the mysterious missing airman, 241
French coast, 183–84, 189–91, 198, 204, 213
Fresno, 261–63, 265–66

G

German fighters, 156, 169, 171, 174, 288
   17 separate missions over the Cherbourg Peninsula, 191
   over 100 ME109s and FW190s rose through solid cloud seeking combat, 156
   attempted to ram the bombers in suicide attacks, 156
   Bomber crews claimed 60 German fighters destroyed, 156
   fighter and Forts were colliding all over the sky, 156
   not a one of which got through the covering escort, 175
   They destroyed a total of 20 German fighters, 191
German radio, 156, 170, 172, 197, 203
Germans, 160, 169–70, 197, 199, 251, 376

Germany, 178–79, 203, 221–22, 227–28, 275–76, 283–84
Good-bye To the Blitz, Leaving London, 11

H
Hamburg, 198, 202, 204, 224–26, 228, 317
Havocs, 184–85, 191, 212, 214–17, 223
Havre, 186–87, 217, 372–73
High Wycombe, 18–20, 22, 24, 26, 31, 323
Holland, 162–63, 165, 194–95, 276
Honour, 239, 267, 325, 330, 379, 387
House of Lords, 330, 383–84
Howe, 326–27, 381–82
Huntley Associates Dallas, 75, 110, 329

I
Invited by Joe Kennedy to attend his sister's wedding, 355
Irving, 75, 80–84, 133, 137, 144–46
Irving Kempner, 79–80, 325
Italy, 179–80, 219, 221, 228

J
James, Ian, 94, 345–46
Janice Morgan, 47, 49, 79–80, 148–51, 328, 330
Jing Zhou, 283–84, 362
Joe Bradshaw, 323–24, 330, 332, 340, 344, 385
Joe Chvala, 113–14, 353–55, 357, 359–60
Joseph Kennedy, 354, 356–57, 370
   Lt. Wilfred Willy, 353
   older brother of John F. Kennedy, 353
   Tomahawk Warrior Connection, 353
Joseph Kennedy Jr, 353–54

K
Kathy Searl, 68–70, 74, 118–19, 386
Kempner, 46–47, 75–76, 83, 148–55, 157, 223–25
   2nd Lt. Saul Kempner's diary, 39
   Kempner family in Detroit, 75
Kempner Diary, 194
   Press Release, 148
   The Return of the Kempner Diary, 148
Kempner family, 47, 75–77, 79–80, 84–85, 147, 150

Kempner family archives, 147
  One of the saddest letters I have transcribed Page 137, 139
Kempner family in Detroit, carefully screening these detailed census records, 75
Kiel, 214, 218–19, 225–26, 228, 275
Knight, Albert, 242, 244, 246, 250, 253, 259–62

L
Late Terry Barker, 309–10
Len, 54, 94–95
Leo C. Walsh, xviii, 30, 32, 34, 270
Liberators, 179, 181, 184–87, 193–94, 197–200, 211–12
Loading Lists' Mission Reports, 254
London, 7–9, 16–20, 26–27, 53, 94–95, 331–32
Lord and Countess Howe, 330, 379–80
Lord Hartington, 356–57
Lord Howe, 330, 332, 341, 379–80, 383, 385
Loudwater, xviii, 8, 17–20, 25–27, 35, 91–92
Lucky Luckadoo, 310, 387
  The greatest hazard we encountered was carburetor icing, 100
  mission was not counted as a "combat mission" unless the crew encountered the enemy, 153
  One of the basic features of the Box Formation, 278
  who flew B-17s for the 'Bloody 100 Bomb Group, 100
Lude Farm, 27–28, 31, 34–35, 91, 93–94, 337
Luftwaffe, 170, 173–74, 188, 190, 203, 205

M
Madera, 262–63, 266
Madera Tribune, 263
Marauders, 184–85, 212, 215–17, 220, 223, 228
Martin, 37–39, 47–50, 77, 148–49, 386
Missions, twenty-fifth, 28
Mission to Berlin, 52, 106, 158, 211
Morrison Shelter, 13
Muspratt, 88, 91, 252, 336–37

N
Navigator, 127–32, 154–55, 159, 213, 297–99, 301

News Reports for July, 214, 216, 218–19, 221, 223
News Reports for June, 181, 183–84, 186, 190, 192, 198–99
Ninth Air Force, 188–89, 200–201, 203–4, 211–12, 216–17, 222–24
Nuthampstead, 3–4, 50–51, 92–93, 97, 122–23, 289–90
  Nuthamstead Airfield Museum, late Geoff Rice was a Trustee of the Museum, 95
  the photo historian for the 398th Bomb Group Memorial Association, 95

O

Ohio, 29, 37–39, 44–46, 75, 244, 249
O'Neal Crew 600th Squadron, 166
  The plane was spiraling down now, going faster and faster, German civilians who had witnessed my descent and were firing at me Page 166
O'Neil, had jumped . . .but had fallen out of his chute, 161
OSS (Open Spaces Society^152), 342
Oxnard, 237–38

P

P38s, 171, 173, 180–81, 203–4, 211–12, 217
P47s, 181, 184–85, 191, 193, 197, 200–201
P51s, 180–81, 185–86, 193, 195, 211–12, 217
Paddy Hopkirk, 341–43, 345, 380
Paris, 103, 108, 182, 184–85, 195, 216–17
Pathfinder Force, 312–13
PBY-1, 354
Penn, village of, 4, 8, 32, 35, 88, 91
Penn and Tylers Green, 339
Penn Church, 33, 93, 324, 336
Penn House Estate, 330, 379
Pennsylvania, 290, 327, 337
Pilot Searl, 190
Plane, 25–28, 91–94, 105–8, 153–57, 159–61, 288–91
Press Release, 148–49
Project Aphrodite, 363–64
Public Footpaths, 8, 341–42, 345
Pyote, 132

R

Radio Beacons, 99, 102
RAF (Royal Air Force), 173–74, 189, 191–92, 201, 203, 312
Rainbow Corner, 245–46

Rapid City, 120, 122, 165
RDX, 227–29, 314–16
 British bombing missions, Cookie" bomb, 315
Reich, 173, 177, 179, 182, 196–97, 199
Return to England, 388
Ridgewell, 123, 189
Rohrer Crew Phil Jones WWII Recollections, Philip H. Jones Tail Gunner, 206
Royal Air Force. *See* RAF
Rumania, 179–80, 219, 228

S
Sacramento, 129–30, 259
Santa Ana, 128–29
Saturday, 54–55, 92, 94, 217, 224, 228
Saul Kempner- B-17 Navigator, 153
Scene, 8–9, 28, 32, 40, 285–86, 333
Scooter, 12
Scrolls of Honour, 239, 267, 379, 387
 British Authorities had awarded to the crew posthumously, 239
 Buckinghamshire, England, Issued on Remembrance Sunday, November 10, 2019, in Penn, Bucks, England, 335
Searl, 52, 91–93, 95, 105–6, 154, 321–22
 crew's 30th mission but only 28 were fully accredited, 28
 flew right over our cottage, 27
Searl
 Davis, 69, 112, 118, 124
 Lude Farm in Penn just above Loudwater, 27
 Tomahawk Warrior and nine young men, 28
Searl's Early Life, 111, 353
SHAEF, 171–72, 192
Snyder, xviii, 30, 251, 254–55, 257–60, 263
Snyder, Frank A., 241–42, 257, 262, 267, 387
Snyder Mystery, 5, 236, 254, 259–60, 262, 266
Sophie, 24–25, 36, 201, 333, 350
Splasher, 99–100, 103
Squadron, 3–5, 98–100, 105–8, 152–53, 205–6, 277
Stearman PT-17 bi-plane, 117, 238
Stelzdfreide crew on arrival in England, 133

T

Texas, xvi, 24–25, 41, 115–17, 132, 347–48
Texas Raiders, 307
Thunderbolts, 211–12, 224, 226
Tomahawk, 61–66, 70–71, 73–74, 76–77, 111–12, 153–54
Tomahawk War Memorial, 65, 387
Tomahawk Warrior (TW), 3–5, 28–29, 36–41, 152–54, 254–57, 383–86
  discovery of the diary, 47
Tomahawk Warrior Crew, 110, 275
  1st Lt. Charles J. Searl, Pilot, xviii
  2nd Lt. Albert L. Dion, co-pilot, xviii
  2nd Lt. Leo C. Walsh, bombardier, xviii
  2nd Lt. Saul J. Kempner, navigator, xviii
  Sgt. Albert W. Knight, waist gunner, xviii
  Sgt. Alfred Bueffel, ball turret, xviii
  Sgt. Cecil E. Kennedy, radio, xviii
  Sgt. Frank A. Snyder tail gunner not on final flight, xviii
  Sgt.Orville M. Wilson, waist gunner, xviii
  Staff Sgt. James A. Beatty, engineer, xviii
Torpex, 314–15, 361, 374
TW. *See* Tomahawk Warrior

U

UK, 25, 32, 94, 385, 388
United Kingdom, xviii, 133, 322–23, 331
United States Army Air Forces, 152, 244
US 8th, 364–65, 367
US Air Force, xv, 364, 387
US Navy, 356, 367–68, 370, 373–74

V

V1, 13, 26, 204–5, 363, 368–69, 373
  Air Raid Precaution Warden (ARP, 13
  the "flying bomb" Fieseler Fi 103 (V1, 363
  rocket planes nick-named by British public as, "Buzz Bombs, or Doodle-Bugs! 200
  rockets or "Buzz bombs" as they were called, 53
  These letters describe the life of an average family, 53
  We had survived the worst of the blitz, 13

when the V2s began raining down around September, 331
V2s, 13, 26, 331, 360, 377
 the German V1 rockets and the V2 menace, 7
 they descended at super-sonic speed from a height of 55 miles, 13
 They took keen interest in the photographs of the bombing, the German V1 and V2 rockets, 62
 The V2s^11 that started in September of '44 were devastatingly different, 13
Vicar, 86, 326, 328, 336, 338–39
Village of Loudwater, xviii, 8, 17, 26, 91, 321–22

W
War memorials, 65, 70, 268, 270–71, 326, 328–29
Warplanes, 228
WWII
 most of those losses were on bomber missions over Nazi Germany in B-17s and B-24s, xv
 Over 50,000 Airmen^139 lost their lives in the four years of WWII, xv
WWII Final Honor, 5, 13–377, 381, 383, 387, 390
 B-17 Flying Fortress heavy bomber, xvi
WWII Hero's Diary Returned to Family, 149

Milton Keynes UK
Ingram Content Group UK Ltd.
UKHW020720301023
431584UK00014B/741